THE BREATHING CATHEDRAL

THE
BREATHING
CATHEDRAL

Feeling our way into a Living Cosmos

MARTHA
HEYNEMAN

Foreword by
Thomas Berry

SIERRA CLUB BOOKS

The Sierra Club, founded in 1892 by John Muir, has devoted itself to the study and protection of the earth's scenic and ecological resources—mountains, wetlands, woodlands, wild shores and rivers, deserts and plains. The publishing program of the Sierra Club offers books to the public as a nonprofit educational service in the hope that they may enlarge the public's understanding of the Club's basic concerns. The point of view expressed in each book, however, does not necessarily represent that of the Club. The Sierra Club has some sixty chapters coast to coast, in Canada, Hawaii, and Alaska. For information about how you may participate in its programs to preserve wilderness and the quality of life, please address inquiries to Sierra Club, 730 Polk Street, San Francisco, CA 94109.

Copyright © 1993 by Martha Heyneman
Pages xi–xii and all permissions cited in the Endnotes (pages 183–198) constitute an extension of this copyright page.

LIBRARY OF CONGRESS CATALOGING-IN-PUBLICATION DATA
Heyneman, Martha, 1927-
   The breathing cathedral / by Martha Heyneman.
     p.   cm.
   Includes bibliographical references and index.
   ISBN 0-87156-687-7 : $25.00
    1. Cosmology—Miscellanea. 2. Human ecology—Miscellanea.
I. Title.
BF 1999.H54 1993
113--dc20   92-34363
                                           CIP

Production by Janet Vail
Book design and jacket design by Amy Evans

SIERRA CLUB NATURE AND NATURAL PHILOSOPHY LIBRARY
Barbara Dean, Series Editor

For my parents, my husband, my teachers—
  in gratitude;
my children, my grandchildren—
  in hope.

Contents

...we need, beyond the political and economic incentives to clean up our land, air, and water, to find ways to cultivate an *imaginative* awareness of man's beholden place in the natural order.

JAROLD RAMSEY, *Reading the Fire*

Acknowledgments

Special thanks to Barbara Dean, without whom this book would not have been written, for her unfailing encouragement; to Pat Harris for her gentle and perceptive editing; to Dr. Richard M. Eakin for permission to tell the story in the Preface; to Professor Jarold Ramsey for the sentence on page *vi*, which so succinctly sums up my aim in writing the book; and to my husband, Alan Heyneman, for his patience and his transcendent cooking.

Some of the material in this book has appeared earlier in a different form in *Parabola* and *A Journal of Our Time*.

Acknowledgment is extended to the following for permission to reprint copyrighted material:

Yale University Press for material from Kent C. Bloomer and Charles W. Moore, *Body, Memory and Architecture*, copyright © 1977 by Yale University Press. All rights reserved. Alfred A. Knopf, Inc., for lines from "Things of August," from *Collected Poems of Wallace Stevens* by Wallace Stevens. Copyright 1947 by Wallace Stevens. Reprinted by permission of Alfred A. Knopf, Inc. Random House, Inc., for lines from "I Think Continually of Those Who Were Truly Great," from *Collected Poems 1928–1953* by Stephen Spender. Copyright 1934 and renewed 1962 by Stephen Spender. Reprinted by permission of Random House, Inc.

Lines from "Sailing to Byzantium" reprinted with permission of Macmillan Publishing Company from *The Poems of W. B. Yeats: A New Edition*, edited by Richard J. Finneran. Copyright 1928 by Macmillan Publishing Company, renewed 1956 by Georgie Yeats. Lines from "The Double Vision of Michael Robartes" reprinted with permisson of Macmillan Publishing Company from *The Poems of W. B. Yeats: A New Edition*, edited by Richard J. Finneran. Copyright 1919 by Macmillan Publishing Company, renewed 1947 by Bertha Georgie Yeats.

Harcourt Brace Jovanovich, Inc. for excerpts from "The Waste

Land" in *Collected Poems 1909–1962* by T. S. Eliot, copyright 1936 by Harcourt Brace Jovanovich, Inc., copyright 1964, 1963 by T. S. Eliot, reprinted by permission of the publisher. Excerpts from "Burnt Norton," "East Coker," "The Dry Salvages," and "Little Gidding" in *Four Quartets*, copyright 1943 by T. S. Eliot and renewed 1971 by Esme Valerie Eliot, reprinted by permission of Harcourt Brace Jovanovich, Inc. Faber and Faber Ltd for permission to reprint excerpts from *Collected Poems 1909–1962* by T. S. Eliot outside the USA.

Foreword

We are presently, in this terminal decade of the twentieth century, experiencing a Moment of Grace. Such moments are privileged moments. The great transformations occur at such times. The future is defined in some enduring pattern of its functioning.

Such a moment occurred when the star out of which our solar system was born collapsed in enormous heat, scattering itself as stardust out into the vast realms of space. In the heat of that explosion the ninety-some elements were formed. Only then could the Earth take shape, life be evoked, intelligence become possible. That supernova event could be considered a Moment of Grace, a cosmological moment that established the possibilities of the entire future of the solar system, the Earth, and of every form of life that would ever appear on the Earth.

Often such moments have a catastrophic aspect, for physical transformations so significant occur amid awesome violence. The world is born into a radically new phase of its existence. Another such moment occurred when newborn cellular life was imperiled by the creation of free oxygen in the atmosphere. The earlier life-forms that produced oxygen could not themselves live in contact with it. While living beings as we know them cannot do without oxygen in its proper amounts, free oxygen was originally a terrible threat to every living form.

For a proper balance to be achieved and then stabilized, a Moment of Grace had to occur, a moment when some living cell would invent a way of utilizing oxygen in the presence of sunlight to foster a new type of metabolic process known as photosynthesis. At that moment, under threat of extinction, the living world as we know it began to flourish until it shaped the Earth anew. Daisies in the meadows, the song of the mockingbird, the graceful movement of dolphins through the sea: all these became possible at that moment. We ourselves became possible. Music and poetry and painting. All began amid such peril.

In human history, also, there have been such moments. Such was the occasion in northeastern Africa some two hundred thousand years ago when the primordial ancestor of all presently living humans began her family. Whatever talent exists in the human order, whatever genius, whatever capacity for ecstatic joy, whatever physical strength or skill, all this has come to us through that mother of us all. It was a determining moment.

There were other moments, too, in the cultural-historical order when the future was determined in some comprehensive and beneficial manner. Such a moment was experienced when humans first learned to control fire. When the first gardens were cultivated. When language was invented. Writing and the alphabet. Weaving and the shaping and firing of pottery. Then there have been the moments when the great visionaries were born who gave to the peoples of the world their unique sense of the sacred, when the great revelations occurred. So, too, the time of the great storytellers, of Homer and Valmiki and other composers who gave to the world its great epic tales.

So now in this last decade of the twentieth century, we are experiencing a Moment of Grace, but a moment in its significance different from and more threatening than any previous such moment. Now for the first time the planet is being disturbed in its geological structure and its biological functioning in a manner and to a degree unequaled in the past sixty-five million years of the Earth's history. We are terminating the Cenozoic era in the geobiological history of the Earth.

We are also altering the great classical civilizations as well as the indigenous tribal cultures that have dominated the spiritual and intellectual development of vast numbers of persons throughout the past five thousand years. These civilizations and cultures that have governed the sense of the sacred and established the basic norms of reality and value and designed the life disciplines of the peoples of Earth are terminating a major phase of their historical mission. Their teaching and the energy they communicate are unequal to the task of guiding and inspiring the future. We cannot function effectively without the traditions, but they alone cannot fulfill the needs of the moment. That they were not able to prevent and have not yet properly critiqued the present situation is evident. Something new has happened. A new vision and a new energy are needed.

This vision and energy must arise from our new experience of the deepest mysteries of the universe that we now have through our empirical observation. We see the universe now as a developmental sequence of irreversible transformations rather than as an ever-renewing sequence of seasonal cycles. We find ourselves living not so much in a cosmos as in a cosmogenesis. If formerly we perceived life as a thoroughly understood sequence of seasonal change, we are now confronted with an ever-changing universe that is never quite the same, a universe of irreversible transformations. Irreversibility is now the central issue in our appreciation of where we are in the total planetary process. In the earlier context any destruction, it was thought, could be renewed as the great cycle of events enabled things to come back to their beginnings. Now we have no such assurance.

As at the moment when the amount of free oxygen in the atmosphere threatened to rise beyond its proper proportion and so to destroy all living beings, so now terrifying forces are let loose over the Earth. This time, however, the cause is from a plundering industrial economy that is disturbing the geological structure and life systems of the planet in a manner and to an extent that the Earth has never known previously. The most elaborate expressions of life and grandeur and beauty that the planet has ever known are now threatened in their survival. All of this by human invention.

So severe and so irreversible is this deterioration that we might well believe those who tell us that we have only a brief period in which to reverse the devastation that is settling over the Earth. Only now has the deep pathos of the Earth's destruction begun to sink into our consciousness. While we might exult in our journey to the moon and in the photographs showing the lunar terrain, we might also experience some foreboding lest through our plundering processes we so denude the Earth of its living forms that we be confronted with a desolate Earth that progressively is becoming more lunar in the erosion of its life-forms. It is tragic to see all those wondrous expressions of life imperiled so wantonly. Those forms of life expression came into being during the past sixty-five million years, the Cenozoic era of Earth's history, a period that might well be designated as the lyric moment of the entire evolutionary process.

In this context we must view the last decade of the twentieth century as a Moment of Grace. It is at such moments that a unique opportunity arises, for if the challenge is so absolute, the possibilities are equally comprehensive. We have finally identified the full difficulty that is before us. A renewal of planetary dimensions is under way. A comprehensive change of consciousness is coming over the human community, especially in the industrial nations. For the first time since the industrial age began we have a profound critique of its devastation and experience a certain withdrawal in horror at what is happening.

Much of this is new. Yet throughout the prior decade studies were made that give us precise information on the situation before us. World Watch and World Resources Institute have identified in endless detail what is happening. The younger generation is growing up with greater awareness of the need for a mutually enhancing mode of human presence on the Earth. Even in the political order we are told by a vice-presidential candidate that concern for the environment must become "the central organizing principle of civilization."

The story of the universe is beginning to be told as a communion of subjects, not as a collection of objects. We begin to understand our human identity with all the other modes of existence that constitute with us the single universe community. In a special way all living beings of Earth are derivative from a single source. We are all cousins to one another. So, too, in the universe entire; every being is intimately present to and immediately influencing every other being. We see quite clearly that what happens to the nonhuman happens to the human. What happens to the outer world happens to the inner world. If the outer world is diminished in its grandeur, then the emotional, imaginative, intellectual, and spiritual life of the human is diminished or extinguished. Without the soaring birds, the great forests, the sounds and coloration of the insects, the free-flowing streams, the flowering fields, the sight of the clouds by day and the stars at night, we become totally impoverished in all that makes us human.

In a corresponding manner there is now developing a profound mystique of the natural world. Beyond the technical comprehension of what is happening and the directions in which we need to change, we now experience the deep mysteries of existence through the wonders of the world about us. This experience has been considerably advanced through the writings of the natural-history essayists. Our full entrancement with various natural phenomena is presented with the literary skill and interpretative depth appropriate to the subject, especially in the writings of Loren Eiseley, who recovered for us in this century the full vigor of the natural-history essay as it was developed in the nineteenth century by Henry Thoreau and John Muir.

It is this mystique of the universe, understood in its full poetic and intellectual dimensions and in its feeling identity, that is the invaluable contribution of this book of Martha Heyneman. A mystique of mutual presence: presence of the human within the universe, of the universe within the human. The comprehensive range of understanding presented here is overwhelming in its power. The poetry of science and science as poetry. Cosmology, imagination, and history. When these turn into each other we have one of our most certain indications that we are now living in a Moment of Grace. That the author should have such appreciation of the *Divine Comedy* of Dante and how he incorporated the science of his day into his great vision, along with the entire course of biblical, classical, and European history, is an impressive achievement. Even more impressive is her understanding of how his vision becomes functionally effective in these times. The universe story as known through our cosmological syntheses fulfills in our times the function of the *Summa theologica* of Thomas Aquinas in the work of Dante. The identity of Dante with the universe of the medieval period is now transformed into the identity in our times of the human person with the emergent universe in its long sequence of transformations.

There is much to be done before this last decade of the twentieth century fulfills its designation as a Moment of Grace in the actualities of the Earth story. What can be said is that the foundations have been established in almost every realm of human affairs. Finally the mythic vision has been set into place. The devastation in process now has its origin in a distorted understanding of the grand mythic vision of an emerging age of blessedness. Until this distorted dream of a technological paradise is replaced by a more viable dream of a mutually enhancing human presence within an integral Earth community, no effective healing will take place, for the dream drives the action. In the larger cultural context the dream becomes the myth that both guides and drives the action.

With this new mythic basis of a celebratory universe presented here by the author we can get on with our human role within that vast liturgy that is existence itself. But even as we identify this final decade of the twentieth century, we must note that moments of grace are transient moments. The transformation must take place within a brief period. Otherwise it is gone forever. That in the immense story of the universe so many of these dangerous moments have been navigated successfully is some indication that the universe is for us rather than against us, that we need only to summon these forces to our support in order to succeed. It is difficult to believe that the purposes of the universe will ultimately be thwarted, although the human challenge to these purposes must never be underestimated.

Thomas Berry

Preface

It is necessary to fly like the hawk in order to understand concretely the geometry of the cosmos.
GASTON BACHELARD, *The Poetics of Reverie*

One day forty years ago, when I was a student in zoology at the University of California, Berkeley, I was looking through the microscope at a section of the kidney, when all at once there came into my head the thought: *I will never understand this thing by this method.* When I tried to make clear to myself what I meant by "understand," the best I could come up with was that I would have to be able to *dance* the development of this remarkable organ from its origin in the fertilized egg to its maturity, and moreover to dance the development of the whole of which it was a part—and of the whole of which that whole was a part, and so on. Since this was clearly physically impossible, I would have to be able to *imagine*, not only in my mind, not only in pictures seen "out there," but in my body, in its sensation of movement, change, and completion—the whole space-time entity that was the kidney.[1] The path to understanding nature, I decided, lay not through science but through poetry.

The idea that poetry might be a path to any kind of valid knowledge sounded as preposterous in that time as it does in this. Science was the only path to reliable knowledge of reality. Poetry was a product of the imagination, which was, by definition, unreality. The thought that had arisen above the microscope in the Life Sciences Building must have been fueled by a very powerful need, else it could not have survived in that atmosphere, where we were being initiated into the unspoken assumptions of the scientific establishment. I could not see, at the time, what that need was, nor could I know that it was not personal to me. Just before this, we had dropped the bombs on Hiroshima and Nagasaki. Soon afterward, manifestations on a large scale would begin to appear, wave after wave, of something unknown that seemed to be trying to restore the balance of the human psyche in order to prevent the destruction of the earth.

When the zoology professor, Dr. Richard Eakin, heard that I had decided to change my major, he called me into his office. He was very kind. He himself, he explained, was fond of verse. But why would anyone want to become a poet instead of a scientist?

He really wanted to know. I really wanted to explain. I knew what I meant but couldn't get it into words. I was miserable, leaning against the wall, hands plunged into pockets, head hanging, staring down at my scuffed penny loafers. He had wanted me to become his research assistant. I felt that I had failed him. Tears splattered onto the front of my lab coat. I have been trying ever since to answer Dr. Eakin's question.

I see now that by "understanding" I meant something different from what science means because I wanted something different from what science wants. I was interested not in knowing how things work in order to have power over them but in knowing why I was here on the earth, in order to know what I was supposed to do. With my fellow science students I shared a passion for observing attentively as much as I could of what takes place in nature. The study of science was bringing us awareness, with wonder and delight, of the inexhaustible multiplicity, variety, and ingenuity of things. But was it not illogical and dangerous to want to have power over things when you had no way of knowing what, in their totality, they were for? And without that knowledge, could you truly arrive at an undistorted view of how they had come to be what they were?

The evidence for evolution seemed to me unassailable—but what was the unifying, patterning force that drew it on, from atoms to molecules to cells to organisms to human beings; who alone of all creatures on the earth had the need to go on trying to understand the whole of it? Was there a verifiable means of *know-*

ing this unifying force at first hand and not just making beautiful words about it out of wishful thinking?

I see in retrospect that Dr. Eakin himself, all unknowing, contributed to my strange notion of what understanding might be. With him, teaching was an art. His ardor for the subject of embryology was such that his body could not help taking part. Each morning when we came into the classroom, we would see on the board a stunning diagram resembling a masterpiece of Art Nouveau —elegant curving lines and swelling spaces—that Dr. Eakin had drawn beforehand in chalks of many colors. Then our long-legged professor himself would stride in, pick up a piece of chalk, and— bending, twisting, with great swooping gestures of his arms, one hand curving over, around, and under the other—*dance* the development of the chick embryo. To borrow a term from psychoanalysis, this was the "latent" content of the course. It was not what we were examined on. It is all I remember.

When I got into the English department, I had to admit that most of the poems we read did indeed seem pretty useless. The lyric outcry was not what I had in mind. Not until we got to the *Four Quartets* of T. S. Eliot did I feel I was getting warmer. Looking at the first few lines of that poem, I had for the first time the experience of acknowledging that although I was looking at words I recognized, I could not imagine what they meant.

> *Time present and time past*
> *Are both perhaps present in time future,*
> *And time future contained in time past.* [2]

I beat my head upon these lines until, standing in the glare of brilliant sunlight on a white Berkeley sidewalk, I experienced what might be called a personal paradigm shift. Suddenly I was able to feel and sense my continuity with everything alive—through space in the present, via eating and breathing and perceiving; and through time, past and future, via the chain of the "immortal germ plasm." I could imagine time speeded up, so that a tree became a fountain springing up out of the earth, spraying out its trembling multiplicity of leaves, materials streaming into it from earth and air and sun, influences streaming out from it, affecting me. I was part of this streaming of materials, this universal exchange, and of the chain of ancestors and descendants.

There was nothing "unscientific" about this. It was just that my other faculties had waked up to perceive in their own mode what my head knew—the simplest facts that everybody knows. When I went to class and read

> *We move above the moving tree*
> *In light upon the figured leaf* [3]

I said, "We do, you know. It's just a fact." My fellow students said, "What are you, a mystic?" This was before the 1960s. I didn't even know what a mystic was. I was thinking of photosynthesis.

Eliot led me to Dante, to the *Divine Comedy,* and this indeed was what I was looking for: a whole world—but a lost one, as it seemed then. It could be entered only through what Coleridge had called "that willing suspension of disbelief...which constitutes poetic faith" because, of course, no one in a post-Copernican world could any longer believe in a naïve geocentric system or in the physics of Aristotle. Still, the *Divine Comedy* seemed to me the only sort of poem worth writing. To imagine the whole with the whole of oneself, mind, heart, and flesh: that would be understanding. That would be a kind of knowledge that could be carried everywhere and applied to everyday life.

Ezra Pound had said that before you can have a *Divine Comedy* you have to have an "Aquinas map." Dante did not have to create the cosmology and psychology that formed the backbone of his great poem. That work had been done for him by Saint Thomas Aquinas, who had created a "theory of everything" for the Middle Ages, having reconciled the recently rediscovered works of Aristotle, which summed up the knowledge of the ancients, with Christian scripture, which had governed thought in the West since the fall of Rome. Aquinas ordered all this—the sum of everything known up to that time—in a system defining, in the language of scholastic reason, man's place and purpose in the universe, and expounded it most exhaustively in his *Summa theologica*, the Aquinas map to which Ezra Pound referred.

Dante's task, equally titanic, was to strike the great skeleton of the *Summa* with his poet's wand and bring it to life in the language not only of reason but also of bodily and emotional imagination. He accomplished that task with such mastery that as reader you feel you are actually accompanying him (for Dante plays the role of pilgrim in his own poem) on his long journey through the whole medieval universe, feeling the hot sands burning the soles of your feet in hell and the love of God piercing your heart in heaven.

So I went looking for an Aquinas map and found, to my great good fortune, the practical teaching of G. I. Gurdjieff, the lucid exposition of its psychological and cosmological theory by his pupil P. D. Ouspensky,[4] and Gurdjieff's own rendition, in *All and Everything*,[5] of the myth of the creation of the universe and the creation, fall, and possible evolution of humankind.[6]

But I could not see how Gurdjieff's cosmology related to Dante's or how either one *could* relate to the acosmic picture of the universe that prevailed at that time in science.

Cosmology should not be confused with astronomy. The proper object of the study of cosmology is not the stars but the universe considered as a whole. In the seventeenth century, a new science that was to become what we call physics altered the position of cosmology to such a degree that it seemed destined to disappear. Early in his career, the great philosopher Immanuel Kant attempted a cosmological synthesis on the basis of Newton's law of universal gravitation, but thirty years later he claimed to prove that the ultimate questions cosmology might raise—whether the universe is finite in space, whether it has an origin in time—are insoluble. In *The Critique of Pure Reason*, he was forced to renounce cosmology for human reason once and for all. This renunciation became widespread among the scientists of the nineteenth century, but despite the warnings of Kant, the infinity of the universe was more and more accepted by science and professed as veritable dogma.[7]

This infinite universe—which could not be called a cosmos,

because it had no form, and hence it was impossible to orient oneself within it—was the one we all unconsciously inhabited during the years when I was growing up. A wordless assumption that the universe was infinite, without beginning or end in space or in time, underlay both science and the world view of ordinary people. This untested assumption reduced all creation myths to the status of pure fiction, although such myths had formed the foundation of every great culture—including the European one, which had been informed by the Holy Bible and had then proceeded to give birth to science itself. My own education had recapitulated this sequence, from Sunday school in early childhood to the premed curriculum of physics, chemistry, and biology in early adulthood.

I kept these apparently contradictory views of the universe—of Christianity (expressed most fully in the *Divine Comedy*), science, and the Gurdjieff teaching—in separate compartments in my mind, unable to arrive at any version of that wholeness of world view that is a necessary foundation for wholeness of being and doing. "Be ye transformed," said Saint Paul (Romans 12:2), "by the renewing of your mind."

I did not become a poet. When I came to myself twenty years later, I discovered that I had been laboring in the service of Nature (whatever we mean by that large abstraction) in her efforts to restore the population after World War II—contributing to the baby boom. I certainly don't regret that. At the time, it seemed to me to be my own personal and individual decision. "Give me children or else I die," I said inside myself, echoing Rachel. Other women of my generation can verify this: we were not conned into multiple motherhood. We chose it freely, going against the whole message of our education, which had been (contrary to what the present generation supposes) "You can be anything you want to be." What interests me is to realize in retrospect that what seemed to be our most personal decisions, made in full consciousness, on our own initiative, turned out to have been, rather, the manifestation of influences at work on a very large scale—something much bigger and more mysterious than social pressure or "stereotyping."

A few years later, again supposing the phenomenon to be peculiar to me, I found my worldly ambition reviving, myself rebelling against the situation I myself had put myself into—and discovered I was part of the women's movement.

> *When had I my own will?*
> *O not since life began.*[8]

All this time I continued to read—science, poetry, mysticism, comparative religion, myth, psychology, philosophy—and to study the theory and try to apply in my daily life the practical methods of the Gurdjieff teaching for strengthening attention and increasing awareness of oneself and whatever is taking place in the moment. But what I read and studied had very little to do with the choices I made or the way I spent my time from day to day—my "religion," in Gurdjieff's down-to-earth definition of the word.[9] I had in fact several apparently incompatible "religions," reflecting the fragmentation of world view that prevailed in my mind and prevails in general in our time.

An almost physical sensation of dismemberment finally aroused me to a rigorous examination of the roots of these "religions" and an ongoing effort to see how they might relate to one another within some larger whole. "There can never be a state of facts," as William James has said, "to which new meaning may not truthfully be added, provided the mind ascend to a more enveloping point of view."[10]

Gradually, over the years, I had come to see—through moments of experience arrived at through its practice—that the Gurdjieff teaching, in its cosmology and psychology and in the path it provides toward wholeness ("harmonious development"), is the same as Dante's, if we understand Dante's poem not literally but in its inner meaning, which becomes apparent in the course of one's own self-exploration. The Gurdjieff teaching, then, although its metaphors are designed for the modern psyche and its methods adapted to the patterns of modern life, in no way deviates in its essence from the ancient and universal tradition of paths to human perfection—for Dante's poem is universally acknowledged, by even the strictest of traditionalists, to be an astonishingly complete and precise expression of the "perennial philosophy" that has reigned in all the great cultures, East and West, since before recorded history.

For myself, I had verified by direct self-observation that the structure of Dante's universe, whether or not it applies to the world "out there," is still the structure of the world "in here," the world of the psyche; and I had verified, by traversing it in its lower reaches and by catching glimpses of its higher ones in my own experience and in the manifestations of others ahead of me, that the path the pilgrim follows in the *Divine Comedy* is still the path that any of us must follow in order to come into the field of action of that influence that can make us whole.

At the same time, the beauty and vividness of the imagery of Dante's great poem, and the geometric unity of its structure, made it possible for me to visualize the path as a whole and to carry the map of that whole with me wherever I went (when I remembered!), in the very sensation of the structure of my own body. As Eihei Dogen said, "The entire body studies all-inclusively the great road's entire body."[11]

Then, in 1980, my friend Marjorie Dickie, who was teaching physiology at Dalhousie University in Halifax, Nova Scotia, sent me a review from *Scientific American* of an article by Mark A. Peterson, of the Department of Physics at Amherst College, called "Dante and the 3-Sphere."[12] Dante's universe not only was not "a naïve geocentric system" but was a "3-sphere," one of the forms currently proposed for the whole of space-time and the one preferred by Albert Einstein, who initiated the rebirth of scientific cosmology in the twentieth century after its hiatus of four hundred years.

It had taken a long time for the big bang theory, which restored the idea that the universe had a beginning, to become generally accepted by scientists, and even longer for news of it to filter down to students and ordinary people. Now the subject of cosmology had reappeared in our textbooks of physics and astronomy. An image of the beginning of things was taking shape again, and its compatibility with Gurdjieff's myth[13] became more and more evident to me—as well as to others who were professionals in one or another of the sciences and at the same time students of the Gurdjieff teaching.[14]

Now all the pieces were assembled. It remained to try to imagine the whole of a world view that could include in harmony all the apparently irreconcilable kinds of knowledge I had absorbed during my life. When Barbara Dean asked me to write something for her Nature and Natural Philosophy Series, that provided me with the occasion and the courage I needed in order to try to answer, at last, Dr. Eakin's question.

This question, fueled by my suffering at being unable to answer it during that interview in his office so long ago, has acted, over the years, as an intense organizing principle behind my search for intellectual clarity, coherence, and comprehension, and in the process has been transformed from an either/or question into the question of how to balance all the parts of the psyche without amputating any of them. After many transformations, the question takes for me the following form: Why are poets—that is, "cosmic storytellers"[15] who comprehend science and mysticism and the incarnation of both in the great, neglected realm of everyday life—essential for the survival of ourselves, of our descendants, and of the earth?

THE BREATHING CATHEDRAL

The Dark Wood

Halfway through the journey of our life
I found myself in a dark wood
Where the right road was erased.

DANTE, *Inferno*

Man does not exist for long without inventing a cosmology,
because a cosmology can provide him with a world-view
which permeates and gives meaning to his every action, practi-
cal and spiritual. THOMAS S. KUHN, *The Copernican Revolution*

In the West, there is no longer one Big Story which we all
believe in, which tells us how the world was made, how
everything got to be the way it is, how we should behave in
order to maintain the balance in which we coexist with the
rest of the cosmos. LOUISE STEINMAN, *The Knowing Body*

Our scientists and historians have already laid out the plot....
The imagery is necessarily physical and thus apparently of
outer space. The inherent connotation is always, however,
psychological and metaphysical, which is to say, of inner
space. JOSEPH CAMPBELL, *The Inner Reaches of Outer Space*

Trying to begin this book, I feel as though I am pushing my way
through thickets of confusion, as my sister and I once pushed our
way through thickets of stiff underbrush, raising clouds of dust
and insects, when we tried to find again the "country home"
where we had spent our vacations as children. I know that what
I am looking for is here somewhere. I feel its immanence. The
book will be an effort to uncover it, to see it clearly—even to move
in, bag and baggage, and live in it.

By the time my sister and I went searching for the cabin of our
childhood, we were both in college. I was about to be married and
depart, never again to be a regular resident of our parents' house

in the city. My sister was to follow the same path after a few years. Neither of us had been to the cabin since I was five years old and she seven.

We were suspended between two homes, one outgrown and the other not yet moved into, as today all of us are suspended between two representations of the universe, at home in neither—the medieval one that is still implied in our religions and the expanding one that has become generally accepted in our science. In history, the two are separated by a period when the universe was assumed to be infinite, without beginning or end in space or in time. Such a universe was like a dark wood or shoreless sea. In it, no one could feel at home.

Some such feeling of alienation and disorientation must have been what sent my sister and me searching for the cabin where both of us had been young enough to perceive the world with the whole of ourselves, as small children do, and to perceive every "chance" event of daily life as full of meaning—as something permanent: a universal law.

Every Friday evening, for example, Mr. Buchanan (our nearest neighbor, who lived several miles away, at the other end of the canyon) would get drunk, seize a gun, and chase his wife toward our cabin. I would stand in the doorway and proclaim in a singsong voice, "Here comes Mr. Buck chasing Mrs. Buck down the canyon with a shotgun!"

This was a law of the universe—something that happened regularly, like Christmas or the rising and the setting of the sun.

Or, one morning, we would arise to find our aunt red-eyed and our uncle (who had bought the cabin for us because he had no children of his own) missing from the breakfast table. When we got outside, we would whisper to each other, "He's gone to the Indian squaw again!"

This event too was one of the regularities of a universe in which we felt at home because (however bizarre it seems to the adult eye) it was something that could be relied upon to recur at regular intervals, an instance of the way things were.

A child regards everything that happens to him more than once as having happened always. That is how he orients himself in time, and that is the importance of rituals like Christmas or Passover, which must be followed exactly or a child will feel himself lost in a vast formlessness.

The annual journey to the country home was for us such a ritual, recapitulating a legendary past. The events and landmarks on the way there were as immortal and unchangeable to us as Ulysses' encounter with the Cyclops or the Land of the Lotos-Eaters, or Dorothy's approach to the Emerald City of Oz.

You had to get up early, when it was still dark. You put on your jeans and ran downstairs to the kitchen. Mother would have made hot chocolate and buttered toast. You dunked the toast in the steaming hot chocolate, which sometimes streamed down your arm to your elbow, to be absorbed by the rolled-up sleeve of your plaid flannel shirt. Having hastily dabbed at your sticky arm, you tossed the paper napkin toward the table and ran out (letting the screen door slam) into the dark front yard.

There you stopped to listen to the dawn wind rustling in the palm tree.

The dawn wind is holy. It is one of the channels of communication between the timeless and time. It flowed delicately over your face. It lifted and rippled your hair so gently that you had to stop dancing with excitement for a moment and listen to the stillness, sniffing like a puppy at the promise-laden freshness of the predawn dark.

Then you piled into Aunt Winnie's Reo—you on your mother's lap in the front seat, your sister, brother, and cousin in the back. Your father couldn't go because there was a Great Depression. He had to go on working to keep you alive.

Aunt Winnie wore tan pigskin driving gloves with round holes over the knuckles. Around her neck she knotted a scarf of chiffon of the color called American Beauty Rose. "Aunt Winnie," said Mother (who didn't know how to drive), "is a *very good driver*."

Then you set off along San Pablo Avenue—silent, deserted, seemingly endless—to the Richmond–San Rafael ferry. Below-decks on the ferry, people left their cars running. Down there the air was was full of the roaring and snorting of engines and the hellish smell of exhaust.

So you beat it up the rubber-matted stairs to the upper deck, where the fresh wind from the sea whipped your hair into your mouth. You brought your dog Sheppie upstairs on the leash to relieve herself in some inconspicuous corner of the deck while you looked apprehensively over your shoulder, hoping no member of the crew would notice what you were up to.

Then you went back down below, got in the car, and prepared yourself to endure the dramatic docking.

The captain aimed in the general direction of the slip, but the ferry always crashed into one side and then into the other, with a terrible creaking and groaning of the silvery, cracked, and weathered piles (festooned with seaweed, adorned with barnacles), a tossing of foot-thick ropes, a chattering shriek of giant chains uncoiling, a revving up of motors, and a hair-raising charge over the flap of metal that bridged the watery chasm between ship and shore, as you visualized, in spite of yourself, what would happen if the captain hadn't got the ferry quite close enough to the dock. Looking down, you saw, in that terrifying instant, the slimy green waters snapping up at you like angry dogs.

Having safely navigated those Symplegades (the Clashing Rocks of classical myth), you sped with relief up the Redwood Highway until you reached the Hopville grade, where you held your breath, and your mother got out the chipped enamel basin and the roll of toilet paper, because your sister always got carsick there. (Your brother and your cousin taunted her unpleasantly: "Pea-Green Squeegie!")

Each fence and tree had a face as distinct for you as the faces of your father and your mother or your well-beloved dog. The names of the towns were as fabulous to you as the Ithaca of Ulysses, or the Thebes of Oedipus, or windy Troy.

Ukiah, Willits, Laytonville—your excitement rose as you drew closer and closer. You competed to see who would be the first to spot the turnoff.

It was a gravelly yellow dirt road on the right, with a gate you had to get out and open (a gate whose countenance you also knew as intimately as you knew each other's faces). You fought for the privilege.

But now, so many years later, my sister and I must have turned off at the wrong place. The road we thought we had found petered out. We got out of the car, walked as far as we could, and then tried to push our way, arms held up in the air, through thick underbrush as high as our armpits. Now we could push no farther.

We had to back out, retrace our steps to the car, look for another turning—just as I am searching now.

For four hundred years, we in the Western world have been without a "home"—an all-embracing communal image of the whole of things and our place and function within it. What we know about the universe has been of no help to us in trying to see how we ought to live our lives. I believe that through the confluence of kinds of knowledge that parted company centuries ago—knowledge gleaned from science, religion, art, and daily experience—such an image is taking shape again. My aim in this book is to perceive it clearly, not just with my mind but also with my heart, muscle, skeleton, and skin, because, although I agree with Joseph Campbell that for an image of the universe "we all turn today, of course, not to archaic religious texts but to science,"[1] and I do not want to deceive myself with pleasant but unverifiable notions, my interest in cosmology is not scientific but practical and poetic. My aim is not to "predict and control" but to make sense of my everyday life. I want to see meaning in what is in front of my nose, and I want to know what I am supposed to be doing here on the earth.

Whatever it is for the physicist as physicist or the astronomer as astronomer, a cosmological image is, for all of us, the frame of order of the psyche, the all-containing skin of the imagination and vessel of our knowledge. It is the house of the mind in which all of us, members of a given culture, live. Within some imagined picture of the whole of things we orient ourselves at any moment, make assumptions about what is real, decide what is possible or impossible. The cosmological image *is* our inner world. Everything we know or imagine is contained, consciously or unconsciously, within it. If the vessel is shattered and the image has no shape, impressions have no meaning. We have no stomach for them—no place inside ourselves to keep them. We are immersed in them, they flow over our surfaces in a ceaseless stream, but we are unable to extract any nourishment from them to add to the structure and substance of an understanding of our own upon which we might base a coherent and deliberate life.

Czeslaw Milosz describes the plight of people in church today, where they go to try to learn how they ought to live:

> They have experienced the collapse of hierarchical space, and when they fold their hands and lift up their eyes, "up" no longer exists. Let no one say that religion can manage without such primitive directions to orient people. Not the theologians' dogma, but human images of the universe, have determined the vigor of religions. The Descent of God and the Ascension are two of the spatial poles without which religion becomes pure spirituality devoid of any toehold in reality, a situation not to man's measure.[2]

"There have always been a multitude of preachers calling for inner rebirth," he says, "a rebirth of the heart....I am not, however, in the least counting on some effort of the will, but rather on something independent of the will—data which would order our spatial imagination anew."[3]

The medieval universe, being a true cosmos, could be spatially imagined all at once and as a whole. Hell was below you, "in the bowels of the earth," and heaven was above your head. As you watched through the night, looking upward, you saw with your own eyes the sphere of the fixed stars revolving slowly and majestically around you and, against that background, the planets running their races—speeding ahead of each other or falling behind—in the track of the zodiac. You imagined each of the planets attached to a transparent sphere and yourself on the motionless earth at the center of that nest of revolving concentric crystalline orbs, trying to hear the music they made as they swept past one another.

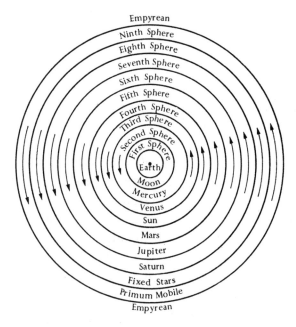

Empyrean
Ninth Sphere
Eighth Sphere
Seventh Sphere
Sixth Sphere
Fifth Sphere
Fourth Sphere
Third Sphere
Second Sphere
First Sphere
Earth
Moon
Mercury
Venus
Sun
Mars
Jupiter
Saturn
Fixed Stars
Primum Mobile
Empyrean

FIGURE 1.1   *...yourself on the motionless earth at the center of that nest of revolving crystalline orbs.* The Heavenly Spheres. (Dante, *Inferno*, Commentary, p. 34, in *The Divine Comedy*, Bollingen Series, no. 80, trans., with a commentary, by Charles S. Singleton [Princeton, NJ: Princeton University Press, 1970]. Copyright ©1970 by Princeton University Press. Reproduced by permission of Princeton University Press.

> There's not the smallest orb which thou behold'st
> But in his motion like an angel sings,
> Still quiring to the young-ey'd cherubins;
> Such harmony is in immortal souls:
> But whilst this muddy vesture of decay
> Doth grossly close it in, we cannot hear it.[4]

Beyond the sphere of the fixed stars was heaven, where God, and the angels, and the souls of the blessed were—though they were in some sense also residing in the various planetary spheres (the seven heavens of sun, moon, and the five planets known at the time), ranked according to their level of being. You could imagine climbing from sphere to sphere as up a ladder, assisted by saints and angels, to union with God, the ultimate goal.

This highest heaven was beyond the material world, not subject to the limiting conditions of space and time. The planetary spheres were somewhere in between. They were the instruments of time (for time was counted by the movements, relative to the earth, of the sun and the moon and, in some ancient cultures, also the planets). Plato called time, and the circling heavens by which it was measured, a moving image of eternity.

In the medieval picture, the spheres were turned by a hierarchy of angels; the speed of a sphere's rotation, like the degree of intelligence of its inhabitants, was in inverse proportion to the sphere's distance from the Empyrean, the utmost heaven (called "empyrean," or "fiery," because it was aflame with divine love), abode of God and the souls of the blessed. The closer to that realm, the greater the ardor to be united with it, and hence the swifter the speed of revolution of the sphere.

Although it was represented as "outside" or "beyond" the sphere of the fixed stars, the Empyrean was not in space but in the mind of God; and although it was still, it was not still with the stillness of earth—the stillness of rest—but was vibrating so fast within that, like the wing of a hummingbird, it *seemed* still.

"You must go out on a starry night," says C. S. Lewis (writing when the "modern" universe was still the infinite one),

> and walk about for half an hour trying to see the sky in terms of the old [medieval] cosmology. Remember that you now have an absolute Up and Down....As a modern, you located the stars at a great distance. For distance you must now substitute that very special, and far less abstract, sort of distance which we call height; height, which speaks immediately to our muscles and nerves.... Because the medieval universe is finite, it has a shape, the perfect spherical shape, containing within itself an ordered variety. Hence to look out on the night sky with modern eyes is like looking out over a sea that fades away into a mist, or looking about one in a trackless forest—trees forever and no horizon. To look up at the towering medieval universe is much more like looking at a great building....[Dante] is like a man being conducted through an immense cathedral, not like one lost in a shoreless sea.[5]

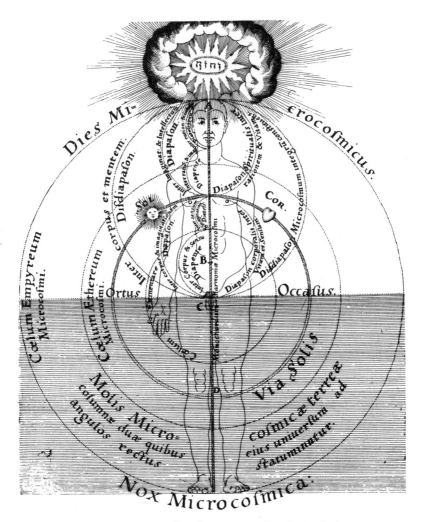

FIGURE 1.2 *It was a pattern of perfection…on all scales.* "The human micro-cosm expresses the musical harmonies of the macrocosm." (S. K. Heninger, Jr., *The Cosmographical Glass: Renaissance Diagrams of the Universe* [San Marino, CA: The Huntington Library, 1977], p.152). Here, the human condition is represented as a microcosm of day and night by Robert Fludd, in *Utriusque cosmi…historia,* 1616–19, p. 83. This item is reproduced by permission of The Huntington Library, San Marino, California. Huntington call number RB 338942.

This medieval cosmological image satisfied the requirements of both the science and the religion of its day. Its structure represented not only the structure of the universe but also the total possible structure of the human psyche. It was a pattern of perfection, or wholeness, on all scales. For the ordinary person, it was a map upon which to chart one's own life's journey to whatever measure of wholeness and understanding one could hope to attain.

Dante's *Divine Comedy* is the story of *his* journey through the universe to a vision of the goal. His poem had a practical purpose: "to remove those living in this life from a state of misery, and to bring them to a state of happiness."[6] Frances Yates suggests that it was a "memory palace," an aid in "the intense effort to hold in memory the scheme of salvation."[7] It was, that is, a kind of navigational chart that made it possible to know at all times where you were and in which direction to steer because the chart included the locus of your destination: a representation of the meaning and aim of existence, the "point of it all."

The goal was holiness, or wholeness—not to leave anything behind but to complete (heal, make whole) your psyche until it mirrored the sphericality and harmony of the cosmos, balanced upon, and revolving around, the point of it all, God, and motivated by "the Love that moves the sun and the other stars."[8]

The loss of this cosmological image was an unexpected side effect of the Copernican revolution. If the earth was turning and not the sky, there was no longer any need to imagine a revolving starry sphere enclosing the whole of the visible universe. With the rupture of this sphere of the fixed stars, no single imagined vessel any longer contained all the different forms of human knowledge, or represented a connection between time and timelessness, or bound together, by virtue of analogous structure, psyche and cosmos, the "inner" and "outer" worlds. As A. O. Lovejoy has pointed out, the significance of the Copernican revolution was not (as we have been conditioned to think) that a naïve medieval, geocentric image of the universe was replaced by a true scientific, heliocentric one.[9] The sun became the center not of the universe but only of the solar system. The universe as a whole ceased to have *any* center or any imaginable shape, and into those infinite spaces that terrified Pascal's *libertin*,[10] the contents of the psyche spilled out like the sawdust from the head of the Scarecrow of Oz.

To some people, this felt like ruin (" 'Tis all in peeces, all cohaerence gone," wrote John Donne); to others, like liberation. In Fontenelle's *Conversations upon a Plurality of Worlds*,

> ...a Philosopher, strolling with a Lady in the moonlight...taught the new cosmology to his apt pupil....
>
> You have made the Universe so large, says she, that I know not where I am, or what will become of me... I protest it is dreadful. But the Philosopher was one of those who delighted in the freedom of the new space, whose imagination expanded with the vast:
>
> Dreadful, Madame...I think it very pleasant; when the Heavens were a little blue Arch, stuck with Stars, methought the Universe was too strait and close, and I was almost stifled for want of Air; but now it is enlarg'd...I begin to breathe with more freedom and think the Universe to be incomparably more magnificent than it was before....[11]

When children play in the sand, girls as a rule make houses and boys make cars, trains, airplanes, rockets—anything to escape confinement; but every one of us, male or female, experiences both these impulses at different times. The longing for untrammeled freedom and the longing for order, relationship, orientation, and understanding alternate throughout our individual lives and throughout political and intellectual history. In the morning—of the day, or of life, or of an era—we long for adventure and set out to seek our fortunes; in the evening we long for order, relationship, harmony, home. Ideally, a picture of the universe would accommodate both these phases—as does, for instance, the Hindu picture of the Breath of Brahma, who exhales a universe every mind-blowing number of milliards of years and then inhales it back home into himself again until it's time for the next exhalation.

In psychoanalytic terms, the lady in Fontenelle's story wishes to remain in the womb and the philosopher fears getting stuck in it. (Even our cosmologies betray our emotional immaturities.) Our psychotherapies have made autonomy their goal, but Evelyn Fox Keller suggests that ideal psychological maturity would go beyond autonomy to the goal of freedom to relate voluntarily. "The ideal described here requires an exquisite balancing act...that the fears of merging, of loss of boundaries, on the one hand, and the fears of loneliness and disconnection, on the other, can be balanced."[12]

> "My house," writes Georges Spyridaki [in *Mort lucide*], "is di-aphanous, but it is not of glass. It is more of the nature of vapor. Its walls contract and expand as I desire. At times I draw them close about me like protective armor....But at others, I let the walls of my house blossom out in their own space, which is infinitely ex-tensible."
>
> Spyridaki's house breathes. First it is a coat of armor, then it extends *ad infinitum*, which amounts to saying that we live in it in alternate security and adventure....Here geometry is transcended.[13]

Or, one might say, geometry becomes non-Euclidean.

"Being is round," says Gaston Bachelard. "Being is alternately condensation that disperses with a burst, and dispersion that flows back to a center."[14] Being breathes.

The mother has no desire to reengulf us. As psychologists reveal, it is our own unconscious *desire* for reengulfment that we fear. There is something valid about this longing, but there is also something valid in the fear, because the longing should lead us not back into the womb (or back to the Middle Ages), which is death, but to a higher equilibrium encompassing all we have learned from experience in the meantime.

In contemplating this ascending spiral, one gets the image of that universal law of octaves that is exemplified in the piano keyboard or the periodic table of the elements. Every octave begins and ends with a *do*, a place of equilibrium, a "home"—in the case of the periodic table, one of the "noble gases," balanced within and encompassing everything that has gone before, from hydrogen on, but (since it has no need of anything) inert. If there is to be a story, or a piece of music, or a material world, the hero will have to leave home—set out to seek his fortune: the music depart from the home tone, the perfect symmetry of the noble gas be shattered.

Having arrived at what seemed an all-encompassing "theory of everything," human beings have always encountered something not taken into account—the unexpected, like the young man at the end of Hermann Hesse's *Glass Bead Game* whose exuberant life energy and the emotion it arouses in the elderly adept shatters for him the perfection of the intellectual system that had explained everything. Similarly, Saint Thomas Aquinas himself, at the end of his life, suffered what must have been not just another syllogism of scholastic logic but a direct experience, since he was heard to remark before he died, "Everything I have written is not worth a straw."

The medieval cosmological image seems to us, in our century of confusion and fragmentation, like one of those *do*s or noble gases—a sabbath in intellectual history—a nest of concentric crystalline spheres, perfectly balanced but inert. As C. S. Lewis says, the medieval model of the universe was itself a supreme work of art, on a par with Dante's *Divine Comedy,* the *Summa* of Saint Thomas, and the great cathedrals of the twelfth century (all of which were incarnations of that model); but "when changes in the human mind produce sufficient disrelish of the old Model and a sufficient hankering for some new one, phenomena to support that new one will obediently turn up."[15] In the sixteenth century, when people began to feel smothered in the medieval model— which had crystallized out in external hierarchies of state and church that eventually grew corrupt and lost connection with the point of it all—they broke out of it, in scientific, religious, and political revolutions, and broke literally out of the Old World in ships sailing into the unknown to discover the New.

The revolution of the sixteenth century, in robbing the universe as a whole of any imaginable form, erased the image of a ladder of spheres up which an individual soul might aspire to climb from earth to heaven; robbed God and the angels of their habitations; and cast them, so to speak, out-of-doors. They might, however,

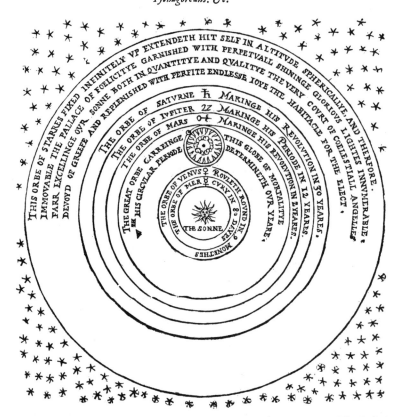

A perfit defcription of the Cæleftiall Orbes,
according to the moſt auncient doctrine of the
Pythagoreans. &c.

FIGURE 1.3   *...God and the Angels...in cosmic Indian territory.* The infinite Copernican universe of Thomas Digges, reproduced from his "A perfit description of the caelestiall orbes," in Thomas Digges, *A prognostication everlastynge* (London, 1576), folio 43. This item is reproduced by permission of The Huntington Library, San Marino, California. Huntington call number RB 53921.

have gone on dwelling indefinitely somewhere out there in infinite space (as Thomas Digges, indeed, portrays them in his diagram of the universe),[16] like tribes of Native Americans in cosmic Indian territory, had it not been for another process that was taking place at the same time. This process, which E. J. Dijksterhuis calls "the mechanization of the world picture,"[17] and Carolyn Merchant, "the death of nature,"[18] transformed the world into a machine that runs by itself, with no need of angels or souls to account for its motions, and God into a "retired engineer."

Symptomatic of the events taking place in the psyche of the West that would bring about the change in the texture of our world picture described by Dijksterhuis and Merchant was Johannes Kepler's decision, somewhere between the 1596 and 1623 editions of his *Mysterium cosmographicum,* to replace the word "soul" (*anima*) with "force" (*vis*) in reference to the planets. "Kepler wished to regard nature no longer *instar divini animalis* (as a divinely animated being), but *instar horologii* (as a clock-work)."[19]

Nevertheless, great transitional figure that he was, Kepler did not renounce the earlier view entirely.

> We read in the histories that "Kepler replaced the notion of soul, the animism of the earlier thinkers, by the notion of *physical energy.*" Such was his effect, yet his passages on "energy" are usually embedded...in others developing his belief that the world possesses both a living body with senses and a soul with memory.... The soul of the earth is a flame "in which the Divine Countenance is imprinted."[20]

Galileo, at about the same time, "...now rejected all questions about the cause of the motions to be studied and confined himself to becoming acquainted, as accurately as possible, with the way in which they took place....It is not the cause of a motion, even less so its purpose, that will interest him."[21] When the question of purpose ceased to be asked, people gradually came imperceptibly (and quite illogically) to assume that purpose does not exist.

> ...with the superstructure from man up banished from the primary realm, which for Galileo is identified with material atoms in their mathematical relations, the *how* of events being the sole object of exact study, there had appeared no place for final causality whatsoever.[22]

At the same time that purpose was being extirpated from our picture of "what is really real," the doctrine of primary and secondary qualities was robbing it of color, sound, taste, and smell. "I feel myself impelled by the necessity," wrote Galileo,

> as soon as I conceive a piece of matter or corporeal substance, of conceiving that in its own nature it is bounded and figured in such and such a figure, that in relation to others it is large or small, that it is in this or that place, in this or that time, that it is in motion or remains at rest, that it touches or does not touch another body, that it is single, few, or many;...but that it must be white or red, bitter or sweet, sounding or mute, of a pleasant or unpleasant odour, I do not perceive my mind forced to acknowledge it necessarily accompanied by such conditions.[23]

It is one thing to define the properties with which the science of mechanics will concern itself and quite another to declare all other properties subjective. As E. A. Burtt points out, in this definition of Galileo's the "secondary" qualities (color, sound, smell, and so forth—not to mention life, sentience, consciousness) "are declared to be effects on the senses of the primary qualities which are alone real in nature."[24]

> ...in the second half of the [seventeenth] century the distinction between the primary, geometrico-mechanical qualities, which were considered to be really inherent in a physical body as such, and the secondary qualities, which were mere names for the perceptive sensations and the feelings of pleasure and pain experienced in consequence of, or in connexion with, physical processes in the external world, was universally accepted, and in fact considered to be almost self-evident. The fact that the primary qualities (size, shape, motion) are after all also presented to us only through sense-perception, so that the whole distinction is really futile, was realized very seldom.[25]

The primary qualities are as dependent as the secondary upon the senses. These qualities amount to a selection of those aspects of sense impressions (though paradoxically, as Erwin Schrödinger points out, the doctrine of primary qualities implies that the senses are not to be trusted)[26] that can be physically measured through the collaboration of sight and touch (or instruments substituted for them) and thus be subjected to mathematical manipulation. In Gurdjieff's terms, these are the perceptions of the "intellectual part of the moving center," that mode of human intelligence that figures out how things work and how to do things and whose mode of thought is mechanical logic. As Ilya Prigogine and Isabelle Stengers point out, "experimental science…is a systematized form of part of the [medieval] craftsmen's knowledge."[27]

This mechanical intelligence, so useful in its proper place, usurped the throne of *nous*, the true intellect, and began to tyrannize over all the other faculties. According to M. C. Cammerloher,

> it all began with Socrates.…Greek philosophy, which before him had been intimation and intuition of the world in its entirety, now surrendered to logic, in the belief that everything could be apprehended and explained with the help of this new instrument.… Aristotle…recognized the fundamental difference between conceptual knowledge and artistic endeavor.….here lay the germ of an insight into the essential diversity of the psychological functions. But…in his *Nicomachean Ethics,* Aristotle went back to Plato's view that the only form of knowledge was the logical procedure of discursive thought.[28]

As for the true intellect, *nous,* we can get some idea of its mode of operation from something J. Krishnamurti (who himself embodied true intellect and spent his life demonstrating it to audiences all over the world) said in a conversation with Ravi Ravindra. "What do you think of that, Krishna Ji?" Ravindra asked, in reference to some idea he himself had just been airing. "You know, sir," Krishnamurti answered, "it occurs to me that K does not *think* at all. That's strange. He just looks."[29]

This is what Beatrice also admonishes Dante to do: "*Look! Look well! I am, I am Beatrice.*"[30] It is our blindness to Beatrice, the soul of the world—that flame in which the Divine Countenance is imprinted—that is destroying both us and the earth.

The events of the sixteenth and seventeenth centuries that resulted in the birth of our science, with all its undoubted accomplishments, had, at the same time, a disastrous effect upon our picture of the universe. From a kind of cathedral filled with life, light, and music, our world was transmogrified—like those dynamited buildings we see pausing for a moment in midair before they break up in a billion fragments and fall to earth—into what Alfred North Whitehead so accurately described as "...a dull affair, soundless, scentless, colourless; merely the hurrying of material, endlessly, meaninglessly."[31]

That formless, meaningless universe is the flood upon which we all have drifted aimlessly for four hundred years—or perhaps an ocean we have been crossing, as our ancestors crossed an ocean to get to a new and unknown land. The picture of an infinite universe is an ocean in time, separating the continents of two cosmologies. At the turn of the present century, after we had drifted for four hundred years at sea in the "infinite" (really indefinite) universe, indications began to appear, first in the equations of theorists like Einstein, then in the telescopes of practical astronomers like Hubble, that the universe has a shape after all, revealing how the tide in our collective psyche had now begun to turn in the other direction, toward a new coherence, a new home.

Today, we see rising before us a new shape. We can see its dim outlines through the fog. We can even smell it, but we haven't yet come ashore. We don't yet *inhabit* our new picture of the universe.

When you are approaching a new continent, first you can make out its general contours; then, as you draw closer to it, you become able to see the creatures that inhabit it—animals, birds, aborigines. Last, you yourself get out of the boat, set foot upon the shore, and enter the new world.

When our new cosmology began to emerge from the mists, first there loomed up like a full moon (or maybe a rising sun) the image of an expanding universe, containing the implication, by extrapolation backward, that it had had a beginning in what we have come to call the big bang. Then, like the animals filing off the Ark, the "particle zoo" of physics entered this picture. Particle physicists, who had been in search of ultimate divisions, found themselves—like the first circumnavigators of the globe, who kept sailing toward the west and found themselves returning to their

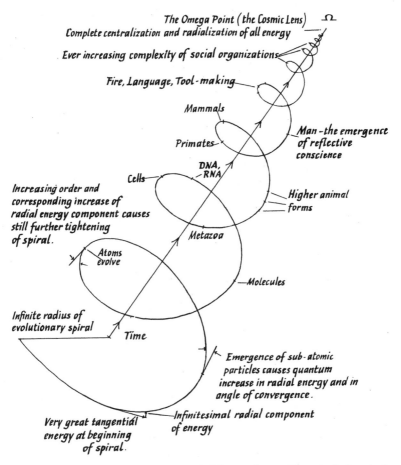

The Omega Point (the Cosmic Lens)   Ω
Complete centralization and radialization of all energy

Ever increasing complexity of social organizations

Fire, Language, Tool-making

Mammals

Primates

Man - the emergence
of reflective
conscience

DNA,
RNA

Cells

Increasing order and
corresponding increase of
radial energy component causes
still further tightening
of spiral.

Higher animal
forms

Atoms
evolve

Metazoa

Molecules

Infinite radius of
evolutionary spiral

Time

Emergence of sub-atomic
particles causes quantum
increase in radial energy and in
angle of convergence.

Very great tangential
energy at beginning
of spiral.

Infinitesimal radial component
of energy

FIGURE I.4   *...ever more intricate and elaborate forms.* The spiral of evolution according to Oliver Reiser, in *Cosmic Humanism and World Unity* (Jill Purce, *The Mystic Spiral: Journey of the Soul* [New York: Avon Books, 1974], p. 128).

starting point from the east—face to face with original unity. The ultimate divisions of matter could exist only in conditions that prevailed in the first microfractions of a second after the big bang.

Then, like the procession of all history that marches past Dante in the Earthly Paradise, there filed into the new picture the "grand evolutionary synthesis," encompassing physics, chemistry, and biology—the whole parade of the increasing organization of matter from quarks to our own brains, the most highly organized entities we know of in the universe. "From the time when the first quarks and leptons materialized out of the undifferentiated cosmic substance, to the present-day pulsars and black holes, red giants and white dwarfs, stars and planets, and more than a million living species that clothe our planet with an ever-changing kaleidoscope of shape, color, and movement—the universe has opened out and blossomed into ever more intricate and elaborate forms."[32]

Theorists laboring to forge the grand evolutionary synthesis usually project the next step in evolution—the next level of organization or "whole-making"—as a new external organization of society, or a planetary mind, but in so doing they skip an essential step: the making whole of the inner world of each one of us, which contains, in a chaos of precreation, more things than are dreamt of in our science.

Now, at last, evolutionary theorists assure us, we can orient ourselves in the universe, both in space and in time. It seems to Brian Swimme that now we can even once more tell the cosmic story:

> A *cosmic creation story* answers the questions asked by children. Where does everything come from? Why do things die? Children want to understand their place in the universe. They wonder about their roles. They have an inherent need for a cosmic story.... Margaret Mead once remarked that she never came across a primal people who lacked a cosmic story.[33]

In all cultures except ours, such a story has given meaning to people's lives, informing the structure of society and the conduct of life. The new story is a story not for just one tribe or nation but for all the people of the earth because it is based on a science that is "already taught and developed on every continent and within every major cultural setting....Instead of building our lives and our society's meanings around the various human stories alone, we can build our lives and societies around the Earth story."[34]

But we can't build our lives around a story of dead matter, however cosmic its scope; and try as we may, we still see earth, ocean, stars, and what was in the beginning—the big bang itself—

as "it." Swimme recognizes that the story has to wait for its poet, as Dante had to wait for Virgil, the last great epic poet before himself, to guide him.

Father Thomas Berry sees that what's missing from our world picture, so that we have been able to lay waste the earth with so little remorse, is, first of all, the *sacred*.[35] To become able to perceive the real presence of the sacred is surely the point of it all. If we came into direct communication with that, we would know what to do: how we ought to care for the earth and what our particular life task might be.

But this perception requires that our psyche be in balance, and for that, Father Berry says, we will have to restore to consciousness and honor all the forms of perception that we think of as "feminine"—those forms of intelligence that, scorned as subjective in the doctrine of primary qualities, came to be rejected at the time of the scientific revolution from the company of human faculties considered reliable instruments in the investigation of reality. These are the forms of intelligence that enable us to *see* the earth as "a living body with senses and a soul with memory." Without them, indeed, we cannot even see these qualities in *each other*.

For Dante, this kind of intelligence is embodied in Beatrice, the girl he fell in love with when he was nine years old and she eight, who died at twenty-seven, and whom he then forgot. It is Beatrice who sends Virgil to Dante when he has lost his way; it is to reunion with her that Virgil leads him; and it is in gazing at her that Dante becomes able to see God.

Richard Tarnas brings into our consciousness even more sharply than Father Berry the effects of the repression of the feminine in the West from the time of the ancient Greeks up to the present. By the "feminine" I mean (and I think Tarnas does too) forms of perception that we all, male or female, are endowed with and the values to which these forms of perception give rise. They are fully functional in all of us when we are children but atrophy as we undergo our education, which recapitulates in each of us, all unconsciously, the intellectual history of the West.

...the evolution of the Western mind has been founded on the repression of the feminine...of any recognition of the soul of the world...a denial of ecological connectedness, a denial of the nonrational, of mystery and ambiguity, of imagination, emotion, instinct, body, nature, woman.[36]

Erazim Kohák is another who sees the root of the ecological problem in habits of perception we acquire in the course of our education—habits that can be broken. "Set aside the learned ways of perceiving the world as dead matter there for your use and see if you can recover again your actual perception of the world as a community of beings to whom you are meaningfully related."[37] In *The Embers and the Stars*, Kohák practices what he is preaching here, setting aside the heavy overlay of theoretical interpretation to look at what is around him in his New Hampshire retreat, and sees in everything not only life and sentience but also *personhood*.[38] In experiments with his students, Kohák has satisfied himself that even we educated adults still see this way, if you take us by surprise. All of us see this way as children, but those of us who grow up in a milieu that is everywhere saturated with the habitual world view of the West (and as Czeslaw Milosz says, "the smallest gadget contains a world view")[39] become ashamed to exercise forms of perception that have so long been looked down upon with contempt.

What is difficult for those of us who have been thus indoctrinated to get through our heads is that the rejection of those forms of perception—all immediate sense perceptions except those that yield measurements; the empathic perceptions of feeling; perceptions gleaned from the bodily imagination's capacity to "turn into something temporarily"; the perceptions of what Cammerloher calls "intimation and intuition"; perceptions arising from the keen, silent attentiveness (free of what he called "thought") embodied and advocated by Krishnamurti—as reliable registrars of anything real, which took place at the time of the scientific revolution, was completely arbitrary and had nothing "scientific" about it. It was not a hypothesis to be tested by experiment but an a priori assumption or unconscious imperative that is buried in the very foundation of the scientific enterprise (and perhaps even deeper in time, if Cammerloher is right—at the level of the ancient Greeks).

The discovery that this is so should lead not to the rejection of science but to the realization that any world picture science can give us will necessarily be a partial one.

Starting from sensory impressions, our only immediate access to knowledge of the world, we can resort to various epistemological procedures to ascertain what is "really real." We can measure, record, analyze, dissect, while regarding knowledge of ourselves—our unconscious motives, the inner turmoil of our unrecognized resentments, fears, desires—as having no effect on our observations, thus ignoring the discoveries of Freud in regard to such unconscious mechanisms as repression and projection that make us fail to see what is really there and see instead what is not. Or we can launch upon a course of self-study and contemplative discipline until we become able, at least at moments, to look at what is in front of us in inner stillness, without preconception, working, over the years, with the help of various practical exercises, to strengthen our attention until it becomes so acute that it penetrates beyond opposites and perceives, as William Blake put it, "the world in a grain of sand, heaven in a wild flower"—the more particular and precise the sensory image, the more powerful the felt presence of the Unconditioned within it.

Attention can penetrate beyond the opposites of particular and general and see that nirvana and samsara, the noumenal and the phenomenal, the one and the many, being and becoming, are one and the same—or rather, as Zen teachers say, "not-two."

"I feel myself impelled..." says Galileo—what kind of science is this? There is an unconscious imperative at work here, and to unearth it is a job for the psychoanalytic historians. "The mentality which was able to reduce nature to 'a dull affair, soundless, scentless, colourless; merely the hurrying of material endlessly, meaninglessly'...is lethal. It is an awe-inspiring attack on the life of the universe; in more technical psychoanalytical terms, its anal-sadistic intent is plain."[40]

For myself, I wish only to do all in my power to shake off the strange spell that has made us accept, without critical scrutiny, the notion that only science can give us an unbiased picture of reality. We do not realize how deeply this prejudice in favor of certain forms of perception still affects us all because it is always invisibly present in the very language we use even as we speak of it—the language I am using right now, advocating attention to the particular in the language of the general.

Tarnas speaks of the feminine in the language of the masculine. Morris Berman speaks of the "reenchantment of the world" in the language that arose in the process of its disenchantment.[41] Brian Swimme tries to tell the cosmic story in language founded on the unverified assumption that matter is neither alive, sentient, nor endowed with personhood. He makes a noble attempt, but it is not possible to tell a story without *persons*—and persons who *act* and *experience*—so that you, the listener, can imagine yourself in that person's skin.

In *The King and the Corpse*, Heinrich Zimmer tells the story of a strange ascetic who every day presents the king with a fruit. The king thanks him, tosses the fruit into a dark storehouse, and forgets about it. Then one day the king's pet monkey retrieves one of these half-rotted fruits and brings it to him. Hidden within this fruit, as in every one of the others lying in a jumbled heap in the dark storehouse, is an incorruptible jewel.[42]

Thus it is with the ordinary sensory impressions of our everyday life, in which the arrogant intellect and ambitious ego see nothing of value. If we wish to recover the intelligence of feeling we were endowed with at birth—what Dante calls the *intelletto d'amore,* the intellect of love—we will have to enter the dark storehouse of memory—the Underworld, where Orpheus sought Eurydice and through which Dante had to pass on his way to reunion with Beatrice and a view of the universe as it is. "We have today to gather our dismembered hearts, as Isis gathered Osiris, piece by piece from where we left the fragments deposited long ago, hidden in the forgotten particular sensations of childhood."[43] As T. S. Eliot recognized in his definition of the "objective correlative," feeling is hidden in, and communicated through, particular sensory images.

Each of us has to make this journey to the Underworld for himself or herself, for we are speaking of the particulars of immediate experience. I myself will plunge into it in chapter 5 of this book—but first I have to throw a sop to the discursive intellect, which, like Cerberus, the ravenous monster dog at the entrance to Hades, must be satisfied before it will consent to keep silence.

There have been many recent attempts to discern and articulate "the new paradigm," but no one seems to have noticed the strangeness of trying to present a "holistic" world view in the language of one small part of the psyche. Thus we have whole books written on the subject of participatory observation in nonparticipatory language, and arguments for the superiority of the intelligence of the body or of the heart written in this same language, as if the discursive reason were trying to talk itself into abdicating.

But discursive reason will have to learn to be still so that we can hear, like the boy in the Iroquois tale, the stories the rocks are telling us—"tongues in trees, books in the running brooks, sermons in stones."[44] The lost language of the whole, in which a whole world view will have ultimately to be presented, is the language of poetry. By that I mean language that does not necessarily make use of rhyme and meter but that embodies idea and feeling in sensory images (and sound, rhythm, relative speeds within sentences, and weights and textures of words are also sensory images, speaking to the inner ear and to the kinesthetic and architectonic senses of the body) and incarnates what is beyond opposites, and hence beyond words, in vivid sensory symbols.

Life does not present itself to us with explanatory placards on its chest, and so we need to learn to perceive meaning directly, by some method quicker and subtler than analysis and explanation—some method that does not "murder to dissect." God is in the details, which we ignore while trying to tease out the meaning of life with the blunt instrument of verbal explanation so that we are always "thinking"—or, in any case, mechanical inner talking is going on in us, taking with it what attention we have—and are deaf and blind to what is shouting at us in front of our noses. *Look. Look well.* Nirvana and samsara are not-two.

True poetry (or any other true art) presents samsara in such a way that you can see nirvana in it, without any need for explanation. This is what James Joyce meant by *epiphany.* The influence of art of this intensity is such that when you look up from the book or away from the painting or emerge from the concert hall, opera house, or theater, you see the world like that for a while, in inner silence, vibrant with meaning.

Poetry has the power to speak from and to the mind, heart, and body all at once and to communicate the experience of unity in multiplicity directly through its form. That form will be the form (or lack of it) of the prevailing image of the universe. Dante's *Divine Comedy* has the form of the medieval universe, which the poet as protagonist explores from bottom to top. T. S. Eliot's "'The Waste Land,' on the other hand, is a series of discrete fragments which...reflects quite clearly the prevalent cosmology of Eliot's day: an infinite universe where motion is relative, where there are no fixed points, in which only the subjective response of the individual percipient gives any sense of order or of limit."[45]

"You know only a heap of broken images," says Eliot to his reader, and his poem has that form or, rather, formlessness: the form of a collection of fragments; whereas Dante's poem is the story of a pilgrimage from a view of the world as a meaningless chaos to a vision of the point of it all—the meaning and aim of existence—and the form of the universe gradually reveals itself to him as he slowly traverses it, two steps forward, one step back, in *terza rima,* until he reaches a height from which he can see the whole at once, of himself and of the world. His pilgrimage through the universe is at the same time an ordering of his psyche, because psyche and cosmological image mirror each other.

Because Dante's universe has a geometric form, the body can also participate in knowledge of it. In order to be of use to you in everyday life, an image of the universe—that navigational chart—has to speak to the body. It has to be portable, to fit into the body's sensation of itself, so that you can learn it by heart and carry it with you at all times in the wordless memory of your muscles, just as you carry an invisible map of the city you live in: it folds up like an umbrella when you go down into the subway, and then, when you come out onto the street, snaps open, so that you know without thinking about it where you are, which way is uptown, which way is downtown, which way to turn to get where you want to go.

The body's sense of itself underlies our sense of structure, of organization, of coherence. Because it is itself a cosmos, the body gives us immediate, wordless experience of what a cosmos is: *e pluribus unum*, a living, functioning unity composed of many parts. By virtue of its flexible, all-enclosing skin, the body imagines topologically, like Martha Graham inside her tube of stretchable jersey (supposing she could have sewn it closed at both ends). Without changing position, it can sense itself in any size or any shape—curled up in a ball, or with an arm poking out here, a leg there, creating a pattern of wrinkles, stresses, and strains in the field of sensation—so long as there is *some* shape, some topological totality it can crawl inside (as into Dr. Dolittle's sea-snail shell) or shrink down and take into itself. This faculty of intentional bodily imagination underlies our capacity to put ourselves in the place of another person or thing and know, not theoretically but in the sensation of our own bodies, what it feels like to be that other.

This is a way of knowing that was familiar to us all as children. ("Crunch! Crunch! I'm a goat out to lunch!" began a book my children once owned.) It is still familiar, Jamake Highwater tells us, to primal peoples. "American Indians...look at reality in a way that makes it possible for them to know something by temporarily turning into it."[46] The whole body becomes an organ of perception. This is the way we would have to know a cosmology if it were to serve for orientation in everyday life.

Thanks to the overall form of Dante's cosmos, it is possible, in what we might call the architectonic imagination of the body, "temporarily to turn into" it and, in what we might call topological imagination, to experience the changes in the way Dante perceives its form as he passes through it. After departing from the formless chaos of the Dark Wood, he descends into Hell: a hollow inverted cone with its apex at the center of the earth, the center of gravity of the whole medieval universe. Then he ascends the island mountain of Purgatory: an upright cone with the Earthly Paradise (the Garden of Eden) on its summit. When he reaches that summit, Virgil will leave him and Beatrice will become his guide through Paradise proper, which is a double set of nested concentric spheres, first increasing, then decreasing, in diameter but always increasing in speed of revolution.

Two cones are topologically equivalent to a sphere. When Dante has traversed Hell and Purgatory and is united with Beatrice, his being is whole. The sphere has always been a symbol of perfection (completeness, wholeness). The cones of Hell and Purgatory were partial views of the same universe that Dante now sees as spherical. Before he could *see* whole, he had to *be* whole. This is something our science forgot.

If, in our search for the country home, my sister and I could have pushed our way back through time, we would have found the cabin itself and the people still alive inside it: our mother, father, and brother; our aunt; and our uncle, who owned the house and tried to pass on to us the lore and skills of the wilderness. That's what the physicists are doing today: in their search for unity, they are pushing their way back through time to the origin of the universe. Their thirst for unity is as passionate as Dante's, and yet it is not the same because it animates only a small part of the psyche. Their cosmology cannot help us see, as Dante's could, how we ought to live our lives and to what purpose. Just the same, it is a cosmology—a shape—which is more than we have had for four hundred years.

As C. S. Lewis says, "In every period the Model of the Universe which is accepted by the great thinkers helps to provide what we may call a backcloth for the arts. But this backcloth...takes over from the total Model only what is intelligible to a layman and only what makes some appeal to imagination and emotion."[47] The

concentric crystalline spheres of Dante's universe were a simplified version of what professional astronomers of the time saw as
a tangle of epicycles, deferents, and eccentrics. The picture of the
universe as a system of concentric circles or spheres, which was
arrived at in the fourth century B.C. and lasted until well into the
seventeenth century A.D., "gives no meaningful indication of relative dimensions of the various orbits, and...makes no attempt to
provide for the observed planetary irregularities. But...the most
influential cosmologies developed in antiquity and the Middle
Ages did not follow ancient astronomy very far beyond this
point...[because] its further development does not provide man
with a home."[48]

A simplified picture of the new cosmology, such as the sphere
Stephen Hawking shows us in his best-selling *A Brief History of
Time* (figure 3.13), with the big bang at the North Pole and the big
crunch at the South Pole,[49] will suffice for us "artists and laymen"
who are trying, not to have power over nature, but to visualize our
place in it as a help to us in our need to understand why we are
here on the earth and how we ought to live.

The sphere that Hawking shows us is really a 3-sphere: a three-
dimensional surface embedded in four-dimensional space, with
time ("imaginary time") treated as the fourth dimension. Mark
Peterson of the physics department at Amherst College has noticed that Dante's universe is also a 3-sphere.[50] This means that
our picture of the universe not only has an imaginable form again
but also has the same form it always had, understood in a new
way. Dante's house is still habitable, though we certainly cannot
use his medieval furniture.

Moving into the new model—the New World—is like the
"mythological process...to which the late Dr. Ananda K.
Coomaraswamy referred as *land nama*, 'land naming,' or 'land
taking.' Through land-nama...the features of a newly entered
land are assimilated by an immigrant people to its imported heri-
tage of myth."[51] In the new terrain we begin to recognize the old
gods, as Greeks entering Rome recognized Zeus in Jupiter,
Aphrodite in Venus, and Hermes in Mercury; or as European

Christians entering America recognized (or should have) the Holy Spirit in *Wakan-Tanka*.

Now we can recognize that what gravity represented psychologically for Dante, entropy represents for us, and what the Pole Star was for primal peoples—the door of "the entering in of time from the halls of the outer heaven"[52]—the big bang is for us. As Joseph Campbell said, "Just bring your old religion into a new set of metaphors, and you've got it."[53]

Verification of the real existence of the sacred has been restored to us through the practice of authentic spiritual disciplines that do not merely sermonize about it but instruct us in practical methods for opening ourselves to its direct presence and influence. Long practice can bring us to moments of inner stillness and immediate experience of a presence that transcends the conditions created by the logical mind, a vibrant living force that is at the same time inner and outer—more mine than anything and yet belonging to everybody. This presence is not subject to space or time or any other conditions and hence was present "before the big bang" and can be schematically represented on our diagram "north of the North Pole." Not being subject to space and time, it is also here and now and amounts to a new way of *seeing*. Father Berry describes it:

> We need only look at the surrounding universe in its more opaque material aspects—look at it, listen to it, feel and experience the full depths of its being. Suddenly its opaque quality, its resistance, falls away, and we enter into a world of mystery. What seemed so opaque and impenetrable suddenly becomes radiant with intelligibility, powerful beyond imagination.[54]

This experience is the product of *attention*.

Accustomed to search for general laws, or ego satisfactions, or material gain—or even "spiritual development"—we have trouble, like the arrogant elder brothers in the fairy tales, in recognizing the cosmic value of particular sensory details. "I want to know how God created this world," said Einstein. "I am not interested in this or that phenomenon...I want to know His thoughts; the rest are details."[55] This same wish was expressed by Galileo and is expressed today by Stephen Hawking.

But God is *in* the details—as well as "before the big bang." His eye is on the sparrow—and in the sparrow. To see God in the details is the task of the poet. To reconnect (*re-ligio*) with the unconditioned power that was before the world began, and is, and ever shall be, is the aim of one who labors and suffers in an authentic spiritual discipline. A theoretical physicist is not qualified to speak about these realms unless his training in poetry or spiritual disciplines matches his training in physics. As Ken Wilber says, "Mathematical knowledge is public knowledge to all equally trained mathematicians; just so, contemplative knowledge is public knowledge to all equally trained contemplatives."[56]

The contempt of an expert in one field for experts in other fields reflects the situation within the psyche of each of us when we have learned to respect some forms of our own perception and intelligence but not others, the physicist but not the poet. "Our gods of reason and truth," notes Ravi Ravindra, "admit physics in their temples, but not poetry and painting."[57] As for the priest, we notice that our parents make jokes about him at the dinner table—as Stephen Hawking pokes sly fun at the pope in *A Brief History of Time*, confident that his reader will share his attitude:

> [The pope] told us that it was all right to study the evolution of the universe after the big bang, but we should not inquire into the big bang itself because that was the moment of Creation and therefore the work of God. I was glad then that he did not know the subject of the talk I had just given at the conference—the possibility that space-time was finite but had no boundary, which means that it had no beginning, no moment of Creation. I had no desire to share the fate of Galileo....[58]

Nevertheless, the pope was right—or nearly so: the expertise of the physicist may extend to the big bang but cannot extend "before" it (or "north of the North Pole," in the "finite but unbounded" supposition) because his knowledge is of events in space and time and not—unless he happens to be at the same time a seasoned practitioner of an authentic spiritual discipline—of the Unconditioned.

The advent of practical spiritual teachers from the East has given us (along with sometimes rueful experience in the course of learning to distinguish between the authentic and the bogus) experience of genuine accomplishment in this realm, manifested not so much in language, though often there too, as in *being*, unmistakably experienced as a silent power of presence and manifested in an overwhelming energy, originality, magnanimity, wisdom, capacity for work, and kindness.

Both poetic and spiritual knowledge are the fruits of immediate experience, without the intervention of any technological instruments, or even of thought, in the sense of "talking about it"— although a great deal of explanatory talk may be necessary at the outset for those of us who are unaccustomed to any other kind of knowledge. Thus, in this book I begin with explanatory talk in order to satisfy that part of my mind (and yours) that feeds on explanations, in the hope that, satisfied, it will then fall silent and allow the holy details to stand forth in an atmosphere of silent attentiveness.

Scrutiny of the history of science reveals how (through no fault of scientists, ever absorbed in their own pursuits) we nonscientists made an epistemological mistake of the first order, humbly accepting a severely partial view of reality for the whole. Thus we learn to be ashamed of whole realms of our own immediate perception until they sink into the underworld of unconsciousness. My hope is that the reader and I will both take courage and return to a religious attentiveness to our own perceptions, pursuing knowledge according to the principle that the most complete knowledge possible to us would make use of all aspects of those perceptions and of the perceptions of all our faculties: intellect, feeling, and the whole symphony of senses, the classical five plus all the subtler ones we become aware of by paying attention to what takes place in the body's sensation of itself.

Take, for example, your grandmother. How can you know her—know the whole truth of her, what she really is?

You can regard her as made of elementary particles moving in accord with the laws of physics, and that will be correct. You can study her in terms of chemistry and biochemistry, and that will also be correct. You can study her anatomically and physiologically, and that too will be correct.

But none of these will give you the whole picture. Even psychology cannot do that—cannot show you *her*. If you want to know *her*, you cannot do better than to sit down opposite her and look at her and listen to her—which is to say, pay *attention* to her, right there before your eyes, and more than your eyes. You talk to her and she tells you about herself, not only in the content of her words but in the quality of her voice, which resonates in your body and transmits information about her. Your body senses her physical presence as a kind of field of force with certain individual qualities, and if you are attentive to what takes place in this sensation of your own body in her presence (here, now, today—on another occasion it might be different), you will gradually realize that certain facts about her inner state are being communicated to you through this form of perception too.

Last, if you have the courage and sufficient self-discipline to shut up and become still inside (and if she will let you), look into her eyes. Then you will understand that with all our sciences we know nothing about what anything or anybody *is*. Before and behind and after and within, there is and was and always will be mystery: the Unconditioned, before which we fall silent.

We can say nothing about it, and yet we can experience it immediately as more real than anything. That Unconditioned is unaffected by changes in our cosmology. It is as present "before the big bang" as it is at the summit and quick of Dante's universe.

This is the way children, poets, and Native Americans (if Jamake Highwater is right) look at the earth and surrounding nature. If you listen, things will speak to you—and the earth is now shouting. Demeter is calling to Zeus to restore her daughter, Persephone, to the light of day, and until we can once more see the daughter—the soul of Nature, see Nature as subject as well as object—the mother, Demeter, will allow us to destroy all she has bestowed upon us.

Psychologists of the school called "object relations" tell us that we fail to reach complete maturity because we never succeed in seeing our own mother as subject—as living, sentient, intelligent, conscious—and the same applies to our perception of nature, and even of other people. This individual failure reflects the collective historical situation, which feminists attribute to the prevalence of patriarchy and I, to the tyranny of one part of the psyche over the rest (though the two articulations amount, *au fond*, to the same thing).

In the psyche there is indeed a rightful ruler, but it is not the mechanical logic that for four hundred years (or maybe twenty-four hundred, if Cammerloher is right) arrogantly usurped the name of reason. This rightful ruler is a kind of silent attentiveness that transcends the distinction between intellect and feeling, is inseparable from caring, looks with an equal eye upon inner phenomena (thoughts, emotions, sensations) and outer, and has on everything it shines upon an ordering and healing effect.

Pursued with enough inner stillness and attention, this kind of knowledge can bring us experience of the sacred in each other, just as it can in nature. What we are after is not power but love, and, according to Wagner in the *Ring* cycle (and we need no Wagner to tell us), the exchange in the other direction is what is destroying us. Ecology and feminism together have brought us the courage to believe in the richness of the whole symphony of our forms of perception and to break out of the prison of the fear of ridicule that our education has built around us, always implying that everything we can see for ourselves beyond the primary qualities is "nothing but" wishful thinking, pathetic fallacy, primitive animism, anthropomorphism, sentimentality, or whatever term of condescension best suits the attitude toward it you felt emanating from the adults around you while you were growing up.

Science must take its place as presenting us with only some, and by no means all, of the aspects of reality accessible to us. It makes use of only a small part of our total human endowment of instruments for perception and action. It is science that must bring us the *form* of our cosmology because we could not believe in it if it came from any other source. The new cosmology has indeed brought us the form of our new poem, our Divine Comedy, and, as we shall see in more detail in chapter 3, it turns out to be the same as the form of the old one.

This does not mean that we once more visualize the universe as geocentric. The places in the pattern are occupied by different entities, but the pattern is the same.

A cosmological image—which, during the period of its hegemony, is the paradigm of wholeness and hence the model for any human enterprise—is born, grows to perfection, disintegrates—or is struck, like the medieval one, a mortal blow—and dies. Then, after a period of chaos such as we have all lived through in this century, a new image—or a new understanding of the perennial one—may germinate and grow. The communal cosmological image rises and falls like a long breath. This curve is its shape (as it is the shape of any living thing) in the dimension of time.

The universe did not change at the time of the Copernican revolution. The way we imagine it changed, and that changed everything.

Now the way we imagine it is changing again. The subject of cosmology, after an absence of four hundred years, has reappeared in our textbooks of physics and astronomy. The physical sciences have restored to us the image of a shape, in space-time, of the whole. Inevitably, this shape is mathematical and abstract—constructed solely of "primary qualities." Can the total imagination, of mind, heart, and sense, move into it, as a living hermit crab moves into an empty shell?

That is the maneuver I intend to essay in this book.

The Meaning of Meaning

His sickness was only part of something larger, and his cure
would be found only in something great and inclusive of
everything.   LESLIE MARMON SILKO, *Ceremony*

...becoming a particle, though an independent one, of every-
thing existing in the Great Universe.
                                    G. I. GURDJIEFF, *All and Everything*

Wisdom is the central form which gives meaning and position
to all the facts which are acquired by knowledge.
                                    NORTHROP FRYE, *Fearful Symmetry*

During the 1960s, great numbers of people began to ask, aloud
and in public, a question human beings have no doubt been asking
themselves since the beginning of time—if they stopped to think,
and if their society had no ready-made answer for them: "What
is the meaning of life?" After a while, the question became a cliché
and then a joke, and now, since it seems to have no answer that
could satisfy the critical intellect, we are embarrassed to ask it.
Nevertheless, if you get to any depth in conversation with anyone,
it turns out that however dazzling our way of life may look exter-
nally, we all suffer from a feeling of meaninglessness.

What is this *meaning* that human beings seem to need as a plant
needs water and an animal, food? If we wish for something so
much as to feel it as a need, we ought to be able at least to *imagine*
what it is, whether or not it is attainable in practical life.

When I was an English major in the forties, on the suggested
reading list there was a book by I. A. Richards called *The Meaning
of Meaning*. Long after the contents of that book had faded from
my memory, its title continued to torment me because it made me
realize that regardless of what "meaning" meant to I. A. Richards,

I could not—although I had a kind of inner sensation of it—define what I myself meant by the word.

After a while, I concluded that what I meant by the meaning of anything was its *place in a pattern*. What I was visualizing was not an allover, indefinitely repeating pattern such as you sometimes see on wallpaper, but a topological entity: something with a boundary, though perhaps a flexible one. ("Form"—or maybe "gestalt"—would have been a better word, but "pattern" was the one that came to me at the time.) If the whole had no pattern, the part could have no meaning. It was lost in a chaos without a center, a principle of unity, a "point."

"Pattern" is one word for the way a multiplicity of things can be, at the same time, a unity. The pattern itself may be invisible. Like one of the hypothetical "morphogenetic fields" that may organize developing embryonic tissues, it is a matrix of tensions, or lines of force, along which the manifest details arrange themselves so that every detail can resonate with every other.[1] The place of the detail in relation to all the others and to the whole defines its meaning.

Its place defines what it is, as with a note in a scale. If the same detail enters the dominion of another pattern, it has a different meaning, just as the note G has the meaning *sol* in the C major scale and *do* in its own scale. Without a sense of the whole, it is impossible to see the meaning of the detail, just as it is impossible to understand the meaning of a foreign word unless you know what language is being spoken. In a different language, the same sound may have a different meaning.

This understanding is not, moreover, a matter of intellect alone. The whole meaning of a word, buzzing and twanging like a bullroarer with the reverberations of thousands of years of human experience, may be forever inaccessible to anyone who is not a native and lover of that tongue. For me, a Chinese character is a momentarily interesting shape, but for the Chinese, as Ernest Fenollosa said, "Their ideographs are like blood-stained battleflags to an old campaigner."[2]

In my long-ago ponderings I concluded that in order to feel that my life had meaning, I would have to feel that I had a place in a pattern. Later, that formulation seemed too static—even imprisoning, as for the lady in Amy Lowell's poem "Patterns": "Christ! What are patterns for?" she cries.[3] The social conventions of her time fit her as tightly as her fashionable corset. She cannot breathe.

That is an interesting case in point. She is confined within a *meaningless* pattern—or one whose meaning she does not understand. If the pattern were *for* something worthwhile, it would not be meaningless, and if, in addition, the lady understood what it was for, it would not be meaningless to *her*.

Here we come to the element of *purpose*. The lady in Lowell's poem is trapped within a pattern that people have gone on repeating long after it has lost all connection with its purpose. That was the case for many people (especially women) in Lowell's time, but beginning with World War I, these long-unquestioned patterns of social behavior began, one after another, to be abandoned, until now, indeed, we are free of them all but don't know what to do—on what basis, beyond "gut reaction," to distinguish right from wrong.

How to be free and at the same time live with meaning? That is the problem.

I decided that for one thing, the pattern had to be *moving*, like a dance—a four-dimensional pattern—or like music, in which an invisible unifying force is everywhere felt (however subliminally to the nonmusician) and exerts a unifying effect upon the listener. A pattern has a total shape in space, and a piece of music or a dance has a shape in time as well, so that if you yourself are participating in such a pattern you can know where you are, not only in space, in relation to the other players or dancers, but also in time—where you are in the sequence. Thus you know what to do—what note to play, what position to take, what move to make—next.

You know what to do not passively, because somebody is telling you, but because, like Nicholas Slonimsky in a story Lawrence Weschler once told in the *New Yorker*, you know the whole pattern by heart:

...as we walked back toward the car I returned to Villa-Lobos. "Were you serious?" I asked. "Have you really not played that piece in twenty years?"

"Well," he admitted sheepishly, "actually, I was cheating there a little bit. It just happens I was thinking about that piece this morning, and I rehearsed it in my head in the shower."

"In the shower?"

"Well, you know, the fingering."

Quite a vision. I asked him what it was he was remembering when he remembered a piece like that. Was it the sound of the music or the sight of the printed page?

"Neither," he replied. "I remember the structure."[4]

To know something by heart really means, first of all, to know it by body. Because the body is, among other things, a structure, it remembers structure. After many repetitions, many run-throughs (for ordinary people, that is—a genius might get it at first glance), the total four-dimensional structure of a dance or a piece of music becomes engraved, as it were, in your flesh.

Although you know that when you perform it, you will unroll it in linear time, you have the impression that what you remember is present inside you all at once: the structure. The body has the capacity to conceive and retain the image of a four-dimensional form—which is not so surprising, since the body is itself a form of at least four dimensions, with a shape in time (entering space-time as a point sphere, expanding to its mature stature, then shrinking, shriveling, falling to dust) as well as in space.

"If you memorize any work," says poet Robert Bly, "you bring it into the body. And then you are participating in space. And then it can become sacred space."[5] And Rabbi Eliezer: "Whoever busies himself with a piece of poetry...in this world is privileged to recite it in the world to come."[6]

If it is only the body that is involved, though, learning is not, properly speaking, by heart but by rote—a dull and automatic process, grudgingly engaged in. (A second meaning of "rote," not officially etymologically related but highly suggestive, is "the sound of the surf beating on the shore."[7] To learn by rote is to learn by attrition.) The body goes through its motions while mind and heart are altogether elsewhere. That, indeed, alas, is usually the case.

But to learn by heart must originally have implied willing participation, *con amore*, with an ardent desire, a longing to take part, an enthusiasm for the undertaking. In the beginning, this ardent desire to participate, and to outdo oneself and play one's part well, usually has its source in one's love and admiration for, and hunger to attract the attention of, a teacher—and the concomitant desire to beat out one's fellow students. In time, though, the participant may begin to experience something else—something less "outer-directed."

For myself, it was participation in the mathematically organized sacred dances created by G. I. Gurdjieff that made me aware of the direct experience (not in words but in immediate bodily sensation) of what I came to call a *patterning force*, and that experience made it possible for me to recognize the same force at work in nature.

Some of the Gurdjieff sacred dances, or "Movements," make a tremendous demand on your attention. There may be, for example, a repeating sequence of six head positions, body bends repeating on counts one and four, a rhythm marked by the feet, and a pattern of eight steps; the left arm may spell out words in Morse code, and the right may be engaged in marking the positions of the periodic decimals corresponding to fractions of one-seventh, two-sevenths, and so forth, on an enneagram (a circle whose circumference is divided into nine equal parts) visualized in the air in front of you. Even in the simpler Movements you must strive to make every position exact, and that means that you cannot take the position automatically but must be aware of it through immediate inner sensation.

The rigor of the external demand is an enormous help in summoning attention, silencing automatic thoughts, and replacing habitual postures—prerequisites to any kind of meditation. When you have struggled until you feel you can do no more, another force may, at rare moments, take over, and the dance seems to do itself while you breathe the clarity and freshness of what feels like another air, permeated at the same time with love and freedom—feelings that, on our usual level of life, may seem contradictory.

It is the rare advent of this "other force" that transforms the psyche from a Rube Goldberg machine into a living creature. It is as if you were struggling to put together the disassembled parts of a robot—springs, screws, computer chips, tangled wires, indecipherable circuit boards, levers—scattered everywhere, when suddenly something from above touches all this mess and it springs up as a living, moving, breathing, human being.

If we are instructed in means of striving toward *it*, there is a force that moves toward *us* in response and has the power to make a harmonious whole out of the cacophony of our thoughts, emotions, and actions. It is experienced from within as an attention of an intensity, penetration, and intelligence of another level that shocks awake and unifies the attention of all our parts so that all of them—ordinarily hankering in conflicting directions—sit up, recognize, and acknowledge this attention as what they have always wanted but could not name.

Once I had tasted a single drop of this patterning, unifying force, there were moments when I could see, feel, and sense it at work in nature, forever creating living forms out of the materials at hand and then breaking them down in order to free the matter and energy contained in them for participation in other living forms. If I ate a carrot or an apple, for example, the matter that had been under the dominion of those forms came for a while under the dominion of the form of my body—just as my body, which had been a drop in the turbulent stream of a rush-hour subway crowd, participated for a while, like a cell in a living organism, in the incarnation of a dance.

After seeing a program of the Gurdjieff Movements, Joseph Campbell remarked, "This is meditation in motion." I think "contemplation" is a better word, because "meditation" has taken on for us the connotation of thinking long thoughts about something, whereas what is described here requires inner stillness—or at least a space of silent listening amid the chaos and din of automatic inner talking that goes on in us all the time. That inner stillness and that ardent attentiveness are conditions for inviting the response of a unifying force from above.

Such experiences, which carry with them the sensation of unification, or inner ordering, are like diagrams drawn in the flesh. One experiences the action of a force with a direction, like an incarnate vector pointing in the direction of "negentropy." Something emotional resonates to this sensation and responds, "*That* is what I have always wished for but could not name!" Something sunlike draws me toward the center and summit of myself. It demands something from me: an effort, a response. So long as I am under that influence, and open to it, the whole of me responds with a willingness to try, fueled by a longing to draw closer to its unseen source.

When I step outside the field of this influence, I fall apart again. Arriving impressions have no meaning for me, and however busily I run around in all directions, I really don't know what to do. Each action has some isolated, short-term purpose, but there is no overriding, all-embracing purpose to which it relates and from which it derives its meaning. I am back in Dante's Dark Wood, or in T. S. Eliot's Waste Land, where, like the third Thames-daughter, "I can connect/Nothing with nothing."[8]

But the experience of harmonization, however momentary, has given me a taste, in feeling and sensation, of what it would be like to live with meaning—to live in a cosmos.

There are other aids in the world, besides deliberate spiritual exercises like the Gurdjieff Movements or Zen "sitting," that have the power to bring you—if you approach them in an attitude of attentive receptivity—a taste of this unifying, harmonizing force. You may experience something like this when you step inside the Gothic Cathedral of Notre Dame at Chartres. You may feel the stab of response to the call of it when you see rising in the distance Mont-Saint-Michel surging up from the sea, with the archangel Michael at its summit, foot on the dragon, sword uplifted toward the sky. There are many places such as these on the earth where the sacred, having first given specifications for the building of a temple or an ark into which it could descend, has dwelt for a time among us.

The sacred itself is impossible to describe because it transcends all our categories and the very conditions of our perception and our language. Nevertheless, the immediate experience of its presence is so real that it makes everything else look wispy and evanescent in itself, though real in the sense that everything alive is an "ark" for the sacred. When I perceive myself as such a vessel, I become able to see the sacred in every living creature.

The specifications the sacred gives for its vessel—for a building and a people (a "church")—amount to a paradigm of wholeness: of unity in multiplicity. Those charged with the responsibility for erecting the edifice have left us accounts of the experience. In addition to the descriptions in the Old Testament of how Jehovah charged Solomon with the building of the Temple and Noah with the building of the Ark (giving, in both cases, the most exact specifications), we have the legend of how, in A.D. 708, Saint Aubert, bishop of Avranches, founded the Benedictine abbey on Mont-Saint-Michel in response to orders from the archangel Michael himself, who appeared to Aubert in three separate visions and who, when the bishop persisted in procrastinating, was obliged to threaten him with the loss of his head.

Closer to us, we have Black Elk's tragic account of how, in his own Great Vision, the Six Grandfathers charged him with repairing the hoop of his nation and how, in his own eyes, he failed.[9]

Sometimes the specifications have been for the transformation of an individual human being, who thenceforth, for a time, has served as that temple or ark and whose life story becomes a model to be followed by others in pursuit of perfection. A creation myth (the *legomenon*) and accompanying ritual (*dromenon*), dictated to the shaman and repeated at the beginning of every communal undertaking as a model of the right way to proceed in bringing any earthly work to perfection, is another kind of ark: participating together in its recitation and reenactment, the tribe is united into one living being.

"But the Middle Ages depended predominantly on books,"[10]

and so, at that time, the sacred built itself a dwelling place not only in the great cathedrals but also in a single great poem, the *Divine Comedy*, which was dictated to the poet, as he tells us, by Love.

> "*I' mi son un che, quando*
> *Amor mi spira, noto, e a quel modo*
> *ch'e' ditta dentro vo significando.*"

> "I am one who, when Love
> Breathes in me, pays attention, and I go along
> Writing it down as he dictates it within me."[11]

I believe that just as the force that draws an apple to the ground—as Newton (or so the story goes) suddenly recognized—is the same force that keeps the moon in orbit around the earth, this unifying force that we can experience directly, immediately, in our very flesh—temporarily, through attentive participation in a ritual or work of art or through inner stillness in the presence of nature or of one of those dwelling-places of the sacred, or in a more sustained way, through deliberate search and long practice of an authentic spiritual discipline—is the same force that has drawn forward the evolution of living forms since the beginning of the universe.

> ...more delicate, elusive, quicker than the fins in water, is that mysterious principle known as "organization."...Like some dark and passing shadow within matter, it cups out the eyes' small windows or spaces the notes of a meadow lark's song in the interior of a mottled egg. That principle—I am beginning to suspect—was there before the living in the deeps of water.[12]

This force cannot be measured by any scientific instrument because we ourselves are the instruments for its detection. Its action upon us depends upon our awareness of its presence, and the measure of that action, upon our degree of openness to it.

The effects of a patterning, unifying, relational force are everywhere apparent in the natural evolution of ever-more-inclusive levels of organization: subatomic particles, atoms, molecules, cells, organs, organisms, and the human brain, which is the most highly organized entity we know of. Physicist and Nobel laureate Richard P. Feynman expressed the reductionist view that has prevailed in science since the time of Galileo when he said, "There is nothing that living things do that cannot be understood from the point of view that they are made of atoms acting according to the laws of physics."[13] But Alfred North Whitehead's philosophy of organism, Norbert Wiener's cybernetics, and now the rapidly developing field of systems theory have made it respectable to acknowledge that isolation of ultimate particles and forces (definition of material and efficient causes, in Aristotle's terms, to the neglect of formal and final causes) can never provide more than a partial explanation of any phenomenon, since—especially in the case of living things—the whole is clearly more than the sum of the parts.

> ...if two particles are put together in an "organized" way, instead of the formula $1+1=2$, we get $1+1>2$, and...this is the basic equation of biology. Thus if an electron and a nucleus come together in an organized way, a hydrogen atom is born, which is more than an electron and a nucleus. If atoms are built into a molecule, something new is born, which can no longer be described solely in terms of atoms. The same holds true when small molecules are built into macromolecules; macromolecules into organelles; organelles into cells; cells into organs; organs into individuals; and individuals into a society or ecological "associes."[14]

"General system theory...is scientific exploration of 'wholes' and 'wholeness.'"[15] (General system theory, then—although I have never heard any systems theorist use these terms—could be defined as scientific exploration of cosmoses and cosmicity, using the term "cosmos" in its broadest sense as referring to a whole on any scale, from submicroscopic to universal.) This exploration discovers the same laws at work in systems on the most diverse scales and in the most diverse realms, from atoms to societies. These laws are reminiscent of Gurdjieff's universal "Law of Octaves,"[16] because they pertain to the state of a system in relation to equilibrium: at equilibrium (*do*), near it (*mi*), far from it but in a steady state (*sol*), or far from equilibrium and fluctuating (*si*), in which state, as Ilya Prigogine and Isabelle Stengers have demonstrated, the whole system may suddenly leap into a whole new order of organization.[17]

It behooves us to study the extremely interesting evolutionary processes now being scrutinized and clarified in systems theory[18] because when evolution reaches the level of the human brain, it crosses the "brain-mind frontier" into the realm of the psyche, and after that the continuation or noncontinuation of the process is up to us and depends, first of all, upon our own understanding. The universe is "self-organizing" up to a point, and that point is in us: the body is self-organized, but the psyche will not be organized unless we hear about, come into contact with, and open voluntarily to the organizing force within and above us.

Understanding evolves in the same way as natural systems do. Each new level, whether of being or of knowledge, encompasses all the previous levels and manifests the inauguration of the dominion of a still more powerful—at the same time more concentrated and more comprehensive—unifying principle. It is as if, as the reach of its organizing power encompasses more and more diversity, the unifying principle itself goes deeper and deeper, approaching closer and closer to the center and unifying principle of the Whole.

This evolutionary process is not continuous but proceeds, when a system reaches a state far from equilibrium, by sudden leaps, as if by inspiration or revelation. The moment of the leap, from atom to molecule, from molecule to cell, from cell to organism, resembles those moments when, after long and anguished searching, there leaps into the mind of the scientist (from he knows not where) a theory that brings into order a vast realm of formerly unrelated data; or into the awareness of the poet the presentiment of a poem—the almost physical sensation that there is now something inside him that will give him no rest until he succeeds in bringing it to birth and precise articulation, and within whose form all the contradictory experiences of his life up to this time will take their places in harmonious relationship so that, at last, their meaning will be revealed to him.

We had the experience but missed the meaning,
And approach to the meaning restores the experience
In a different form, beyond any meaning
We can assign to happiness.[19]

"Harmonizing" is a better word than "unifying" for the evolutionary ordering principle, since its action is not homogenizing.
Its products are not monoliths but living organisms. "Things
composite," as Saint Augustine puts it, "imitate unity by the
harmony of their parts";[20] and according to Julian Huxley, "the
trend is towards more harmonious integration of the individual
organism as a whole. Progress, from this aspect, is characterized
by an increase of variety-in-unity."[21] This is the same criterion
that James Caldwell, one of my Berkeley English professors, gave
us for judging the relative value of poems—that is, the greater the
variety of experience the poet had succeeded in encompassing and
harmonizing within it, the greater the poem.

We go along perceiving, experiencing, studying, trying to understand. We eat ideas, information, and experiences. Just as the
matter or energy that was once in the dominion of the form of a
carrot or cow comes under the dominion of the form of my body,
information that was part of a book, or impressions that were
part of an experience, can be digested (but only through my own
active effort) into my own "body of thought"—can be, but aren't,
because without a cosmology we can have no single body of
thought. Partial and mutually exclusive world views, unrelated
bits of knowledge, and isolated fragments of memory lie about in
us like the ruins of old civilizations, or like the pieces of the chess
game that, after the Flood, a new generation of Norse gods finds
lying about in the still-wet grass.[22] A resurrected body of thought,
in which all these fragments have a place and thereby a meaning,
will require a new cosmological image as its all-encompassing
skin.

In my groping for clarity about what I meant by meaning, I
eventually began to understand that in order for our lives to have
meaning, the pattern in which we participate must also be *alive*.

That makes the meaning of the part its function—the role it was designed to play somewhere in the dynamic hierarchy of the structure and functioning of the living organism of the whole. Beyond that, this organism would have to be a *conscious* one, with an aim. If the whole has no purpose, the part can have no ultimate purpose either.

Finally, the organism of the whole has to be in some sense a person: it has to be *some one*, in order for the part to feel related to it. It is not possible to feel related to an *it*, as Martin Buber has pointed out to us, but only to a *thou*—a *you*, as we would say.[23]

Meaning is the relation of the part to the whole. In order for the part to know that its existence has meaning, it needs to have some vision of the whole and of its own place and function within it and to feel and sense a reciprocal relationship between itself and the omnipresent unifying principle, however unknowable, of the whole. Our feeling of meaninglessness is a consequence of the way we have long accepted to imagine the universe: as formless, dead, devoid of sensitivity, consciousness, or purpose—an endless desert of swirling dust.

To be able, like the poor, disposable girl in T. S. Eliot's poem, to connect nothing with nothing is absolute meaninglessness, and absolute meaninglessness, according to Maurice Nicoll, is hell.[24] That is where we have been living for four hundred years.

What is the meaning of, say, a liver cell? It has to maintain its own life, of course, but that would not give it meaning. No isolated entity may be said to have meaning. It may have a good time, but it has no meaning.

Besides, there is no such thing as an isolated living entity. We are all "open systems," enmeshed in the biosphere, totally dependent upon it to keep us supplied with food, air, and impressions. The biosphere, in turn, is dependent upon the energy of the sun and the substance of earth and air, as well as upon that whole intricate network of mutual relationships and delicately adjusted balances among its constituent parts that makes it a single living being—*Gaia*, as James Lovelock calls it. Within the body of Gaia we ourselves, insofar as we are living creatures like other animals, live and move and have our being. Outside it (or conditions created in imitation of it—and how long we could exist in artificial conditions without going insane is not yet known) not one of us is even conceivable.

Why do we almost always forget these things? Hardly anybody any longer even says thanks, *grazie*—grace.

Even if we regard the creatures who become our food as alive, we certainly don't think of them as conscious beings, let alone persons.

Why say thanks?

As for the sun and the earth, we don't even think of them as alive.

Who says thanks to a *thing*?

This is an example of how something as vast as a cosmological image affects the very way we live our everyday lives—and, one suspects, our quality as human beings as well.

"My son," says Old Lodge Skins, the Cheyenne chief, to Little Big Man, his white adopted son,

> "...white people...are strange and do not seem to know where the center of the world is....The Human Beings [i.e., the Cheyenne] believe that everything is alive: not only men and animals but also water and earth and stones....But white men believe that everything is dead: stones, earth, animals, and people, even their own people. And if, in spite of that, things persist in trying to live, white men will rub them out...."

"That," he concludes, "is the difference between white men and Human Beings."[25]

And when, one night under the stars, Allardyce Meriweather, the white bunco artist, reminds Little Big Man of the prevailing view (which you and I, in spite of ourselves, still share), that those stars move in the void, the young man rightly concludes that if that is the case, it doesn't matter what he does, and so (for a time) he stays drunk.[26]

Meriweather keeps losing parts of himself—an eye, a leg, an arm—and that, indeed, is what has happened to us. We think of ourselves as having progressed beyond "primitive animism," but maybe in that thought we are like those docked foxes Ananda Coomaraswamy spoke of (making an analogy with the attitude of the West toward ancient and "primitive" cultures), who look down pityingly upon foxes who still have their tails.[27] In gaining a wilderness of gadgets, we may have lost (while our backs were turned, as it were) something much more important.

If we imagine the universe as "it"—a universe of "dead matter and blind force"—something in us goes dead and blind. We can engage without remorse (until we understand that our own existence is threatened) in the wholesale destruction of nature. If we imagine, moreover, a purposeless universe, we suffer, in the letdown that follows the momentary elation of achieving a proximate goal, from a baffled feeling of depression. If the universe has no meaning, can my life have any ultimate meaning? If the whole has no purpose, can the part?

There is at least a proximate meaning and purpose in the liver cell's existence. Its own life is maintained in order that it may squirt its drop of juice. That would have no meaning either were it not that the whole tissue of which the cell is a part has the purpose of producing a certain volume of juice, which has the purpose of transforming a certain substance in the food...and so forth. There is a hierarchy of purposes subordinate to the purpose of maintaining the life of the whole organism.

But we heirs of the Western intellectual tradition have suppressed our immediate awareness (although we may have had it as children) of being part of the organism of Gaia, much less of the whole universe. We may work for the purpose of maintaining our own organism, bringing it to a state of ideal fitness and beauty, but that enterprise can suddenly seem to have no meaning either if we ourselves, whose vehicle this organism is, serve no purpose beyond "stayin' alive."

If a human being is to serve a purpose, he or she has to serve voluntarily, else the psyche splits into one who obeys outwardly and another who resents and hates inwardly and awaits the chance to escape or rebel. In order to serve voluntarily, the part has to understand intellectually, feel emotionally, and sense immediately its relation to the whole.

Supposing the liver cell were to serve voluntarily and not automatically, as we assume it does (although we don't really know), it would have to have a sense of the whole and of its own place and function within it. Next, it would have to understand that its own life depended upon the life of the whole, that it was itself almost synonymous with its place and function within that whole. Still, it would feel like a slave-cell unless it felt that it had some choice in the matter. It might prefer death to this subordination unless it were able to feel that the whole and its maintenance were important.

It would have to *care*. It would have to have some sense of relationship to the person for whose sake the whole mind-boggling complex of functions was being maintained. It would have to love and respect that person—however vast the difference in the quantitatively measurable dimensions of their physical vehicles. For this, it would need to be equipped with some capacity for perceiving the real existence and quality of the person—some awareness of the presence of *some one*, within itself and all around it—and a sense, moreover, that this someone *knows* it—that is, that the relationship is reciprocal.

The quality of a person must produce something like a chemical that permeates all the tissues of the body, since you and I, who are built on the same scale as other human beings, can sometimes sense that quality. A small child always can. A dog can smell it. Personhood has this characteristic of uniqueness, and we too have the capacity to recognize a person we know as this one and nobody else. We experience this particularity almost as a fragrance, an essence, a resonance, a kind of uniquely shaped pattern of tensions in the ether that stamps, more unmistakably than a monogram, everything that person has touched.

Look at the well-worn shoe of someone you know intimately, for instance, and you will see what I mean; or put on the sweater with the frayed elbows that your mother always wore in the last years of her life; or the black leather jacket your son wears when he rides his motorcycle; or his helmet with the skull and crossbones on it.

In order to feel that your life has meaning, then, you need to feel, first of all, that you are part of something bigger than yourself that has a shape, however vast, that you can imagine, so as to have a sense of orientation within it; that you have within that larger something a job to do that may be microscopic but is nonetheless indispensable (like the liver cell's production of its drop of juice); that what the larger something does, or is, is important and valuable; and that the whole is saturated through and through with a quality to which you respond with love and unforced respect.

Then you will take care how you do your microscopic job. You will do it the best you can and take some satisfaction in so doing it. You see for yourself that your life depends upon the successful functioning of the larger something, but know that at the same time you have chosen to serve voluntarily, on the basis of your own understanding and valuation (rather than commit suicide, on the one hand, or be dragged through each day in blind slavery on the other), because of the feeling you have (love, respect, gratitude, loyalty) toward the principle that animates the whole.

It is evident that this degree of understanding and participation would require the full exercise of *all* our faculties and *all* our senses. Although those that are employed in the perception and manipulation of "primary qualities" would certainly be needed, they alone would not suffice.

There has, moreover, in the case of human beings (unlike liver cells or angels) to be room for advancement. There has to be a vertical dimension, a sense of which way is up, a scaffolding of ever-increasing responsibility that corresponds to an individual's capacity for growth in comprehension and in strength.

Japanese auto manufacturers know as much as this about keeping their worker-cells content. But in the end, it is not enough. When you have served the company forty years, rising steadily through the ranks to a position of maximum realization of your potentialities for functioning in that context, after the fine dinner and the speeches and presentations, you go home to the empty house, take out the gold watch, and say, "Well, what was it all for?"

For a human being, it is not enough to feel part of a family, or a company, or a community, or even of organic life on earth— although all these are essential, as the tissue, organ, organ system, body, are to the liver cell. All these have a longer duration in time and greater reach in space and power than the individuals that compose them. But human beings need a vision of *everything*— the whole of space and time, the whole universe, how it works, what it's for, where it came from, where we are in it, and why.

We need, in short, the image of a cosmos, and one that is not only mathematical but also animate and conscious and that exists, moreover, for a purpose.

Beyond that, since we know in advance that our bodies die, nothing will finally satisfy us but to know, and feel related to— and even that our own unknown inmost center coincides with— something timeless: something that does not die.

The Breathing Sphere

*The imaginative image returns by the seed of Contemplative
Thought.*   WILLIAM BLAKE, in Roger Cook, *The Tree of Life*

I. BODY

*Stand still. The trees ahead and bushes beside you
Are not lost. Wherever you are is called Here,
And you must treat it as a powerful stranger,
Must ask permission to know it and be known.
The forest breathes. Listen. It answers
I have made this place around you.
If you leave it, you may come back again, saying Here.*[1]

My husband and I have come out in the evening, into the country,
to look for Halley's comet. We turn the car off the road. Tall,
untended grasses flash green in the sudden yellow beams of our
headlights, as if two eyes, startled awake, look back at us. Then
we turn off the lights and the engine, and everything returns to
blackness and silence. We sit for a moment, allowing the unaccustomed emptiness to penetrate our tense bodies and buzzing brains.
Then we get out of the car and walk out under the sky.

We do not really have much hope of finding the comet, but
tonight is the last night it can be seen with the naked eye in our part
of the world. Last time it came around, it was brilliant and unmis-
takable. This time, it's less clear—at least for people like us, who
own no special equipment. The morning paper has instructed us
to look for it toward the southwest, twenty-seven degrees up from
the horizon, between sunset and ten o'clock, when the full moon
will rise and wipe out our last hope of a sighting.

Right now, there is still a streak of apricot above the black
horizon in the west; above that, pale green, turquoise, lavender,
and, at the zenith, dark purple. In the east, a low layer of clouds,

still lit by rays from below the opposite horizon, glows like the coals of burning roses. Against the western turquoise hangs the evening star, immense, liquid, and golden.

Down here on the earth, we can't see much in the dim light, but the slant of our feet and faint tug of our muscles tell us we are climbing up a gentle slope. When we come to the top, where a lone tree stands, we turn and look around. Our son, who directed us to this spot as a likely place for viewing the comet, told us that here, where the meadow slopes away toward the evening, a farmhouse once stood. We can see no trace of it now.

We sit down under the tree and wait. It is not cold. A breeze, soft and moist, stirs the hairs on our arms and the sparse grass on the ground around us.

Looking up, we vie with each other as to who can see the first real star. A faint one appears against the greying lavender, then another and another, until at last there are too many to count.

Turning my head and scanning the sky, I begin to recognize the few constellations my uncle showed me when I was a little girl: Orion, with his belt and sword; Cassiopeia in her chair; the Big and Little Dippers. Remembering what my uncle taught me, I trace out the line of the Big Dipper's front lip and find the North Star.

The sky darkens. My husband and I joke with each other a little in low voices.

"There it is."

"Where?"

"There."

"Oh."

"Why are we whispering?"

We see now that we will never be able to single out the comet amid the numberless swarms of stars in the southwest, but we are grateful to it anyhow, for bringing us out to attend to the night sky for the first time since we were children. There has been no reason for us to look at the stars. They have had nothing to do with our lives. Except for dutifully pointing them out, as part of the necessary cultural equipment, to our own children, we have paid no attention to them since we worked for merit badges in the Boy and Girl Scouts.

When I was four or five and looked at the stars, the stars looked back. That was the way I saw them. They looked interested, concerned, amusedly affectionate, like my mother's eyes.

By the time I became a Girl Scout, word had somehow reached me that I should not trust my eyes. The universe was infinite, without beginning or end in space or in time (remember, this was before ordinary people had heard about the big bang), unconscious, inanimate, and certainly uninterested in me.

On our first campout, when I slept out under the stars for the first time, I lay flat on my back in my sleeping bag, stared straight up into the black sky, and experienced the terror of infinity.

This was not the simultaneous terror and adoration one might experience at suddenly realizing (like Job) the presence of an infinitely great being, but just terror: terror at being a nothing dissolved in an infinitely great nothing.

It was like being suspended upside down over a bottomless well of black water. If you let go, you would fall and fall and fall and fall and fall and fall...

I quickly flipped over onto my stomach and scrunched down farther into the sleeping bag. I looked at my hands, my fingernails with the little moons in them, the pebbles, the blades of grass. An ant was crawling there, wiggling his feelers, feeling his way in the dark, grasping with his two front legs an enormous cookie crumb from the stash in my sleeping bag, being bowled over on his back by the weight of it, struggling onward, trying to get home with what he came for. The crumb was a boulder to him. He went on struggling, oblivious of my vast face hung dimly glowing, like a rising moon, above him.

The ant's perceptive equipment had not prepared him to be aware at all of anything built on so large a scale as I, much less to surmise that I might be alive or conscious. It did not occur to me at the time to speculate as to whether the same might not apply to me in relation to the heavenly bodies or the universe as a whole; but I did understand—not in words but in feeling and sensation— something else.

In the organization of the ant's body—his slender waist; the delicate hinges of his legs; the fine, constantly palpating threads of his two sentient feelers—there was something greater than any endless universe of lifeless dust. The ant was a cosmos: a living unity composed of many parts.

The infinite universe was not a cosmos. It not only was not alive but had no imaginable shape. It was impossible to orient oneself within such a picture (actually, neither "picture" nor "universe" can be properly applied to it), and since it developed in isolation from the question of purpose, it was impossible to live in it with meaning as I tried to define that word in chapter 2. Neither body nor heart could participate in imagining an infinite, purposeless universe. There was no up and down in it, no *place*, no *there* there—and certainly no land of heart's desire.

When the universe ceased to have any relation to the way we live our lives, we lost interest in it. This explains what was so puzzling to scientists: how quickly we lost interest in the attainment of travel to the moon. Paradoxically, the result of that attainment was a sudden uprush of interest not in the moon but in our own native planet, seen for the first time as a whole in all its imperiled loveliness—and seen as *alive*,[2] animated by that dynamically patterning force I was groping to describe in chapter 2.

The moon, finally seen firsthand, was clearly dead—or perhaps not yet alive, since there was no evidence it had ever *been* so. The shocking contrast between the two heavenly bodies was evident to all the faculties, so that valuation of the earth awoke in feeling perception, which indeed is alone equipped to perceive value and is one of the faculties rejected (by implication) in the doctrine of primary qualities.

Not since I was a Girl Scout have I sat and watched the night sky for as long as I am watching, like an ancient shepherd, tonight. While I have been thinking, Orion, the giant hunter with his dog, has slid lower in the west. Golden Venus has vanished behind the black horizon. Slowly, majestically, imperceptibly, the great, transparent sphere of the fixed stars has been revolving, pivoting on the still point of the North Star.

Of course, I know there is no sphere of the fixed stars. It is the earth that's turning, not the sky, and what seems from down here under our tree so breathlessly hushed, so slowly, soundlessly, and geometrically revolving, is in fact, according to present views, full of immense violence: exploding supernovae, black holes, pulsars, quasars, galaxies all rushing apart at breakneck speeds.

I do not imagine any God out there, his white beard blown by the interstellar wind, nor my mother and father singing in the high spheres of Dante's Paradise, nor my uncle (who ended up shooting himself) among the leafless, bleeding trees in the sad grove of the suicides in Dante's Inferno under the earth. Astronomy has long since ceased to have anything to do with heaven, and geology never did have anything to do with hell. Virtue does not vary directly with altitude.

I take it for granted that what's really out there are particles of inanimate matter of various sizes, burning or not, moved without meaning or purpose by unconscious, inanimate forces. There is a precision clockwork solar system ticking away to no purpose within a sort of whirlpool of stars called the galaxy, and there are billions of other such galaxies scattered at random throughout black space, all rushing away from one another, impelled by the unimaginable force of the big bang, the explosion in which they— and space and time themselves—had their origin.

Why, then, does the night sky have such a profound effect upon me, evoking an inner stillness, piercing me with its beauty? Looking up at the stars, I long for something, but I don't know what it is—not to escape from time, which here under the stars presents itself, as Plato said, as "a moving image of eternity"; but to reconnect myself with timelessness.

The heart does not see as the mind sees, and neither does the body. Being itself a cosmos—a unity in multiplicity, a purposeful, hierarchical order composed of many parts, each fulfilling its function for the benefit of the whole—the body continues to perceive in terms of ancient cosmologies everywhere, which must have had their origin in the body's sensation of itself—or were, in any case, in harmony with it. "Revelation descended not only into the souls of the Prophets but also into their bodies."[3] "Within this

FIGURE 3.1   *They called that central point the* omphalos, *or navel of the earth.*
Apollo seated on the omphalos at Delphi (Jane Harrison, *Prolegomena to the
Study of Greek Religion* [New York: Meridian Books, 1955], p. 319).

fathom-long body, equipped with mind and sense perception, O
monks," said the Buddha, "I declare unto you is the world, the
origin of the world, the cessation of the world, and the path to its
cessation."

"Here," said every tribe (wherever it was located, according to
our present notions, on the surface of the earth), "is the center of
the universe." They called that central point the *omphalos*, or
navel of the earth.

> ...Delphi, where
> Phoebus, on earth's mid navel o'er the world
> Enthronèd, weaveth in eternal song
> The sooth of all that is or is to be.[4]

Just below our own navel lies the *hara*, the center of gravity of
our physical body and the center of its power. When, in the inner
sensation of your body, you take your stand on the *hara*, you are
unshakable, as students of Japanese martial arts well know.

> Physiologically speaking...[the swordsman] must have been thor-
> oughly trained in keeping his *kokoro* way down in the abdominal
> region....[There are] two kinds of *kokoro*: one is the physical

"heart" and the other is the true "heart." The heart susceptible to emotionality is the first kind. When it is kept down below the navel, it becomes immovable. Unless this takes place, all the skill the swordsman may have acquired is of no use.[5]

When the priest or shaman took his stand at the navel of the earth, his upright body coincided with the axis of the universe. The North Star—the only still point in all the turning heavens and hence the doorway to timelessness—was the "north nail," the point where the upper end of this *axis mundi* turned in its socket or passed through the dome of the sky to the unconditioned realm beyond. In the daytime, the sun at the zenith became the doorway in and out of time (the Sundoor). On the scale of the body, this role was played by the opening in the top of the skull through which the spirit was supposed to enter the body at birth and depart at death.

The axis pierced our world at its center and passed on through to the underworld, so that this place where the preist or shaman stood was both the center of the earthly plane and the place of communication with the levels above and below. This underlying image, of an axis passing vertically through a central place on our level, uniting it with the worlds above and the worlds below, was envisaged as the unifying principle of structures on three scales alike: cosmos, body, and house, or temple. The image can be discerned, fleshed out in the physical details of the particular scale, time, and place in question, in myths, scriptures, and works of art and architecture from all over the world, from prehistoric times up to the Copernican revolution.

> The centre is, first and foremost, the point of "absolute beginning" where the latent energies of the sacred first broke through....it is also imagined as a vertical axis, the "cosmic axis" or "axis of the world."...Ultimately all creation takes place at this point.[6]

> The Buddhist stupa...is an image of the sacred centre of the world, that still point from which all creation emanates. The cosmic axis or Axis Mundi, the linear extension of this cosmogonic point, passes through the various planes of being....It was here at the

centre, beneath the Cosmic Tree, that Prince Siddhartha, the future Buddha, attained enlightenment. At one with the Axis Mundi which ensures communication between these planes, the Buddha could transcend the human condition at will, and enter into intimate and compassionate communion with all beings at all levels.[7]

Sometimes a tree, with a spring or a stream or a well of water underneath it, represented the axis. At the foot of the tree was an altar, where the libation or the blood of the sacrifice could find its way to the world below, and the rising smoke of the incense, to the world above.

> Trees were writing their own Divine Comedy about the ascent from hell to the high spheres of heaven long before Dante wrote his.... The thrust of the trunk, from roots beneath the earth, through our middle dimension, to the sky, where the leaves sway, has always lent credence to the division of existence into three zones.[8]

Trees could not write their own Divine Comedy were it not that these zones are established in the kinesthetic awareness of every one of us as soon as we stand upright on the earth. Then we feel, in the deep proprioceptors of our muscles, the downward pull of gravity and, at the same time, that upward longing of our ancestors which must resonate in our very genes, since if nothing goes wrong, we can't help struggling up at some point in our infancy and standing erect. Willy-nilly we plant our feet on the ground and direct our heads toward the sky, despite the obvious absurdity, from an engineering point of view, of trying to balance what is going to become fifty, or a hundred, or two hundred pounds upon the soles of two smallish feet.

From the very beginning of our lives, we have immediate knowledge in our muscles and bones that we are pulled between two forces, a downward one from beneath our feet and an upward one from—where? within ourselves? above our heads?—and that between the two stretches a scale of sensations of density, increasing toward the body's center of gravity, decreasing toward the top of the head.

We feel the faithful support of earth pressed against our

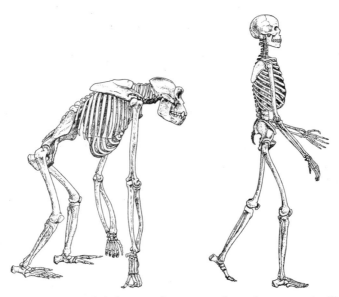

FIGURE 3.2   *...we can't help struggling up...and standing erect.* Gorilla and man. From "The Antiquity of Human Walking" by John Napier. Copyright © 1967 by Scientific American, Inc. All rights reserved.

footsoles—without having to think about it, we understand that our muscles would have no strength were it not for the necessity of maintaining ourselves upright against the pull of gravity; and we feel an upward reaching inside ourselves so that the sight of a great tree may make us want to stand up straight and raise both arms toward the sky.

Most of the metaphors for character development and moral integrity stem from our struggle to stand upright in the field of earth's gravity and keep our balance—not to be always swayed by outside influences but to remain vertical, accessible to the whispering wisdom of the ancestors in the streams below the earth and to the high, singing stillness of something that is always calling us (if we listen) from above.

Then we can orient ourselves from within (be inner-directed) and walk clear-eyed in inner stillness, open to that unknown which is always there in front of our noses, as well as accessible from within.

Out of the sensation of the body standing upright at the central

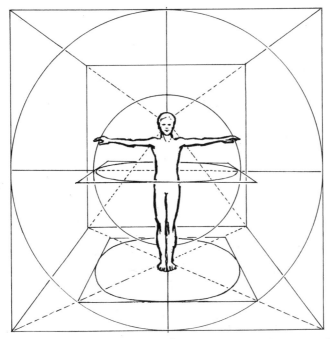

FIGURE 3.3   *To orient oneself in space was to orient oneself in time and in the stillness at the center.* Sacred space. "The circle's four points, where the two axes meet it, are seen to be the four turning-points in the sun's path [the equinoxes and solstices]…" (Maria-Gabriele Wosien, *Sacred Dance: Encounter with the Gods* [New York: Avon Books, 1974], p. 22).

place on the face of the earth bloomed the whole three-dimensional flower of spatial orientation: forward, back, to the right, to the left, up, down, inward (toward the center), and outward (away from it); north, south, east, west, zenith, nadir, and the central point where the three axes of the six directions intersect, "in the centre of man, the 'cave of the heart.'"[9]

To orient oneself in space was to orient oneself in time and in the stillness at the center—"the still point of the turning world"—that transcends both time and space. From where you were standing, you could mark the points where the sun would rise at the equinoxes and solstices on the circle of the horizon and at the same time on the circle of the zodiac, then trace these points as they circled across the sky in the night.

These were the "doors of the year," points—like the North Star

FIGURE 3.4   "...this seventh ray will evidently coincide with the Axis of the Universe." The Seven-Rayed Sun, from the Nativity in the church of San Matorano in Sicily: "...the long shaft of the seventh ray extends downward from the Sun to the Bambino in the cradle" (Ananda K. Coomaraswamy, "The Symbolism of the Dome," in *Coomaraswamy: Selected Papers*, vol. 1, *Traditional Art and Symbolism*, Bollingen Series, no. 89, ed. Roger Lipsey [Princeton, NJ: Princeton University Press, 1977], p. 421). Copyright © 1977 by Princeton University Press. Reproduced by permission of Princeton University Press.

and the Sundoor—of entry into, and egress out of, time, whereas the point in the heart where the axes of the six directions cross— the "seventh ray"—corresponding to the Holy of Holies in the temple, is the residence of the Unconditioned within us. "When the separated essence can be thought of as returned to the center of its own being, on whatever plane of being, this seventh ray will evidently coincide with the Axis of the Universe."[10] This point of no dimension where the axes cross is the empty space of the heart where, Ananda Coomaraswamy tells us, God can be brought to birth: Emmanuel, God with us.

Houses, temples, cities, kingdoms were designed and constructed in imitation of this cosmic image, which seems to have been *secreted* by the body's sensation of itself, as naturally as a nautilus secretes its shell. The dome of a temple corresponded to both the dome of the skull and the dome of the sky, and the round opening in the dome, to both the fontanelle (the space between the sutures of the skull that is open at birth) and the North Star or Sundoor.

The rectilinear axes, intersecting within the body and defining the four corners of the earth and the cube of space, were at the same time the axes of the spheres of heaven. In his very body, a human being could sense himself as a citizen of both earth, where everything is in motion and change, and heaven, which looks from here to be immune to change. "While the celestial bodies measure the passage of time, yet they and their patterns are immutable....They are both timely and timeless."[11]

In every traditional culture (every culture, that is, except our own "heap of broken images"), the North Star or Sundoor was the doorway out of time altogether, to immortality, to union with the Unconditioned Source. In one's own house, this same locus was incarnate in the central smoke hole in the roof, directly above the hearth, the heart of the house. This intimate relation of body, house, and cosmos was the armature for a rich array of correspondences, so that the small details and repeated acts of everyday life, and the pageantry of the communal cycle of rituals and festivals, hummed and resounded with meanings on every scale. This was as true of the Catholic church (before it chose to cling to a discredited cosmology, an event that cast a cloud over the whole enterprise of religion in the West)[12] as of the Dogon of Africa, or the Celestial Empire of China, or the vanished inhabitants of Teotihuacán.

As noted earlier, traditional guiding principles for right living seem to stem from the bodily sensation of trying to keep one's balance, to walk upright, remaining aligned with the axis of the universe. We speak of equanimity, of well-balanced natures. We symbolize Justice as a woman holding an upright sword in one hand and a pair of scales in the other. We still use the phrase "to justify" in the sense "to make vertically straight" when we apply it to the margins on a page.

As P. D. Ouspensky remarks, the relation of one world to a world that contains an additional dimension is the relation of zero to infinity.[13] The secret aim of right living is the realization of one's own nothingness in order to reconnect with the genuinely infinite—which is to say the Unconditioned. When the weights in the two pans of a scale are balanced, the pointer points straight up toward zero, toward timelessness, like the *axis mundi*, like the tops of our heads when we stand erect, weight equally distributed between two feet. We have balanced our accounts. Our debts are forgiven, as we have forgiven our debtors. We have added up all the forces acting upon us and canceled out the sum.

These are not mere metaphors. As well as a kinesthetic sense, the body has an architectonic one, of forces in equilibrium, thrust and counterthrust, the delicate adjustments required for keeping perfectly still—for sitting or standing in the posture most conducive to opening to the influence of something from above, something timeless, something that does not die. If, for an instant, that connection is made, one has no doubt of the real existence, power, and intelligence of that "something" that is nothing—no thing.

According to modern unified field theories,

> ...all the interactions we see in the present world are the asymmetrical remnant of a once perfectly symmetrical world. This symmetrical world is revealed only at very high energies, energies so high they will never be accomplished by human beings. The only time that such energies existed was in the first nanoseconds of the big bang which was the origin of the universe.[14]

Through the door of broken symmetry, time entered in from the halls of the outer heaven. Through moments of restored symmetry, I reconnect my mortal life with timelessness.

I straighten my back and sit in silence at the base of this tree.

II. BREATH

> Across three times nine countries, in the thirtieth Tzardom, there is a green garden, and in the garden is a mill which grinds of itself. It winnows the grain and throws the chaff a hundred versts away. By the mill stands a golden column, and up and down the column climbs a learned cat. As it goes up it sings songs, and as it comes down it tells stories.[15]

> I am in a world which is in me.[16]

My body is beginning to ache from sitting still for such a long time on the cold ground. I place my hand on my husband's shoulder and heave myself up onto my feet. We smile ruefully into each other's eyes, acknowledging our common subjection to the growing stiffness of age.

He returns to his own thoughts. I walk around for a while to restore my circulation. Then I sit down on the other side of the tree.

The Big Dipper is right in front of me. The zenith is over my head. Polaris lies like a cold jewel between my eyebrows.

FIGURE 3.5   (A) The thread winding around the spindle. Reprinted with the permission of Macmillan Publishing Company from *New Key to Weaving: A Textbook for Hand Weaving for the Beginning Weaver* by Mary E. Black. Copyright © 1957 by Bruce Publishing Company, renewed 1985 by Mary E. Black.

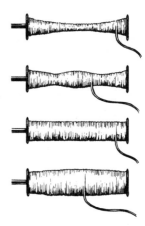

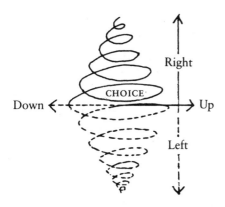

(B) "…in three dimensions, the spiral may be imagined either as the aspiring upward spiral or as the downward vortex" (Jill Purce, *The Mystic Spiral: Journey of the Soul* [New York: Avon Books, 1974], p. 9).

(C) "The first vibrations of the egg of the world, which unfold to the confines of the universe…are seen by the author…as both expanding and contracting, emerging from the source and going on to disappear into it, on a *spherical vortex*" (Jill Purce, *The Mystic Spiral: Journey of the Soul* [New York: Avon Books, 1974], p. 96).

I straighten my back again, aligning my backbone with the tree trunk. My breath slides up and down along the axis of the universe.

At the beginning of chapter 1, I compared my struggle through thickets of confusion toward a clear view of something whose immanence and importance I feel but whose exact nature I can't define to the struggle my sister and I once made through stiff underbrush toward the country home of our childhood. What I glimpse so dimly through the shrubbery is an image of one of the patterns of wholeness itself, on whatever scale it manifests. It is something like an invisible spindle that descends and ascends, spinning all the while, picking up the disconnected fibers of whatever medium it has descended into, spinning them into a coherent thread, winding the thread around itself.

As the wound thread builds up around the revolving spindle, it grows at first into the form of two cones—the apex of one pointing up and the other down—with a common base.

Continuing, it grows for a moment into a perfect sphere.

Then the thread begins to unwind, the form is undone, and the spindle itself, axis of the image, is pulled out of the vertical, becomes distorted, falls to the horizontal, and breaks into pieces. Its fragments swirl down and around in a great whirlpool (a negative cone) that leads to the underworld—the subconscious, or world of the dead.

After a while, the point of the spindle reappears, like the seedling of a tree, and begins to grow upward into a new connection between above and below—a new covenant. It is as if the whirlpool were being turned right side out, pushed up from underneath its apex, until the hollow vortex has become a solid cone.

One must think of the spindle as never ceasing to turn, even when (like the axis of the whirlpool) it is invisible; and of the winding as forever moving, however imperceptibly, either toward the above or toward the below—except at three points: first, at the bottom, when it seems all movement has come to a stop forever, since we expect that things will fall, or run down, spontaneously but not that they will rise, or start up, again spontane-

FIGURE 3.6   (A): "Mount Meru, the world mountain [the axis of the universe], rising from the sea, surmounted by holy radiation, with sun and moon circling around it, as depicted in an old Buddhist cave sanctuary in Chinese Turkestan" (de Santillana and von Dechend, *Hamlet's Mill*, p.61); photograph from Albert Gruenwedel, *Altbuddhistische Kultstätten in Chinesisch-Turkistan* [Berlin: G. Reimer, 1912], p. 216). (B) ...*the axis...breaks into pieces.* "The collapse of the hourglass-shaped Meru, caused by Buddha's death, with sun and moon rolling down..." (de Santillana and von Dechend, *Hamlet's Mill*, p. 61); photograph from Albert Gruenwedel, *Altbuddhistische Kultstätten in Chinesisch-Turkistan* [Berlin: G. Reimer, 1912], p. 46).

ously (death is natural; resurrection, a miracle); second, at that hushed moment at the top, before the direction is reversed, when ascent and descent are of equal force and cancel each other out, and contact is made with something beyond time; and third, at the moment of perfect sphericality or completion, before the thread begins to unwind.

The thread seems to represent time, and the direction of its winding or unwinding (pulled toward the center or pulled toward the periphery) represents the tendency toward order or disorder, negentropy or entropy; or the predominant direction of attention: toward unity or multiplicity, toward subjectivity or objectivity (that is, study of oneself and work toward self-completion, or study of the "outside" world and work toward gaining power over it) during any given historical epoch, stage of life, or moment. The alternate turning toward center and circumference, unity and multiplicity, is also a turning from belief in the primary reality of the inner world to belief in the primary reality of the outer one. "Line and plane are combined in a gyre which must expand or contract according to whether mind grows in objectivity or subjectivity."[17]

The figure of the spindle that rises and falls and the thread that winds and unwinds around it, making and then unmaking shapes of cones and spheres, is the same as the figure of the *axis mundi* but with another dimension added: the dimension of time. Like a mathematical formula, or like music or a dance, this moving form underlies both physical and psychological phenomena on all scales of time: cosmological, historical, biographical; year, week, day, breath.

With the spread of Christianity after the fall of world-conquering Rome (A.D. 560), attention turned inward. The real world was the inner one, and ardor was directed toward attaining self-perfection and experiencing timelessness. The image of cosmic order grew until it attained its perfection during the twelfth and thirteenth centuries and was embodied in such works as the great cathedrals, the *Summa theologica* of Saint Thomas Aquinas, and Dante's *Divine Comedy*.

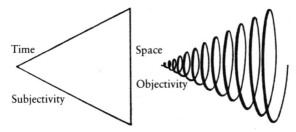

FIGURE 3.7   (A): "Line and plane are combined in a gyre which must expand or contract according to whether mind grows in objectivity or subjectivity." Yeats's gyres. Reprinted with permission of Macmillan Publishing Company from *A Vision* by W. B. Yeats. Copyright 1937 by W. B. Yeats, renewed 1965 by Bertha Georgie Yeats and Anne Butler Yeats.

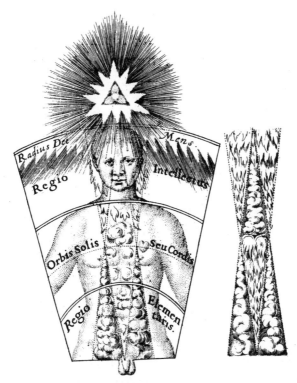

(B) "The balanced, intersecting gyres (as triangles) centred on the heart, form the Perfect Man" (Jill Purce, *The Mystic Spiral: Journey of the Soul* [New York: Avon Books, 1974], p. 119). From Robert Fludd, *Utriusque cosmi...historia*, 1616–19, 3:175. This item is reproduced by permission of The Huntington Library, San Marino, California. Huntington call number RB 338942.

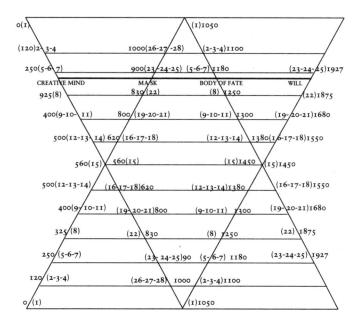

FIGURE 3.8   ...*this moving form underlies both physical and psychological phenomena on all scales of time: cosmological, historical, biographical.* The historical cones. Reprinted with permission of Macmillan Publishing Company from *A Vision* by W. B. Yeats. Copyright 1937 by W. B. Yeats, renewed 1965 by Bertha Georgie Yeats and Anne Butler Yeats.

At the time of the Renaissance, Reformation, and scientific revolution (A.D. 1450)—the age of exploration—there was a reversal of direction. Attention turned toward the outer, the multiple, the things of time. The thread that had wound around the central, vertical axis that points toward the timeless began to unwind. When the axis fell to the horizontal, heaven, the state of perfection, which had been felt to be in some sense "above," was cast into the future, in the form of an ideal society on the level of the earth or of unbounded material progress.

Events of the twentieth century shattered that image and broke up the current that had oriented our hopes toward the future. Now, not knowing which way to turn, we pursue fragmentary, short-term, contradictory goals, "every one to his own way," "stayin' alive."

But a new current begins to be felt so that the psyche, which, like agitated water, has reflected only fleeting, broken images, begins to quiet down. Since the 1960s, many of us in the West have learned, through the practice of contemplative techniques recovered from the East and rediscovered in our own traditions, how to grow, at moments, attentive and still. Reflected in the medium of that stillness, a new, collective, coherent image of the whole of things is, I believe, beginning to appear. With the return of the idea that the universe had a beginning, the principle of unity—"the point of it all"—has reentered our world view.

The thread pulled straight as it unwinds (clockwise) is linear time, as our schooling has habituated us to imagine it and as we do in fact experience it when our attention is out of balance. The origin of the idea of linear time, as opposed to the repeating cycles of pagan time, is often attributed to Christianity, since Christ died "once for all" rather than dying and resurrecting annually, like the old fertility gods. But the birth, life, death, and resurrection of Christ are reenacted annually in the calendar of the church, and Christian time as a whole is a great circle, returning at its end to Christ, who is alpha and omega, beginning, middle, and end, and who, partaking of both the timeless and time, gives the things of time their significance. In contrast, linear time as we, having lost connection with timelessness, experience it, is "just one damned thing after another," with no discernible pattern or purpose. In a given week, we can't remember what covered the front page of the newspaper the week before.

The large and small circles the thread makes around the spindle—smallest at the apices of the double-cone figure, greatest at its waist—are the cycles of organic time: systole, diastole; breathing in, breathing out; morning, evening; spring, fall; childhood, maturity, death, and (by analogy with cycles on other scales) rebirth. Although of different relative durations, all these cycles have the same inner form and pass through analogous sequences. This is the kind of truth revealed by metaphor:

> That time of year thou mayst in me behold
> When yellow leaves, or none, or few, do hang

> Upon those boughs which shake against the cold,
> Bare ruin'd choirs where late the sweet birds sang.[18]

Far from being a mere decorative fancy, this is a statement about isomorphisms: the formal equivalence of phenomena (seasons of the year, ages of man, epochs of history) on vastly different quantitative scales.

Metaphor is a mathematics of the whole man, engaging the intelligence not only of intellect but also of feeling and sensation. It was that mathematics of proportion, or ratio, that interested Pythagoras and Plato: $a:b=b:c$, "a is to b as b is to c." In Shakespeare's poem, autumn is to the year as late middle age is to one man's life span, as the destruction of one stage of a given culture (here, Roman Catholic Great Britain) is to the total history of that culture. The word "reason" (Latin *ratio*) must originally have referred to this sense of a proportion or harmony among all the faculties, and not, as it does today, to the mechanical logic of discursive thinking only. Plato's proposed system of education, based on music and gymnastics and directed toward philosophy—the love not of knowledge for its own sake but of wisdom, the balanced conduct of life in imitation of the harmonious movements of the heavenly spheres—seems to point in that direction.

An intact mythology, which tells the whole story of the universe, living creatures, and human beings, from Genesis to the Apocalypse, is a paradigm of wholeness—"the fullness of time." In a traditional society, the creation myth is recited at the beginning of any undertaking because living wholeness—a process carried through to completion—has the same inner form on any scale. In possessing this power to reveal the inner identity of phenomena on vastly different scales and of completely diverse external appearances, myth resembles mathematics; but whereas mathematics is an activity of one aspect of the intellect, myth is an activity of the whole psyche, acted out in ritual drama by the body as well, in this case becoming an activity of the whole community.

Nevertheless, the hidden structure of myth, its skeleton, is mathematics—the mathematics of proportion or harmony, which Pythagoras and Plato discerned in music and in the apparent movements of the planets and the stars, and which systems theory is rediscovering in the global behavior of dynamical systems on all scales. The playing of process upon this keyboard is the music that underlies all natural beauty, ringing the changes on all possible relations of the Many to the One, from Creation to Apocalypse, when "there shall be time no longer."

With the advent of systems theory, the ancient approach to unification of the mind through the perception of analogies is being restored to respectability, since the global behavior of dynamical systems on all scales, from atom to ecosystem and before and beyond, is found to display certain universal features. These features relate to conditions at equilibrium, near equilibrium, far from equilibrium but at steady state, or far from equilibrium and fluctuating, this last condition pregnant with the seeds of evolution—possibilities for total reorganization of the system on new principles.[19] These universal features of dynamical systems begin to resonate with what Gurdjieff calls the Law of Octaves, one of the fundamental laws of the universe, for these features recall the inner sensations of the various notes of the octave, as distinguished by Victor Zuckerkandl in his *Sound and Symbol*:

> Speaking...of the major mode, we could say that the tone $\hat{7}$ [*si*] gravitates toward $\hat{8}$ [high *do*] just as $\hat{2}$ [*re*] does toward $\hat{1}$ [low *do*], but even more urgently. We could further single out two tones and distinguish them from the rest: $\hat{3}$ [*mi*] and $\hat{5}$ [*sol*]. The tendency toward $\hat{1}$ is clear in them both; yet the striving seems less outspoken here. Unlike $\hat{2}$ or $\hat{7}$, these tones are not, as it were, torn from their places; they are more firmly rooted in themselves. Their condition might perhaps be described as outer equilibrium together with noticeable inner tension. Owing to their greater stability, $\hat{3}$ and $\hat{5}$ serve their more unstable adjacent tones, especially the higher, as the nearest points of support. Thus $\hat{4}$ [*fa*] gravitates to $\hat{3}$, $\hat{6}$ [*la*] to $\hat{5}$, in the same way as $\hat{2}$ to $\hat{1}$; $\hat{4}$ points toward $\hat{1}$ across $\hat{3}$, $\hat{6}$ across $\hat{5}$....Expressions like stable and unstable equilibrium, tension, attraction, gravitation, and the like, can give a *general* conception of the phenomena with which we are dealing....Besides itself, a tone also expresses its personal relation to the tone $\hat{1}$, its place in the tonal system as a whole.

A system in which the whole is present and operative in each individual locus, in which each individual locus knows, so to speak, its position in the whole, its relation to a center, must be called a dynamic system.[20]

Zuckerkandl notes, further, how motion up the scale is motion toward completion.

The motion follows the general schema: advance toward... attainment of a goal....The beginning $\hat{1}$–$\hat{2}$ runs counter to the will of the tones; it is a step *against* the forces in operation, "away from...." The close $\hat{7}$–$\hat{8}$ does what the tones want to do; it is a step *with* the forces in operation, "toward," a step that leads to the goal....Is it possible to determine a point at which the reversal takes place, at which "away from" becomes "toward"?...It is the tone $\hat{5}$. Up to $\hat{5}$, all motion is a departure from...; after $\hat{5}$ it is an advance toward...; $\hat{5}$ is the turning point....All motion from $\hat{1}$ to $\hat{5}$ is motion against the forces in operation....With the attainment of $\hat{5}$, however, the view opens in the other direction, in the direction of $\hat{8}$. Tone $\hat{5}$ itself points in both directions—hence the "knife-edge balance" characteristic of this tone....Tone $\hat{7}$, on the other hand, is unmistakably and wholly under the spell of $\hat{8}$....Here there is no "away from"...beyond $\hat{5}$; with $\hat{5}$, so to speak, the greatest possible distance from $\hat{1}$ is reached; after $\hat{5}$ it is an approach again. Approach to what? The tone toward which we look in the descending segment of the curve is always the same tone we left behind us in its ascending segment. We go toward a tone by going away from it....But the point that we thus approach and reach as our goal is not the starting point....The going away becomes *an arrival, not a return.*[21]

The moment of arrival is also felt as a moment of completion. The sphere into which the thread winding around the spindle grows is spherical time, a moment of perfect balance and harmony, when motion is so perfectly regulated as to be indistinguishable from stillness, and the sense of being alive in time raised to such a ringing pitch that it cannot be distinguished from a sense of deathlessness—as in the experience of love at first sight.

...when we came back, late, from the Hyacinth garden,
Your arms full, and your hair wet, I could not
Speak, and my eyes failed, I was neither
Living nor dead, and I knew nothing,
Looking into the heart of light, the silence.[22]

The spherical waves expand and contract simultaneously, center unfolding to become surface, surface infolding and reappearing at the quick to unfold again—as when a great bell, struck, sounds, resounds. This is an audible diagram of a hypersphere, in which the inside is continually becoming outside and the outside inside; and that, I believe, is the form of the universe, perceptible to us only when we too are whole and still.

There is thus a kind of geometry underlying myth, a mathematics of wholeness, as there is in music. The hero sets out from home to seek his fortune and in the end returns, "with bliss-bestowing hands," bringing back the fruits of his struggles and discoveries for the benefit of those who have remained at home. The storyteller unfolds the story, and simultaneously, in those who partake

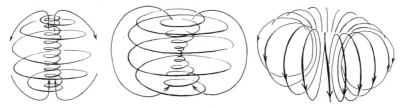

FIGURE 3.9   The spherical vortex. "The universe and man's consciousness (the macrocosm and the microcosm) consist in a continuum and a dynamic whole; this can be expressed by the spiral when, instead of ending, it is drawn either round a sphere or a doughnut ring, so that it joins up with itself by spiralling through its own middle. This symbol, which is perpetually turning in on itself, expanding and contracting, has an interchangeable centre and circumference, and has neither beginning nor end: it will be referred to here as the spherical vortex....In a science he has called *geometrodynamics*—the dynamics of the geometry of curved empty space—one of our foremost cosmologists, J. A. Wheeler, describes how the structure of our universe is none other than the vortex ring—a manifestation of the universal spherical vortex" (Jill Purce, *The Mystic Spiral: Journey of the Soul* [New York: Avon Books, 1974], pp. 7, 32).

of it, the story infolds toward its origin until the listeners have "got the point." What was inside the teller—known "by heart"—is becoming outside and, simultaneously, in the hearer, becoming inside. This is the pattern of any living exchange; the feeder at the same time is subtly fed. The tale reverberates between teller and hearer, and both are awakened to ponder its meaning, for themselves and for the community in which it has arisen and been handed down from generation to generation.

This geometry, which is closely allied with the sensation of the body (itself a cosmos—a paradigm of living wholeness), is what I call "mythematics." We carry living diagrams of it in the sensation of our heartbeat and our breathing, in the vertical sense of the upright body in the field of gravity, in our sense of where we are in our life cycle and in the history of our civilization—whether in its exuberant youth, self-satisfied maturity, catastrophic dissolution, or, as now, interregnum, the interval between two lives, two breaths, as we wait for the appearance of a new dispensation, a new covenant between the timeless and time. This interval is like the Flood that separates two ages—not only in the Bible but in the mythology of many cultures—or like the ocean that lay between the Old World and the New.

In their remarkable book *Hamlet's Mill*, Giorgio de Santillana and Hertha von Dechend began to discern in shards of myth from all over the earth the outlines of an image like my spindle. They called it "Hamlet's Mill," after one of its incarnations (in the original story of Hamlet in Icelandic legend), or, in general, "the frame of time."

> Amlodhi (Hamlet) was identified, in the crude and vivid imagery of the Norse, by the ownership of a fabled mill which, in his own time, ground out peace and plenty. Later, in decaying times, it ground out salt; and now finally, having landed at the bottom of the sea, it is grinding rock and sand, creating a vast whirlpool, the Maelstrom...which is supposed to be a way to the land of the dead. This imagery stands, as the evidence develops, for an astronomical process, the secular shifting of the sun through the signs of the zodiac which determines world-ages, each numbering thousands

of years. Each age brings a World Era, a Twilight of the Gods. Great structures collapse; pillars topple which supported the great fabric; floods and cataclysms herald the shaping of a new world.[23]

A mill is a machine for grinding something coarse into something fine. It consists of a lower, or "nether," disk-shaped millstone, which is fixed and remains still, and a matching upper stone that revolves and rubs against it, grinding the grain fed between the two into flour. (You often see these old millstones resurrected as front stoops in country places.) The upper millstone is attached to a revolving axle empowered, via a series of gears, by wind (captured by such vanes as we see on Dutch windmills) or water (pushing against the paddles of a water wheel) or some other source of power—in the case of a coffee mill, the power of your arm turning the handle.

In the image of Hamlet's Mill, the axle is vertical and represents the *axis mundi*. The combination of vertical axis and rotary motion are what my spindle and this mill have in common. In the mill, the axle revolves; in spinning, the spindle revolves, with the rotary motion made visible in the thread.

In some bodies of myth, instead of a mill the central image is of a tree or a mountain; in both of these we recognize the *axis mundi*, but in the mill this is seen to be the central axis not only of space but also of an epoch of time, since to the image of the three-dimensional cross formed by the vertical axis of the universe and the two horizontal axes, the image of a mill adds motion—not only the rotary motion of its turning but also, in the case of Hamlet's Mill, the motion, perpendicular to that rotation, of its rise and fall, its alternating growth and collapse.

Whether tree, mountain, or mill, this "frame of time" has three roots: one in heaven, one on earth, and one in the underworld. In whatever form it appears, its axis grows up, arising in response to a descending power from above, makes connection with the Pole Star ("the still point of the turning world"), gathers everything into a whole structure, ordering all the details it has encompassed (so that each has a place, function, and hence meaning, within the

FIGURE 3.10 *...this "frame of time" has three roots: one in heaven, one on earth, and one in the underworld.* The Scandinavian World Tree, Yggdrasil (Richard Folkard, Jr., *Plant Lore, Legends, and Lyrics* [London: Sampson, Low, Marston, Searle, and Rivington, 1884], facing p. 2).

whole), prevails for a while, then grows rigid and cannot adapt to the forces of change.

A pin is pulled out or some small part dislodged, and the whole gets out of kilter. The sap of life can no longer circulate through the structure and drains down into the underground, while the dry sticks of the old order continue impotently to try to rule the daylight world by the imposition of force. "The time is out of joint," as Shakespeare's Hamlet said, thus demonstrating how poetry can be prophecy. Shakespeare knew very well what time it was in his own day, the Renaissance—a "little bang" when immense energy erupted out of the old forms, which had been broken by the Copernican revolution, the Reformation, and the discovery of the New World.

"Myths are not distorted records of historical events," said Ananda Coomaraswamy; "...so far from that, events are demonstrations of the myths."[24] A true myth is not just a fairy tale but is a representation of the pattern of forces that underlies real events. We have an abstract representation of all such mythic patterns possible in the I Ching.[25]

Eventually, the dead skeleton of the old order collapses, like Poe's House of Usher (there was a maiden buried alive in the cellar of that house, as the soul of the earth is buried in the subconscious of our old, mechanical world view), and sinks into the cosmic ocean. All the king's horses and all the king's men cannot put this old order—this collapsed Hamlet's Mill—together again. Attempts to do so prove futile, and all must submit to the purifying flood that intervenes between the ages. The corrupt old establishment must be brought to a final end and the debris cleared away.

In some versions of the universal myth of the creation and destruction of worlds or world ages (a concept that includes the shape of a world in time: its conception, birth, growth, prime, disintegration, and death), an infant hero pulls out the plug ("The emperor has no clothes!") and the polluted waters swirl down in a great whirlpool to the bottom of the sea, where the ghostly mill may continue to grind but grinds out nothing useful—"rocks and sand"—an image reminiscent of Gurdjieff's characterization of the modern mind as "a real 'mill for nonsense.' "[26]

Then the timeless seeds of order must be recovered from the depths of the cosmic ocean or the ends of the earth or the farthest recesses of the cave, or they must be carried over out of the destruction of the old order and planted in the virgin soil of the new, so that fed by fresh energy, the new world tree will grow again toward the source of light, establishing once more the connection between becoming and being, time and the timeless, earth and heaven. "The measures of a new world had to be procured from the depths of the celestial ocean and tuned with the measures from above."[27]

At the same time, the maiden must be rescued from the underworld. Persephone must be restored to the light of day. Awareness that nature has a soul—is alive, sentient, and conscious—must be restored to daylight consciousness, so that life on earth will not perish forever. "According to Koyukon teachers, the tree I lean against *feels* me, hears what I say about it....There is no emptiness in the forest, no unwatched solitude."[28]

Sometimes instead of a mill, tree, or mountain the image is of a dying and resurrecting god or cosmic person, living and dying not on the scale of the year, as with so-called fertility gods, but on the scale of world ages. In this case, there is an implication that the one who rises and falls and is the key to the order of the age is alive and conscious, can know us and be known. With the Sufis, it is a great teacher who is the Axis of the Age, and with the Hasidim, the Just (which is to say, upright, balanced) Man, whose life serves, as did Christ's, the Buddha's, or Mohammed's, as a model to be imitated according to one's strength and understanding. Both divine and human, citizen of both the timeless and time, both spindle and thread, he is Aion, the incarnation of the myth, the paradigm of the wholeness of the world age he informs with his presence and his teaching.

After finding that something like Hamlet's Mill appears in stories from all over the world, de Santillana and von Dechend began to suspect that myth was the technical language of ancient astronomers, that the Mill was the revolving sphere of the starry

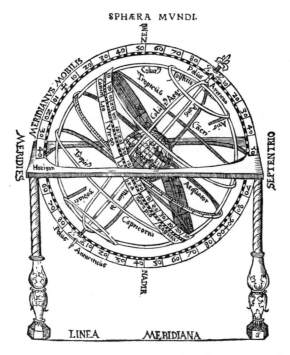

SPHÆRA MVNDI.

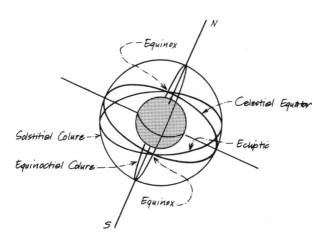

FIGURE 3.11 *...the structure of great celestial circles (equinoctial and solstitial colures, celestial equator, and ecliptic).* (A) Armillary sphere, from Peter Apian, *Cosmographicus liber,* 1533, folio 5, verso. This item is reproduced by permission of The Huntington Library, San Marino, California. Huntington call number RB 14138. (B) The colures. Drawing by Richard Sharpe (Martha Heyneman, "After the Flood," *A Journal of Our Time,* no. 3 [1982]: 21).

heaven itself, and that the story of the Mill's rise, completion, and subsequent disjointing, collapse, submersion, and resurgence referred to the structure of great celestial circles (equinoctial and solstitial colures, celestial equator, and ecliptic) that is the system of coordinates for locating any point in the heavens.

> The equinoctial "points"—and therefore the solstitial ones, too—do not remain forever...at the same spot with respect to the sphere of the fixed stars. Instead, they stubbornly move along the ecliptic in the opposite direction to the yearly course of the sun, that is, against the "right" sequence of the zodiacal signs....
>
> This phenomenon is called the Precession of the Equinoxes, and it was conceived as causing the rise and cataclysmic fall of ages of the world. Its cause is a bad habit of the axis of our globe, which turns around in the manner of a spinning top, its tip being in the center of our small earth-ball, whence our earth axis, prolonged to the celestial North Pole, describes a circle around the North Pole of the ecliptic, the true "center" of the planetary system....
>
> The sun's position among the constellations at the vernal equinox was the pointer that indicated the "hours" of the precessional cycle—very long hours indeed, the equinoctial sun occupying each zodiacal constellation for about 2,200 years.[29]

During each of the twelve zodiacal ages, the precession of the equinoxes slowly skews the structure of great celestial circles until that structure can no longer serve as a frame of reference for priest, farmer, navigator—for the conduct of life. Whereas before it was right to plant at the heliacal rising of certain stars, it is no longer so. If you try to navigate with reference to the old map at this time, you will go astray. The doors to heaven, at the solstices and equinoxes, where the great celestial circles meet the earth (the "four corners" of the earth) have shifted to new places and can no longer be found in the old ones. Even the Pole Star has moved from its place. To try to cling to the old structure has become counterproductive. It must be allowed to disintegrate and sink into the baptismal waters of the underworld.

A hero has to dive to the bottom of the sea and find a new opening to timelessness. He has to turn the hourglass over to initiate a new direction of time.

I believe that Hamlet's Mill, as well as being de Santillana and von Dechend's astronomical figure of the heavens, is the image of the universe that is carried in the minds of the members of a given culture, the coordinate system in relation to which each of us arranges (probably unconsciously) his particular experience and interprets its meaning. Such an image slowly grows to relative comprehensiveness and coherence, taking root in the three realms of intellect, feeling, and senses, so that the three all contribute to, and are bound together within, the world image. De Santillana and von Dechend rejected the psychological interpretation of myth in favor of the astronomical, but I believe there is no contradiction between the two. Psyche and cosmological image mirror each other. The psyche can find completion and coherence only when it lives within, or has living within itself, a complete and coherent image of the universe.

Conversely, as Dante shows, objective knowledge of the universe is impossible without self-knowledge (*Inferno*) and self-change (*Purgatorio*). In order to *see* whole, we must *be* whole.

Having its origin in mathematics—an initially wordless sense of the relation of the Many to the One—the cosmological image has in the past become incarnate in communal myth and ritual: in poetry, music, dance, and spectacle and, ultimately, in an order of daily life—in the way the humblest act is performed. This is total language, speaking to intellect, feeling, and senses all at once, including the kinesthetic senses of structure, weight, motion, rhythm, so that it can be learned by heart (which is to say, by body); chanted by bards; danced; dramatized; painted; carved in stone; recited in daily, weekly, or yearly cycles; sung in hymns; or recalled in prayer five times a day or before every meal.

The founding myth is the paradigm of perfection, as the story of Christ once was (before the discrediting of its underlying cosmology disharmonized the teaching) for Christians. We have learned from such accounts as Black Elk's[30] and such studies as Marcel Griaule's of the Dogon[31] how other traditional cultures have also been informed by their founding myths, so that Shelley's assertion that poets are the unacknowledged legislators of the race becomes comprehensible. European culture was once so informed by the Bible, as a glance at the history of art in Europe immediately demonstrates. In the twelfth century, when rediscovered classical learning seemed to contradict the Bible, a great labor of intellectual reconciliation and assimilation ensued, culminating in the *Summa theologica* of Saint Thomas Aquinas. The new world image did not enter popular consciousness through the *Summa*, however, but through the mediation of artists like Dante and the architects of the great cathedrals, who imagined the whole world story with mind, heart, and flesh and embodied it in forms perceptible to the imagination of the reader or to the senses of the worshipper in church.

> ...none of [Dante's] ideas are novel, though he clothes the traditional teaching in a vernacular form of incomparable splendor, *splendor veritatis* [the splendor of the truth].[32]

A coherent world image like the medieval one governs, for a time, the organization of society and daily behavior; then suffers a blow (as medieval cosmology suffered the blow of the Copernican revolution) from which it cannot, with intellectual honesty, be recovered. The "discarded image"[33] breaks up into isolated, contradictory fragments and sinks, finally, into chaos, taking with it the hubris of the ego and leaving us, as Simone Weil said, "waiting for God," acknowledging our need for grace, while having no assurance that such help from an unknown level of life exists.

This is the moment of waiting in the Ark for the return of the dove (*O my dove that art in the clefts of the rock, in the secret places of the stair, let me see thy face*); the moment of the Virgin's waiting in openness and simplicity (*...behold, he standeth behind our wall, he looketh forth at the windows, showing himself through the lattice*), assuming—even expecting—nothing.

> *...the faith and the love and the hope are all in the waiting.*[34]

After the long winter of waiting, the first delicate signs of the possibility of a new coherence begin to emerge, themselves constituting evidence of the real existence of a unifying influence that cannot be dictated to but enters "in the fullness of time."

He cam also stylle
  Ther his moder was,
As dew in aprylle
  That fallyt on the gras.[35]

Since this process of rise and fall is like a breath, occurring over and over, Hamlet's Mill has a form in time (that is, it is a figure of at least four dimensions), and visualizing the process as a whole makes it possible for us—even in the period of confusion that intervenes between two ages—to know where we are.

The last intact image of the Mill was the medieval one, which was at the same time an image of the universe, the psyche, and the social and biological order ("the great chain of being"). The breakup of medieval cosmology can be traced in the history of science and corresponds exactly to de Santillana and von Dechend's representation of the bending and collapse of Hamlet's Mill—because the medieval image, displayed with greatest perfection in Dante's *Divine Comedy*, itself had the form of the whole of Hamlet's Mill. The whole structure stands there in four-dimensional simultaneity, while its skewing, undoing, swirling into the underworld, and reconstitution are represented by the course of Dante's journey through this medieval cosmos, which journey at the same time represents the process of the soul's perfecting. The four-dimensional form of the individual soul in its possible completeness is the same as the four-dimensional form of the universe.

In the destruction of the medieval cosmology, much more than astronomy was at stake, as some historians of science have recognized.[36] The cosmological image corresponded to the image of the possible wholeness of the psyche and revealed the cosmological function of that enterprise of self-perfection that was the goal of human life. This aim was the axis—the central current of aspiration—around which the structure of society had crystallized out, as rock candy will crystallize out, informed by an otherwise invisible lattice, when a string is lowered into a supersaturated solution of sugar. The medieval cosmological image was the invisible pattern that underlay, and gave meaning to, all the forms of daily life. With the dissolution of this image, we all lost our way and returned to that Dark Wood where Dante found himself at the beginning of the *Divine Comedy*. Only late in the present century have large numbers of us come to ourselves and realized that we are going nowhere and don't know whether there's anywhere to go.

> Life goin' nowhere
> Somebody help me
>   Stayin' alive, stayin' alive.[37]

III. 3-SPHERE

We make, although inside an egg,
Variations on the words spread sail.

The morning-glories grow in the egg.
It is full of the myrrh and camphor of summer

And Adirondack glittering....[38]

Is the point the physicists and astronomers are beginning to envision, at the instant of origin of the physical universe, when all four forces (strong, weak, electromagnetic, gravitational) are one, different from the point Dante saw at the end of his poem, where the scattered pages of the universe are bound into a single volume by love? Or is it the same point imagined with a different selection of human faculties?

Here is Timothy Ferris, speaking to a television audience and trying to extrapolate from the latest scientific theories what the universe must have been like at 10^{-40} seconds, when it was ruled by a single primordial law:

> The universe, everything that there is or can be, was contained, we think, at this point, within a single spark of energy....[39]

And the Kabbalah, in the *Book of Zohar*:

> When the Concealed of the Concealed wished to reveal himself, he first made a single point: the Infinite was entirely unknown, and diffused no light before this luminous point broke through into vision.
>   Beyond this point nothing is knowable....[40]

And Dante, as he approaches the quick and origin of the universe:

> ...I saw a point which radiated a light so keen that the eye on which it blazes needs must close because of its great keenness....

And Beatrice explains:

> From this Point hang the heavens and all Nature.[41]

In the context of Dante's poem, which speaks to the whole human being and not just the intellect, this is seen to be the point of it all, in every sense of the expression. Thanks to Saint Thomas Aquinas, Dante had a "theory of everything" (T.O.E.) such as present-day theoretical physicists seek—but not altogether thanks to that philosopher of unprecedented systematic comprehensiveness. When Dante tried to unfold his understanding of the medieval T.O.E. in didactic prose (in the *Convito*), he came abruptly to a stop in front of the problem of death, leaving the work unfinished. He could not succeed in his exposition until he had reunited himself with Virgil, rejoining the company of poets, who speak not just to the mind but also to the emotions and the senses; and with Beatrice, "the intellect of love," which listens not only to reason but also to the voice of God.

What physics and astronomy offer us for our purposes since the discovery that the universe as a whole is expanding is the restoration to respectability of the idea that the universe had a beginning. The layman's natural question, "What, then, was there before the beginning?," only irritates the physicist, since the question has no meaning within the realm of his expertise. The same question, according to popular wisdom, also irritated Saint Augustine.[42] "Then," "there," and "before" are meaningless words outside of space and time, which had their beginning (another problematic word) in the big bang. As theoretical physicist Stephen Hawking has said, "To ask what happens before the Big Bang is a bit like asking what happens on the surface of the Earth one mile north of the North Pole. It's a meaningless question."[43]

That realm "north of the North Pole," beyond the confines of the phenomenal world, is the realm of expertise of the mystic. Just as the matter in our bodies was there in the beginning, when all the matter in the universe was contained in a single point, so also do we all bear within ourselves that which was "before" the beginning—a "particle," to be discovered and nurtured by each one of us, of something that transcends all opposites and is not subject to the conditions of space and time.

What has perhaps not yet been noticed is that the big bang theory is the harbinger of a new covenant between the timeless and time—or, rather, is the outward sign of an inner event. It is like the first fine thread thrown out by a spider across the void to begin the spinning of her web. Through that delicate fiber that has reconnected the intellect with the timeless can begin to flow the knowledge and power to reorder our thinking, and subsequently our behavior, into a new coherence, so that the minute particularities of our daily lives may begin once more to glow and pulse with meaning and, like the humble, disguised helpers in a fairy tale, point us the way that we must go.

As noted earlier, Professor Mark Peterson has noticed that Dante's universe, so far from being a naïve geocentric system, is a 3-sphere, which, in modern cosmologies, is considered a possible configuration of the universe. "Einstein's preference for the spherical cosmology...is well known."

> The belief that the earth must be round goes back at least to Aristotle....
>
> The belief that the universe as a whole might be round (or more generally, curved) is a much more recent one. It seems to require mathematics of the 19th century (non-Euclidean geometry) even to formulate the notion.
>
> It is therefore a considerable surprise to find, on closer reading, that Dante's cosmology is not as simple geometrically as it at first appears, but actually seems to be a so-called "closed" universe, the 3-sphere, a universe which also emerges as a cosmological solution of Einstein's equations in general relativity theory.[44]

A 3-sphere is a three-dimensional "surface" of spherical form embedded in a four-dimensional space, just as what we usually think of as the surface of a sphere (which topologists call a "2-sphere") is a two-dimensional surface of spherical form embed-

ded in a three-dimensional space. If the big bang is followed by a
big crunch (that is, if the expanding universe eventually begins to
contract and ends, as it began, in a point or "singularity"), a 3-
sphere is the simplest way to imagine the form of the whole of
space-time.

If an ordinary sphere passed through a plane (a two-dimensional space), it would appear as a point that expanded to a circle,
grew to maximum size, then shrank to a point again and disap-
peared. As the Sphere said to the Square, a native of Edwin A.
Abbott's Flatland,

> "...your country of Two Dimensions is not spacious enough to
> represent me, a being of Three, but can only exhibit a slice or
> section of me, which is what you call a Circle.
>
> "The diminished brightness of your eye indicates incredulity.
> But now prepare to receive proof positive of the truth of my asser-
> tions. You cannot indeed see more than one of my sections, or
> Circles, at a time; for you have no power to raise your eye out of
> the plane of Flatland; but you can at least see that, as I rise in Space,
> so my sections become smaller. See now, I will rise; and the effect
> upon your eye will be that my Circle will become smaller and
> smaller till it dwindles to a point and finally vanishes."
>
> There was no "rising" that I could see; but he diminished and
> finally vanished. I winked once or twice to make sure that I was not
> dreaming. But it was no dream. For from the depths of nowhere
> came forth a hollow voice—close to my heart it seemed—"Am I
> quite gone? Are you convinced now? Well, now I will gradually
> return to Flatland and you shall see my section become larger and
> larger."[45]

Similarly, a 3-sphere passing through our three-dimensional
space would appear as a point-sphere that expanded to a sphere
of maximum size, then shrank to a point-sphere again and disap-
peared.

Note that these are abstract definitions of surfaces, as if we
were to speak of the earth as a smooth and naked hollow billiard
ball, whereas we know that its surface, marked by mountains,
valleys, oceans, and deserts, teems with the whole bewildering

variety of living creatures and its restless interior boils with molten magma, iron, and shifting continental plates.

In the case of the expanding universe—if it is a 3-sphere, a "closed" universe—on its surface lives the whole phenomenal world, and its poles are alpha and omega, genesis and apocalypse, the beginning and the end (which becomes, if it is a breathing universe, "the recurrent end of the unending").[46]

But as Steven Weinberg says, the big bang was "...an explosion which occurred simultaneously everywhere"[47]—which is the best one can do in trying to express it, though there was no "where," since the big bang was the origin of space as well as time—so these "poles," the point of beginning and end, coincide, and the point

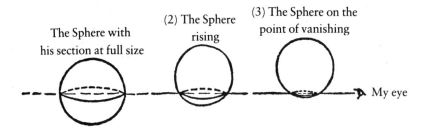

FIGURE 3.12   The Sphere passing through the two-dimensional space of Flatland (Abbott, *Flatland*, p. 85).

or zero doorway between the timeless and time, the spaceless and space, is also here and now, everywhere and always.

To postulate a beginning and possible end of space and time raises once more the question of the philosophical status of the categories space and time, which Immanuel Kant concluded were not "primary"—not "out there"—but were categories of our perception. Experience with Eastern disciplines has revealed to us that space and time are not unavoidable, natural, innate conditions of our perception but rather are learned preconceptions that can be transcended. Experience, even for moments, of an open, unconditioned awareness reveals that all such categories as space and time—and, indeed, all opposites—are mental constructs.

There is a Gurdjieff Movement called "The Big Circles," seen

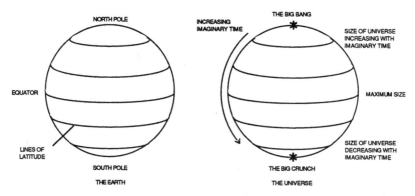

FIGURE 3.13   The earth (a 2-sphere) and the universe (a 3-sphere) (after Stephen W. Hawking, *A Brief History of Time: From the Big Bang to Black Holes* [New York: Bantam Books, 1988], p. 138).

(in part) at the end of Peter Brook's film *Meetings with Remarkable Men*. You are seated cross-legged on the floor. With your right arm, you describe a large circle in front of you in eight counts, being careful to adjust your speed so that your outstretched fingertips arrive precisely one-eighth, two-eighths, three-eighths, and so on, of the way around precisely on each beat. Your left arm, moving exactly twice as fast, completes two smaller circles in the time it takes the left arm to complete one. It is somewhat as if (although the ratios are different) your right arm were the hour hand and your left arm the minute hand of a clock, or as if you were the earth with the planets (from earth's point of view) moving around you in mathematically harmonious periods. Head turns, eyes move up and down, and legs unfold and refold at other precise intervals, demanding that you intensify your attention to be aware of all the parts moving at once, while your voice marks the regular beat by repeating "Om, om, om, om..."

Most of the time you are floundering, losing touch with one part or another, panicking, losing attention, finding it again, and so on.

But there can come a moment when the movements of all your parts suddenly continue by themselves, with no physical effort on your part, attention continues to embrace the whole like a globe of light, and you experience, directly, how motion, when it is mathematically regulated, is the same as stillness.

Maybe this is what the old watchers of the sky were after, in Egypt and Babylon, when night after night they kept track of the movements of the heavens.

There is another Gurdjieff Movement—a Women's Movement called "The Sacred Goose"—in which the dancer experiences, with echoes of all the attendant emotions, all the stages of a woman's life: girl, nubile young woman, mother, and woman past childbearing; and at the same time experiences how, like those liberated yogis of India called Wild Geese, she is free and always has been. There is an arm position like a broken wing feather, but that will mend. While being a woman immersed in life, with all its weight of entanglement and responsibility—sexuality, childbirth, cares and anxieties—she is at the same time one of those heavenly maidens who appear in mythologies all around the world: she stays for a while here on the earth and then, one day, puts her feathered cloak back on and returns to her other home (for both are our homes), in the realm of timelessness.

> Time is but the stream I go a-fishing in. I drink at it; but while I drink I see the sandy bottom and detect how shallow it is. Its thin current slides away, but eternity remains.[48]

Our physical body is an incomplete 3-sphere. It makes its first appearance in the three-dimensional world as a point-sphere (the fertilized egg) and proceeds to expand to maximum size, into a topological sphere (topologists ignore such protuberances as arms, legs, head, and so forth, provided the "skin" does not break). It does not itself, however, then proceed to contract symmetrically back into a point-sphere and disappear but shrivels up and disintegrates, so that from the point of view of the isolated individual the "time-body" has the form of a "3-cone" wrinkling up and fraying out irregularly at the base, while the material that participated in this particular form goes on to serve in the incarnation of other forms, weaving a "3-net" incorporating, by the time the world ends, everything that has ever lived on the earth.

Also, within each form at its maturity, sex cells continue to be produced, so that in one sense the body (or rather two bodies) may be said to shrink once more into a point-sphere (a new fertilized egg) and in this way complete the formation of a 3-sphere, and a breathing one at that: seed and fruit and seed again; concentration, expansion, concentration....

Hamlet's Mill is like this. The cosmological image grows to maturity and then begins to crack up, but even when the official cosmology has become "a heap of broken images," seeds of new cosmologies continue to form "at the bottom of the sea," in the subconscious, as experiences of the poet William Butler Yeats and the psychologist Carl Jung suggest. Both of these men lived and worked in the interval when there was no official cosmology but only the formless ocean of the unimaginable infinite universe. One night, Yeats's wife, Georgie, began to talk in her sleep. In this way, and later through automatic writing, she unfolded to him the all-encompassing psychocosmological system of gyres that he describes in *A Vision*. At about the same time, Jung's patients began to dream and draw those quadripartite circular diagrams he called mandalas—eggs of cosmologies that could never grow to maturity and transform waking life until the official, conscious, scientific cosmology began to take on mandalic form. That's what it seems to be doing today, when we begin to envision the universe as an expanding sphere and the four forces—strong, weak, electromagnetic, and gravitational—as having their origin in timelessness, like the four rivers issuing out of Eden.

There is not yet sufficient evidence to conclude whether the universe will contract symmetrically back into a point-sphere (whether the big bang will be followed by a big crunch). If we do not wish to wait for the Day of Judgment, however, the return is inner and on a different quantitative scale—that is, it is not cosmic, or universal, but individual.

One of the ideas current in science today is that the universe began from nothing by a process of broken symmetry. Nothing is the only "thing" that is symmetrical. As soon as there is something, there is an asymmetry between something and nothing.

A perennial idea in traditional spiritual teachings is that the individual, in order to return to his origin in the unmanifest, must restore that symmetry within himself—add himself up and cancel out the sum; so balance his psyche that the pointer on the scale becomes vertical and still, pointing to zero, the needle's-eye entrance to the kingdom of heaven, a realm (or way of seeing) not subject to the conditions of space and time.

This is the balancing act, the *contrapasso*, that the souls are engaged in on Dante's conical mountain of Purgatory: the "justification" (in its original meaning of straightening out and straightening up, which is preserved in our expression referring to the margins on a page) "of the ungodly"—of those, that is, who are unable to see God, to see the point of it all, to see meaning.

Like the thread that winds around the spindle, the path of the souls in Dante's Purgatory winds around the mountain, having previously unwound on the descent into Hell. (This path is not precisely a spiral, since the circles of hell and the terraces of Purgatory are discontinuous, like the quantum levels within an atom or the notes of a musical octave.) This unwinding and rewinding represent the death of the "old man" and birth of the new, the growth, on the individual scale, of a new spindle, a new "backbone" or will.

The growth of a new will means that you come in fact to *want* something different from what you wanted before. This new "backbone" or central axis is a palpable current of aspiration—a new understanding of what is possible, conviction that the possibility really exists, attendant hope, and energy experienced as a wish of growing ardor that gradually subordinates all other wishes and desires into harmony with itself.

"Set these loves in order, O thou that lovest me," says God to the soul entering Dante's Purgatory.

The figure of the spindle with the thread that winds and unwinds around it is the same as the gyres that inform the later poetry of William Butler Yeats and are explicitly described in *A Vision*. Like Hamlet's Mill, Yeats's gyres are a diagram of the inner form of time, the sequence of stages of the working out of any process to its completion, or, if we view all time as simultaneously present, the total assemblage of aspects of any whole phenomenon—all possible types, for example, of human beings.

Yeats pictures the gyres as a double conical spiral movement such that while one cone is expanding, the other is contracting. When the circling movement around one cone reaches its widest extent, the apex of the other cone appears at its center and the direction of movement reverses.

> An aged man is but a paltry thing,
> A tattered coat upon a stick, unless
> Soul clap its hands and sing, and louder sing
> For every tatter in its mortal dress.[49]

The return is inner.

Yeats quotes Empedocles:

> "When Discord has fallen into the lowest depths of the vortex"—
> the extreme bound, not the centre...—"Concord has reached the
> centre, into it do all things come together so as to be only one, not
> all at once but gradually from different quarters, and as they come
> Discord retires to the extreme boundary....In proportion as it
> runs out Concord in a soft immortal boundless stream runs in."[50]

Like Yeats's gyres or the thread wound around the spindle, Dante's Hell (Inferno) and Purgatory also have the form of two opposed cones or spirals. Inferno is a hollow cone with its apex downward, at the center of the earth. This point was the center of gravity of the whole medieval universe. Dante, as pilgrim, and Virgil, his guide, descend this cone, from circle to narrowing circle, clockwise (in the direction of entropy, the arrow of time), and when they reach the bottom—the hole in which Satan is fixed, like the plug in the drain—manage to squeeze through this zero past the devil and turn completely over, pointing their feet in the direction toward which their heads had been pointing before, then continuing in the same direction, begin to climb, since—just as from the South Pole every direction is north—from this point every direction is up. This very literally portrayed "conversion" corresponds to the reversal of direction in Yeats's gyres or to the

historical moment when interest and belief in the outer and multiple, in explanations by ultimate division (elementary particles),
reaches an extreme, and interest and belief in the inner, in relationship and unity, in the whole as greater than the sum of the
parts, reappears.

Dante and Virgil then enter a dark tunnel, climbing against the
current of the river of forgetfulness (time and entropy), and emerge
("through a round opening seeing again the stars") onto the outer
surface of another cone, the island-mountain of Purgatory.

There Cato orders Virgil to take Dante down to the shore
(where the island is widest) before the two can begin to climb
(counterclockwise, in the direction of effort and order, against
entropy, undoing time in order to return to the timeless) toward
the summit, where Beatrice, Dante's beloved, whose image has
become for him the vehicle of Divine Wisdom and Saving Grace,
awaits him.

Professor Peterson omits consideration of Purgatory in his article
announcing his observation that Dante's universe is a 3-sphere,
but the complete traversal of the opposed cones of Hell and Purgatory corresponds (as well as to the gyres of Yeats and Empedocles)
to one of the methods he describes for constructing an ordinary
sphere. The base of an ordinary cone is a circle. Two ordinary
cones ("2-cones") with their bases "glued together" are topologically equivalent to a sphere.

The base of a 3-cone is a sphere. Two 3-cones with their bases
glued together are topologically equivalent to a 3-sphere. Although
Dante does not portray the bases of his Hell and Purgatory as
literally contiguous, the bases of both lie on the surface of the
terrestrial globe—that is, the entrances to both lie right here beside us. If we regard the whole surface of the terrestrial globe as
the common base of the two opposed cones—that is, if their
common base is a sphere rather than a circle, with the apex of one
cone inside the sphere, at the center (the bottom of Hell), and the
apex of the other outside it (the summit of the mountain of Purgatory)—then together they form a topological 3-sphere.

Dante's Paradise—the third division of his universe—consists

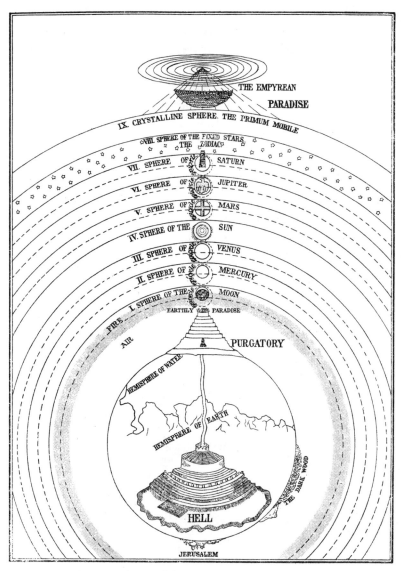

FIGURE 3.14   Dante's scheme of the universe (Charles Singer, ed., *Studies in the History and Method of Science* [Oxford: Oxford University Press, 1917], p. 31).

of a double set of nested spheres. "Division" is not the right word, though. Paradise is a more nearly complete view of the same universe the pilgrim and his guide traversed in their journey through Hell and Purgatory. It was their own position in those realms that made possible only a partial view. Their winding path along linear time was all the while traced out within a structure that was there before, and remained after, they traversed it, just as the earth remains present before and after we trace out our journeys over its surface.

When Dante's self-knowledge is complete ("Now we have seen all," Virgil, his guide, tells him when they reach the bottom of the Inferno), and his will is "single, whole, and upright" (as Virgil declares it to be when they reach the top of the mountain of Purgatory), Dante perceives spherically: he now sees the universe as a nest of concentric planetary spheres, with the earth at the center, and himself and Beatrice ready to ascend from the summit of the mountain on its surface.

When he *is* whole, he *sees* whole. It is as if the journey through

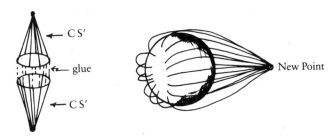

FIGURE 3.15 (A) Two cones with their bases glued together are topologically equivalent to a sphere (Peterson, "Dante and the 3-Sphere," p. 1033). Courtesy of the *American Journal of Physics*. (B) "If we try to suspend the 2-sphere to get the 3-sphere, we must choose where to imagine the two new points. One new point can go inside the 2-sphere....The other new point must go outside....There must be a 'part' somewhere, like the cowlick on a head of hair. The 'part' is a flaw in the method of visualization and is not a property of the 3-sphere itself." Dante avoids the "part" by imagining himself journeying first to the point inside the sphere (the center of the earth), then to the point outside (the summit of Purgatory), thus incorporating into the figure the dimension of time (Peterson, "Dante and the 3-Sphere," p. 1032). Courtesy of the *American Journal of Physics*.

Hell traced out its winding path around the narrowing circles of the inner surface of the Southern Hemisphere, and the journey through Purgatory wound over the narrowing circles of the outer surface of the Northern Hemisphere, until the figure of the sphere was complete.

To reiterate: this double 3-cone and this double set of nested spheres, which are two ways of seeing the medieval universe according to the degree of completion of one's knowledge and being, are, Professor Peterson tells us, two ways of constructing a 3-sphere, a form of the universe that also emerges as a cosmological solution of Einstein's equations in general relativity theory and has now entered the public mind through Stephen Hawking's best-selling book *A Brief History of Time.*

When they take off from the summit of Purgatory, Dante and Beatrice ascend without effort from one planetary sphere to another, each sphere enclosed within a greater one, until they reach the sphere of Saturn and, beyond it, the sphere of the fixed stars and the Primum Mobile, upon whose outer surface they pause to look back along the way they have come and forward to the Empyrean (*Paradiso*, canto 28).

This is the moment in the poem that has most caught Professor Peterson's attention, as well it might, since here Dante has answered, in vivid images, a question that still burns today, as we may see in the encounter described in the next paragraph between Stephen Hawking and the pope.

Professor Peterson frames the question in terms of space:

> It is the same problem every child has wondered about: unless the universe is infinite, it must (the argument goes) have an edge—but then what is beyond?[51]

This is the same as the question put to Saint Augustine, cited earlier, in terms of time: What was God doing before he created the universe?

This ancient question arose again in the conversation between Stephen Hawking and the pope. Let us recall Hawking's account of how, at the end of the conference on cosmology organized by the Jesuits in the Vatican, the participating scientists were granted an audience with the pontiff:

> He told us that it was all right to study the evolution of the universe after the big bang, but we should not inquire into the big bang itself because that was the moment of Creation and therefore the work of God. I was glad then that he did not know the subject of the talk I had just given at the conference—the possibility that space-time was finite but had no boundary, which means that it had no beginning, no moment of Creation.[52]

Hawking then proceeds to describe the universe of space-time as "finite but unbounded"—that is, as a 3-sphere, in which time ("imaginary time") is treated as a fourth dimension of space, the big bang is represented as the North Pole, and the big crunch is represented as the South Pole (figure 3.13).

> The universe starts at the North Pole as a single point. As one moves south, the circles of latitude at constant distance from the North Pole get bigger, corresponding to the universe expanding with imaginary time.…The universe would reach a maximum size at the equator and would contract with increasing imaginary time to a single point at the South Pole. Even though the universe would have zero size at the North and South Poles, these points would not be singularities, any more than the North and South Poles on the earth are singular. The laws of science will hold at them, just as they do at the North and South Poles on the earth.
> The history of the universe in real time, however, would look very different.…
> …In real time, the universe has a beginning and an end at singularities [big bang and big crunch] that form a boundary to space-time and at which the laws of science break down.…Which is real, "real" or "imaginary" time? It is simply a matter of which is the more useful description.[53]

Either way, that realm, whether we locate it "before the big bang" or "north of the North Pole" of the 3-sphere, is the realm of the Unconditioned and as such is not subject to the laws of physics, although the big bang or the North Pole itself may be. Nor is this realm discoverable through the application of our scientific method, though, as we have seen, it is discoverable through application of appropriate methods, preserved in the inner sciences of the East and at the root of the authority of the pope's church, whether or not they are still alive within it. In recent years, we have watched such notable Christians as Thomas Merton humbly apply to practitioners in the East in order to recover those methods for that church.

Dante's description of the boundary that is no boundary and of the realm "north of the North Pole" transcends and reconciles science and religion, the partial descriptions of cosmologist and pope, and restores to us knowledge of a right relation between intellect and body that has been lost since the time of Descartes.

It is Beatrice, a lady who has intelligence of love, who leads Dante across this universal "mind-body frontier," revealing (as does the cosmology of G. I. Gurdjieff) an unbroken continuity between what we have divided into body, psyche, and spirit until in the end we have come to believe in the reality of the physical alone and have attempted to reduce the other two to epiphenomena, probably illusory, of that supposed sole reality—which, on closer scrutiny, can be seen to be a fabrication of the groping, measuring eye and hand in alliance with mathematical logic, to the exclusion of all the other faculties.

In the *Convito* Dante had described the heavenly spheres thus:

> Aristotle...believed that there were only eight heavens, of which the outer one, containing all the rest, was that of the Fixed Stars, that is, the eighth sphere;...Ptolemy afterwards, perceiving that the eighth sphere had more than one motion [due to the precession of the equinoxes]...and constrained by the principles of philosophy (which necessarily demanded a perfectly simple *Primum Mobile*), supposed another heaven to exist beyond that of the Fixed Stars....So that according to him...the movable heavens are nine....And the order of position [of the heavens] is this, that the first one enumerated is that where the Moon is; the second that where Mercury is; the third that where Venus is; the fourth that where the Sun is; the fifth that where Mars is; the sixth that where Jupiter is; the seventh that where Saturn is; the eighth that where the Fixed Stars are; the ninth [the Primum Mobile] is that which

is not perceptible to sense (except by the motion spoken of above), and which is called by many the Crystalline, that is, the diaphanous, or wholly transparent. However, beyond all these, the Catholics place the Empyrean Heaven, which is as much as to say the Heaven of *Flame*, or *Luminous* Heaven; and they hold it to be immovable, because it has within itself, in every part, that which its matter demands....And this is the reason that the Primum Mobile moves with immense velocity; because the fervent longing of all its parts to be united to those of this [tenth and] most divine and quiet heaven, makes it revolve with so much desire that its velocity is almost incomprehensible. And this quiet and peaceful heaven is the abode of that Supreme Deity who alone doth perfectly behold himself....This is the supreme edifice of the universe in which all the world is included, and beyond which is nothing; and it is not in space, but was formed solely in the Primal Mind.⁵⁴

By the time Dante wrote the *Divine Comedy*, when his prose had been transfigured by poetry and his reason by revelation and love, he had changed the order of the planetary spheres somewhat and, more important for us, portrayed the Empyrean, or highest heaven, in a new way. It remains, however, not in space or time but in the mind of God ("this heaven has no other *Where* than the divine mind," says Beatrice), beyond the reach of the scientist but not of the contemplative.

Professor Peterson summarizes Dante's picture of this highest heaven:

Dante...endows the Empyrean with a detailed and precise geometric structure. This structure is described in Canto 28, as if seen from the Primum Mobile [on whose outer surface Dante and Beatrice are standing], as a bright Point representing God, surrounded by nine concentric spheres representing the various angelic orders. The details which follow leave the almost inescapable impression that he conceives of these nine angelic spheres as forming one hemisphere of the entire universe and the usual Aristotelian universe up to the Primum Mobile as the other hemisphere, while he is standing more or less on the equator between them.... In Canto 27 Dante looks down into the first semi-universe and sees the earth ("this little threshing floor") far below him. At the beginning of Canto 28 he *turns around* and *looks up* into the second semi-universe. This means the two hemispheres are positioned exactly as they should be....Standing at the top of the Primum Mobile and looking first one way, then the other, is the way to see the entire universe in one sweep....Taken all together, then, his universe is a 3-sphere.

...the various heavenly spheres revolve faster in proportion as they are bigger, while just the reverse is true of the angelic spheres: the innermost and smallest of these are revolving the fastest, and the outer ones are slower....The innermost angelic sphere turns faster than the other angelic spheres because it ranks higher, just as the Primum Mobile turns faster than the other heavenly spheres because it ranks higher. In other words, the spheres have a ranking, a "greatness," which does not necessarily correspond to their size (although for the first nine it does), but is rather indicated to the eye by their speed. This explanation strongly suggests our construction of the 3-sphere as sliced up into 2-spheres which first grow and then diminish in size, labeled by a fourth coordinate ...which simply increases. Indeed Dante has actually introduced such a fourth coordinate to label the spheres as they grow and

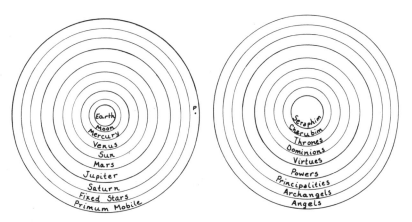

FIGURE 3.16 "In Canto 27 Dante looks down into the first semi-universe and sees the earth...far below him. At the beginning of Canto 28 he *turns around* and *looks up* into the second semi-universe." The two semi-universes of Dante's universe (Peterson, "Dante and the 3-Sphere," p. 1034). Courtesy of the *American Journal of Physics*.

diminish, namely their speed....Dante embeds the model in four dimensions....His fourth dimension is speed of revolution.[55]

Interestingly enough, Stephen Hawking comes to an analogous conclusion but in the opposite direction. With regard to his 3-sphere model, representing the universe as a sphere that has the big bang at the North Pole, expands toward the "equator," then diminishes to the big crunch at the South Pole (figure 3.13), Hawking tells us that he thought at first that "if and when the universe stopped expanding and began to contract," the thermodynamic arrow would reverse and disorder would begin to decrease with time—time, that is, would run backward.[56] Later, he realized he had made a mistake. While the universe first increases and then decreases in size, entropy continues to increase in the direction of increasing imaginary time, indicated by the arrow on Hawking's diagram as a descent from North Pole to South Pole. Hawking's "fourth coordinate" in Peterson's sense of the expression is entropy, or disorder. Hawking's view of the history of the universe therefore corresponds to Dante's descent into Hell. After he has made the turn at the bottom of Hell, Dante is moving in the direction *against* time, against entropy.

"Conversion," the astonishing turn Dante and Virgil make at the bottom of Hell to begin their journey in the direction against time, entropy, and forgetfulness, is the origin of evolution, symbolized in Christian myth by Christ's descent into incarnation and then into the underworld, where he makes the turn that overcomes Death, opening a new path to the world above for all humankind after the fall of the Hamlet's Mill of the previous age.

Es war ein wunderlicher Krieg....[57]

It was an awe-inspiring fight to turn and swim against the direction of time. This does not mean, as Hawking visualizes it, that the pieces of broken cups would leap together or that we would remember the future and not the past. The direction against time is not toward the past but toward timelessness, and the return is not physical but inner: a waking up to timelessness, a rebirth of *attention* within ourselves.

It will be only in chapter 4, when we expand our view to embrace the sciences of biology, psychology, and the spirit, as well as physics, that we will become aware of the real existence of the current in the universe—against entropy, toward higher and higher levels of order or organization—that corresponds to this possible evolutionary current in the inner development of an individual, toward the total attentiveness that is timelessness.

One must stop thinking of Dante's universe as a static structure in three-dimensional space and understand that it also includes all time—all entropy and negentropy, the unwinding and rewinding of the thread. At one pole, in the beginning, *en archē*, at the origin and source, is God: the Point of it All, that Love, absolute Intelligence, maximum acuity and penetration of Attention—that unifying, harmonizing force—that binds the scattered pages of the universe into a single book. At the other pole is Satan: ultimate division, multiplicity, absence of meaning or relationship, the "center of entropy"—a "hydrogen," in Gurdjieff's terms, "without the Holy Ghost"—but also, like the *hara* on the scale of our own bodies, the adamantine foundation of the whole.

One must recall that in Christian iconography, the Virgin is also given the place at the bottom, as "most lowly," and that she too is "without the Holy Ghost" until that Divine Energy descends and unites with her to conceive the New Man, axis of the New Age—or, on an even greater scale, the Logos, the very principle of order in the universe throughout all the ages. Satan and the Virgin occupy the same place, but he is upside down and she is right side up. They resemble those dolls in which Red Riding Hood is hidden under the skirt of the Wolf and the Wolf under the skirt of Red Riding Hood, so that turning one upside down and the skirt inside out reveals the other. Satan is our illusion of being the center of the universe; the Virgin is the liberating realization of our own nothingness that makes room in us for God. This place "at the bottom" corresponds to the point of reversal in Yeats's gyres. It is the place where the universe turns right side out.

Dante, too, when he has issued out of Hell, must be confirmed in the realization of his own nothingness. Having squeezed through two round holes in a graphic image of rebirth, and before he can begin to climb the island-mountain of Purgatory, he must descend to the shore at the bottom and be girded round with the reed of humility, which surrounds his waist in the form of yet another zero. As Charles Singleton has pointed out, the reed is the goal of the journey through Hell.[58] The aim of self-knowledge is the realization of one's own nothingness.

One must also recall that Christ is born below the ox and the ass, in a manger, the place where the animals feed. Like Satan, Madonna and Child are located at the bottom of the universe, the end of time, but whereas he is upside down and represents the end of something, they are right side up and represent a new beginning—that miracle at the bottom of the spindle or breath, where descent reaches its limit; ascent begins, against all expectation; and time turns around and runs toward timelessness.

Realization of one's own nothingness is prerequisite to union with the All. The relation of one cosmos to another, as mentioned earlier, quoting P. D. Ouspensky, is the relation of zero to infinity, since the more complete cosmos has one more dimension than the less complete.[59] The "bottom," on all scales of time's spindle, is one of the turning points. On the scale of the year, the bottom is the winter solstice, and that is where the church, with mythological correctness, placed the birth of Christ. The Fall of Man was the fall into dualism ("knowledge of good and evil"), and redemption is a healing or making whole. Holiness (wholeness) is not a sterile, one-sided purity but is the reconciliation of opposites, embracing both poles and all the teeming levels of interwoven lives and deaths between.

Between poles analogous to these—God and Satan, center of relationship and center of entropy—intellectual history also breathes: first seeking Being in the unity of the whole, as in medieval philosophy, then seeking it in the atoms, the indestructible ultimate divisions of matter, as in the history of the philosophy of science. During the present century, it has become clear that there are no such indestructible ultimate divisions: the atoms have vaporized in the quantum vacuum, and those who sought the ultimate divisions have come full circle to face the original unity. Interest has also turned toward systems theory, with the renewed realization that the whole is always greater than the sum of the parts.

This turn took place during the 1960s, accompanied by astonishing psychological phenomena that we are still trying to understand—revolutions of the young against the "establishment" all over the earth. At that time, the psyche came to the end of its tether and the reality of the inner world forced itself upon our attention, at first (with the psychedelic revolution inaugurated by widespread ingestion of LSD) with a formless, submarine craziness, a shout arising from the land of the dead, as the thread began to wind itself once more around the central, vertical axis. Then came a sober search for the authentic among the bewildering variety of spiritual and pseudospiritual teachings that suddenly migrated from the East, as if there had taken place a reversal of East-West polarity like the reversal of up-down polarity Dante and Virgil accomplished at the bottom of Hell.

All the geometric abstractions I have attempted to describe and illustrate suddenly spring to life when we notice that the motions of these opposed and connected gyres, and the expanding, contracting, turning-inside-out spheres, are two ways of experiencing in immediate sensation the motion of our own respiration: breathing in, breathing out. Our own breathing is our paradigm of wholeness in the dimension of time, the breathing of the universal 3-sphere comprising the breathings (sleeps, wakings; lives, deaths) of all the living creatures, on all scales, that it contains.

Although he certainly had never heard of the non-Euclidean geometries of the nineteenth century, Plato describes this universal 3-sphere, and the hierarchy of wholes implied in systems theory as well:

> ...he made this world a single complete whole, consisting of parts that are wholes, and subject neither to age nor to disease. The shape he gave it was suitable to its nature. A suitable shape for a living being that was to contain within itself all living beings would be a figure that contains all possible figures within itself. Therefore

he turned it into a rounded spherical shape....And he gave it a perfectly smooth external finish all round....For it had no need of eyes, as there remained nothing visible outside it, nor of hearing, as there remained nothing audible; there was no surrounding air which it needed to breathe in, nor was it in need of any organ by which to take food into itself and discharge it later after digestion. Nothing was taken from it or added to it, for there was nothing that could be; *for it was designed to supply its own nourishment from its own decay....*[60]

This is what Gurdjieff calls the Trogoautoegocratic principle by which the Whole is governed: "I eat myself"; whereas within the Whole, every living creature feeds on the deaths of other living creatures and becomes in turn food for somebody else, "everything issuing from everything and again entering into everything";[61] "dying each other's life, living each other's death."[62] Nothing can live independently except the Whole, and each of us has being only insofar as we become aware of the real presence of the being of the Whole within us. Like consciousness, being is a singular that has no plural. These are aspects of the Unconditioned.

Like the cones of Inferno and Purgatory, which are partial views of the spherical whole, Yeats's gyres can also be seen as spherical. Jill Purce represents the universal motion as a spherical vortex (see figure 3.9). "Empedocles seems to have conceived a period when love was predominant, and all the elements formed one great sphere."[63] "Michael Robartes [chief character in the story Yeats tells to introduce his *A Vision*] called the universe a great egg that turns inside-out perpetually without breaking its shell."[64] (That is, it is a 3-sphere, "finite but unbounded.") The earth, likewise, is continually extruding from its interior, along the oceanic trenches, molten rock that solidifies into the continental plates, which, at their opposite margins, plunge again under adjacent plates and into the interior, so that the whole is turning inside out perpetually, inside becoming outside and outside becoming inside, simultaneously.

Thus, if instead of riding my breath up and down with my

attention, I remain at the center, I experience breathing as a sphere that expands and contracts, as does the universe. At the same time, if I am attentive, I notice that something else, something subtler, moves toward the center as the sphere of the breath expands and that as the sphere of breath contracts, this something subtler moves outward, as if through the pores of my skin.

> We imagine that our body is opaque, even dream sometimes of transforming it into something more subtle. But the subtlety is already there. Nothing is dense except the wall of inattention, of insensitivity and passivity which prevents us from seeing.[65]

Dante's Inferno, corresponding to that state in which we believe that only the outer, material world, the world of "primary qualities," is real (or, as Gurdjieff puts it, "take the ephemeral for the Real") may be said to be his Purgatory upside down and inside out. When Dante (as pilgrim-protagonist of his own poem) turns right side up (is "converted") and emerges from his closed world to see again the stars, he perceives the equal reality of his inner world, the world of the psyche, and the necessity for ordering, balancing, and completing that world so as to be able to see differently—to see the point of it all.

Then everything and everyone he knows finds its place and meaning within a structure—a "magical memory cathedral"[66]—that is in harmony with the sensation of his own body upright in the field of gravity and with the rhythm of its breathing and its walking—in *terza rima*, two steps forward and one step back.

Breath is our paradigm of wholeness in the dimension of time. What we call the big bang the ancient Hindus, approaching from the "other end"—the inside rather than the outside—and by way of different methods of investigation and means of verification (that is, by looking inward rather than outward), called the Breath of Brahma.

> *God made sense turn outward, man therefore looks outward, not into himself. Now and again a daring soul, desiring immortality, has looked back and found himself.*[67]

Whether we call it the big bang or the Breath of Brahma makes no topological difference but makes enormous psychological difference in the way we imagine the whole and hence conduct our lives. Are we accidental results of an automatic explosion, or is there, at the origin of the phenomenal universe, prior to space and time (and therefore here and now, closer than the neck-vein), a consciousness that is aware of us, whether or not we are aware of it, and an intentionality that lay behind the creation of the world and has for each of us, this instant, a job to do, a part to play, upon which a great deal depends? The former view justifies despair, callousness, wanton destruction; the latter leads to questioning, self-examination, search.

Is there a Watcher waiting for us to wake up to why we are here? How can we know? Not just believe, but *know*?

The way we imagine the world—to articulate which was once the business of poetry and storytelling—is of gravest importance and is prior to science and technology, which are themselves based upon one way (and that a partial one) of imagining the world. If we come into genuine contact with the timeless source of the universe, we become points of entry of wisdom and love into the world (otherwise to talk of such things is mere sentimental twaddle), and it does not matter how we imagine the shape of the whole of things. But if the way we imagine the universe precludes the possibility of such a contact, we are not likely to search for it.

Physicists are distressed when we, in our need, grasp at each new theory and proclaim that physics now proves our religion. It is not the business of physics to prove religion. But it is the business of each of us—say, rather, the opportunity, for there can be no compulsion in this—to try to arrive at wholeness and harmony: of mind within itself, of heart with mind, of action with heart—and the beginning of this journey is to see, and suffer, the fact that we are not now whole; that we make, as Gurdjieff said, "cacophonous music"; that we are, as was Dante at the beginning of his journey, "lost in a Dark Wood."

Our awakening to this fact is at the same time the recurrent beginning of the Great Adventure, which never appears in the same guise twice but is a sortie into the Unknown in every one of its incarnations.

The cosmology of the physicists and astronomers will change almost daily as they make new discoveries and try out various models—the inflationary model, the eleven-dimensional model that would reveal the four forces as aspects of a single superforce, and so on—with the aim of arriving at simplicity and elegance. But if our aim is not to "do science" but to inaugurate the healing of our psyche by arriving at a unified world picture, a simplified image will serve, so long as it is not so completely out of keeping with the scientific view as to compel the fragmentation of the psyche into ironclad compartments—as is the case now, when, for example, we have to forget what we know about science (or, indeed, try to stamp it out with militant zeal in our own minds and the minds of others) before we can sit peacefully in church.

That simplified image, embracing religion and the physical, biological, and psychological sciences in harmony, is already present in embryo, but we have not yet imagined it as a whole with the whole of ourselves or understood how it relates to our own lives. In order to move into our new cosmos, we will have to summon up the languages of feeling and senses as well as of true intellect (which *just sees*) and of what we have called intellect heretofore: mechanical logic, which is really the intelligence (not to be sneezed at) that unconsciously imitates the way the body moves and hence knows "how things work."[68]

Under this tree where my husband and I are sitting, a house once stood, where people nobody now remembers were born, sometimes looked up at the stars as I do now, and died. Of their house there remains not a trace.

The medieval universe was such a house. It rose up around the central pillar of the universe, conceived not just as a physical vertical dimension but also as a scale of qualities, of density of matter, and, inversely, of speeds of revolution and degrees of intelligence—the "great chain of being," from minerals to God, with human beings halfway up, "a little lower than the angels."

People made their home in this universe, which still corresponded to the body's sensation of itself and contained a locus for the heart's desire, a *telos* represented as "the point of it all," the goal of the intellect as well as of the heart. To sin was to miss the mark, to miss the bull's-eye of the target, to miss the point of life.

The body, which understands geometry without any lessons, could easily represent to itself a universe of concentric spheres. It can just as easily relate, through the sensation of breathing, to the image of an expanding universe. We can regard the concentric spheres of the ancients as epochs in the expansion of the universe—"cross-sections" of the 3-sphere taken at various moments in its history when one or another parameter reached a critical value so that a new level of organization could appear. Thus, we can distinguish the epoch or sphere of the quarks and leptons, the epoch or sphere of the nucleons, of the neutral atoms, of the molecules, and so on, and the simultaneous epochs of emergence of large-scale structures:

> Evolution acts in the sense of simultaneous and interdependent structuration of the macro- and microworld.... It is not adaptation to a given environment that signals a unified overall evolution, but the coevolution of system and environment at all levels, the coevolution of micro- and macrocosmos.[69]

Within the expanding universe, something like the "great chain of being," a hierarchy of increasing levels of organization, from quarks to our own brains, each living in its corresponding world, its macrocosmos, was, and still is, evolving—if we ourselves do not fail. And as in Dante's universe, the energy—the "speed of revolution"—increases as we ascend upward and inward, in Dante's terms, or extrapolate backward, in present-day cosmologists' terms, toward the Source.

Now the moon has arisen and erased the stars. Startled out of my reverie by her brightness, I see her for a moment, as Erazim Kohák predicted, just as if, startled awake, I looked up and saw my mother's face smiling gently down upon me.

Then my habitual mode of perception closes in again. If I confessed to my first impression, people, brainwashed into assuming without question that the prevailing world view constitutes "common sense," would think I was a sap—a silly female telling fairy tales, not to be taken seriously.

When I look again, the moon is a cold stone.

I begin to hear a rumbling from the other side of the tree. My husband has fallen asleep. I wake him gently, so as not to startle him (what would he see?), and we make our painful way back through the moonlight to the car.

The Grand
Evolutionary Synthesis

This connectedness of our own life processes with the dynamics of an all-embracing universe....

ERICH JANTSCH, *The Self-Organizing Universe*

A crow stands on the yellow median line of a grey highway. He stands on a bloody rag of smeared meat and tattered fur that was once a rabbit, holding it down with his claws, tugging at it with his beak. When a shred of meat tears loose, his head jerks back, and he looks at me.

He looks back along the highway stretching without a curve behind us, then he swivels his head and looks in the other direction, along the highway stretching without a curve ahead of us. The string of meat swings in his beak like a pendulum. The western desert is featureless, the sky a white glare. The gleaming, purple-black crow on the yellow line and the smear of brown and red he stands upon are the only colors anywhere.

With another jerk of the crow's head, the shred of meat disappears down his throat. A rabbit is turning into a crow. As the energy that once animated the rabbit slowly infuses into his living flesh, the crow keeps gazing at me with his round black eye, as if to ask me whether I understand.

I turn and look down the highway behind me, the way the crow was looking before, in the direction from which I have come. The sun is rising on the far horizon. It looks enormous, quivering and sweating, its molten gold spreading out over the rim of the earth like a pair of arms. The yellow median line leads directly into—or issues directly from—its heart.

Then I turn and look in the other direction. Where the highway meets the horizon there, the yellow line is broken into rippling, dancing fragments that ride the rising waves of heat like salamanders of old—spirits that live in the flames—ascend, writhing, from the earth, break up, disappear, reform, and vanish once more.

When I face the crow, I can see in both directions at once. I look at him again and feel, unaccountably, the energy in my own body slowly changing, like water into nectar, into some unknown new substance that has the quality at the same time of understanding and of love.

We are all in this together.

Those are the first words that come to me, but they are not just words. They carry a feeling of kinship—no, it is something more than kinship; it is continuity. And it is something more intimate than a feeling; it is a sensation. The sensation of the entrance of this energy that tastes like love is as immediate as the flow of honey over the tongue. Either kind of energy—the kind that is entering the crow through his beak or the kind that is entering me through my eyes and (so it feels) through my skin—has come from the sun. It has come from the heart of the sun. We are all in this together, interwoven with one another and woven, as if by golden threads, into a single space-time fabric by the love of the sun.

That is how a part of our total endowment of faculties—feeling and sensation together, feeling arising from immediate sensation—perceives the situation. Now let the part of the mind that figures out how things work join the chorus—but not drown the other voices out, as it has for four hundred years.

In the sun's core, its "nuclear furnace," four protons (hydrogen nuclei) combine in a series of steps to make one atom of helium, with a loss of 0.7 percent of the proton mass, which is converted to energy in accordance with Einstein's equation $E=mc^2$. This energy, in the form of photons, wanders 50 million years finding its way from the sun's heart to its photosphere, then speeds in eight minutes from there to the earth. To get into the rabbit, and from there into the crow, it has to go another long journey, first landing on a leaf or a blade of grass, where a molecule of chlorophyll persuades it to raise electrons to a high energy level and store them in high-energy chemical bonds.

What this tastes like to you and me and the rabbit is sweetness: in a silent, invisible sacred dance performed in the sanctuary of a leaf cell, tasteless, odorless water and air have been transformed into sugar.

That's transubstantiation. Divine energy enters into virgin matter to become our food: God with us—God *in* us, on the tongue, down the throat, in the belly, infusing into our flesh like wine.

The energy of the electrons in the high-energy chemical bonds is lowered step by step through the chemical reactions of life until it reaches the level of water, the waste product of all living things— and one of the raw materials too—which is then recycled by the green plants, the energy level lifted up again by a new influx of photons from the sun.

We are all plugged into the stream of descending energy, like those old factories along New England rivers in which every sort of contraption—water wheels, driving belts, turning spools, rattling looms—was harnessed to the energy of the stream descending from the mountain springs to the sea; only here, the factories are known as sweet grass, alfalfa, willow tree, sagebrush, jackrabbit, crow, Martha Heyneman.

I push my cart into the supermarket. Arrayed before me are a thousand shapes of things: rows of green peppers, red peppers, yellow peppers, green and yellow squashes, purple satin eggplants, onions, mushrooms; pyramids of apples, peaches, pears; casual heaps of grapes, green, purple, and bronze; the fishes in their plastic packages (but in Japan, the shrimps and squids were piled up higher than my head, row upon orderly row, still glistening from the predawn sea); the cut-up chickens; the chunks of muscle of cattle and pigs.

Other shapes like myself are pushing other carts. We pile them high with the shapes of things—God's bottles, containers for energy. We dump the shapes in paper bags and lug them home, there to slice, chop, boil, and roast them, flavor them with many-shaped leaves of aromatic herbs, and serve them up with lemon slices, parsley, and paprika, accompanied, for the grandchildren, by the mammary secretions of cows and, for us, by the tenderly fermented juices of crushed grapes, come from afar in space and time. Then we all sit down and chew and swallow, and the many shapes vanish—all but our own, laughing, talking, animated, beloved.

Shapes are broken down by other shapes into their simplest elements, to be built up again into the new design, as if temples and cathedrals and mausolea came daily under the wrecker's ball and were reduced to bricks and stones, then built up again into the also-temporary fabric of another architecture.

> Old stones to new building, old timber to new fires,
> Old fires to ashes, and ashes to the earth
> Which is already flesh, fur and faeces,
> Bone of man and beast, cornstalk and leaf.[1]

What was once alive fertilizes lives to come. The energy that one creature has to relinquish another snatches up. Interrupting entropy, all of us are kept alive by an insignificant fraction of the energy the sun throws away. Descending, the energy lifts other things up, as Niagara Falls lifts up elevators in far-off Manhattan. Descending, the energy fuels the building up of all these fantastic forms and fuels their activities until they themselves disintegrate, releasing their energies for the use of others. "There is a reality which is making itself," said Henri Bergson, "in a reality which is unmaking itself."[2] The unmaking of the hydrogen in the sun is the making of the helium, and the leftovers from that process sustain the whole of organic life on earth. The unmaking of a blade of grass was the making of a rabbit. The unmaking of the rabbit is the making of the crow. The unwinding gyre empowers the winding-up one, which in turn will empower, in its unwinding, the winding up of a third—"dying each other's life, living each other's death." The parents expend themselves in nurturing the children, who become parents in their turn. This "perpetual motion machine" is another manifestation of the gyres, spindle, or mill described in chapter 3. But here, enmeshed in it myself, feeling the heat of the sun on my right cheek and the grave regard of the crow in front of me, I experience this network of processes not as anything mechanical but rather as something passionate and sexual, heavy with grief and adoration: intercourse and childbirth and death—"Everything issuing from everything and again entering into everything."[3] We are all in this together.

> Morowitz has presented the case, in thermodynamic terms, for the hypothesis that a steady flow of energy from the inexhaustible source of the sun to the unfillable sink of outer space, by way of the earth, is mathematically destined to cause the organization of matter into an increasingly ordered state. The resulting balancing act involves a higher and higher complexity, and the emergence of cycles for the storage and release of energy. In a nonequilibrium steady state, which is postulated, the solar energy would not just flow to the earth and radiate away; it is thermodynamically inevitable that it must rearrange matter into symmetry, away from probability, against entropy, lifting it, so to speak, into a constantly changing condition of rearrangement and molecular ornamentation. In such a system, the outcome is a chancy kind of order, always on the verge of descending into chaos, held taut against probability by the unremitting, constant surge of energy from the sun.[4]

If this were translated into music, Lewis Thomas proposes, it would sound like the Brandenburg Concertos of Johann Sebastian Bach.

One part of the psyche can stand back and admire the process aesthetically, having explored it mathematically, feeling itself to be separate from it. Another part is deeply engaged in all the births and deaths, joys and sufferings involved in it and is able to feel the joys and sufferings of the other participants. These aspects of the psyche screen each other, suppress each other, argue with each other like men and women, sometimes fear each other, have contempt for each other, and alternately dominate in successive historical epochs, but both are needed to make a whole human being. Bach himself was able to objectify in his music dynamical systems

THE GRAND EVOLUTIONARY SYNTHESIS *121*

theory before it was discovered by science and to communicate at the same time the anguish, aspiration, and ecstasy involved in what was being represented: the laws of creation, maintenance, transformation, and evolution of the universe, which are at the same time the laws of creation, maintenance, transformation, and possible evolution (redemption, salvation) of an individual human being. *Wachet auf!* says the cantata: "Sleepers, awake!" Another says that Christ is himself the sun.

Unlike the energy that is entering the flesh of the crow, that which is entering my eyes has come direct from the sun—or almost so—in the form of light. Reflected off rabbit, crow, and highway, light is the medium that carries an impression of their forms and colors into my eyes—and more than their forms and colors, or so it seems, into my eyes and also through the pores of my skin. The crow in his eating and I in my seeing are in communion with the sun. The rabbit too is dissolving back into sun: into warmth, strength, and transforming power—the power that is changing a pattern of rabbit molecules into a pattern of molecules of crow. Being, knowledge, and power all come to us courtesy of the sun.

And how did the energy get into the protons in the sun? The new cosmology, like the ancient and medieval ones, and unlike what went between, is a gold mine of metaphors for seekers of the point of it all. Darwin's observation at the close of his *Origin of Species* about the history of life on earth—

> There is a grandeur in this view of life, with its several powers, having been originally breathed by the Creator into a few forms or into one; and that...from so simple a beginning endless forms most beautiful and most wonderful have been and are being evolved.[5]

—has been extended to embrace the whole history of the universe:

> ...even at this early stage it's possible to discern the grandeur and beauty, and the extraordinary explanatory power of what is, after all, the ultimate history story—the history of the universe, the story of how a single kernel of energy could have become everything that there is.[6]

The new history of the universe links us back (*re-ligio*) to unity, to the point of it all, and beyond that to the Unmanifest, the perfect symmetry of the No-thing out of which everything has come. This sounds like metaphysics, but it's physics—the "theory of vacuum genesis." It is also a new covenant, a bridge uniting the things of time to timelessness. Something begins to stir deep inside us: *It's all true. It's all really true after all...*

But still we cannot feel it. We do not think of the sun as a god because—at least in our grown-up, fallen condition—we are unable to perceive life or consciousness in it. The sun is the source of our life, but we do not think of it as alive, conscious, or a *person*, and cannot, therefore, feel related to it. For that, we will have to go "east of the sun and west of the moon," beyond the sun to the source of this source of our life, which, being unconditioned—everywhere and nowhere—is closer to us than our neck-vein.

How did the energy get into the protons in the sun?

"It is generally believed that all the protons which exist naturally today—at least one in every atom in the universe—were created in the first one hundred millionth of a second after the Cosmic birth."[7] "The legacy of the Big Bang is still with us. The heat released by the sun and other stars represents a fraction of the energy stored in the nuclei of atoms at the outset of time."[8] The energy remained bundled up in the protons for 15 billion years until the sun (Far-Darting Apollo!) untied the package and flung the energy toward the earth in the form of photons, which the chlorophyll in a blade of grass bound up in the bonds of a molecule of sugar, which the rabbit undid and spent in leaps or stored in muscle until a speeding car and a carrion crow undid it again—"cycles for the storage and release of energy."

Other photons—other arrows of the sun—are bringing the vision into my eyes and from there into my brain, which is another kind of organ of digestion. I ruminate—chew on the vision to extract its meaning, a kind of nourishment I cannot live without—and vision, meaning, and power to extract it have all come to me, courtesy of the sun, from the beginning of the world. We are all plugged into the stream of energy that was released in the big bang, stored in forms, released again, stored in more elaborate forms, released again....

This is the "soul's history."[9] Having, like the prodigal son, departed from simple unity in the direction of the ferment and excitement of multiplicity, we arise, impelled by a yearning for inner harmony, and seek unity again and again in *forms* : unities within unities, "forms balanced upon forms" (Louise B. Young), embracing greater and greater realms of multiplicity.

> To be, is no other than to be one. In as far, therefore, as anything attains unity, in so far it "is." For unity worketh congruity and harmony, whereby things composite are, in so far as they are: for things uncompounded are in themselves, because they are one; but things compounded, imitate unity by the harmony of their parts, and, so far as they attain to unity, they are. Wherefore order and rule secure being, disorder tends to not-being.[10]

The unceasing release, capture, recycling, and degradation of energy are inseparable from the building up of levels upon levels of *form*, which we may think of as hierarchies of standing vibrations, ripples, wavelets, and waves, since no embodiment of form is permanent. A form is a pattern of movement—a dance, a dynamical system—that begins, is maintained for a while by "cycles for the storage and release of energy," and then subsides, its energy consumed by other forms or dances, or slipping away from all participation in form down the drain of entropy, there to remain until the big crunch—until Brahma draws in his breath again. "It was designed to supply its own nourishment from its own decay."

> From the time when the first quarks and leptons materialized out of the undifferentiated cosmic substance, to the present-day universe with its almost infinite variety of things—galaxies and quasars, pulsars and black holes, red giants and white dwarfs, stars and planets, and more than a million living species that clothe our planet with an ever-changing kaleidoscope of shape, color, and movement—the universe has opened out and blossomed into ever more intricate and elaborate forms.[11]

The ascent of form, from quarks to the human brain, in coevolution with galaxies and solar systems, ecosystems and societies, is what we call the grand evolutionary synthesis. The developments in science during the twentieth century have revealed that evolution is not confined to organisms on the earth but reaches back almost to the beginning of time. "Biology," said Alfred North Whitehead, "is the study of the larger organisms; whereas physics is the study of the smaller organisms,"[12]— and we are all in this together, the living and the dead, who are alive in another part of time.

> When we look at subatomic particles, and when we look at the stars and galaxies, we see evidence from every direction that the universe is all of a piece, and that it began as a single seed smaller than an atom.
>
> And in a very real sense, you and I were there. Every scrap of matter and energy in our blood and bones and in the synapses of our thoughts, can trace its lineage back to the origin of the universe. The natural laws that fragmented and multiplied as the young universe expanded and cooled continue to operate today in the beating of our hearts, as well as in the trajectories of the stars....The evolution of the universe goes on, not just around us, but within us. Our thoughts and feelings, after all, are part of the universe too. And its story is our story as well.[13]

And "in a very real sense" you and I and the crow are there *now*, "before the beginning." Science, which is a method for studying phenomena, cannot penetrate beyond the big bang, but the crow's eye can and did. When the crow looked at me in silent attentiveness, and I at him, One looked at One. "Consciousness," said Nobel Prize–winning physicist Erwin Schrödinger, "is never experienced in the plural, only in the singular."[14]

> The spiritual world is one single spirit who stands like unto a light behind the bodily world and who, when any single creature comes into being, shines through it as through a window. According to the kind and size of the window less or more light enters the world. The light itself however remains unchanged.[15]

Each one of us too
Has a moon of enlightenment
That shines on unclouded
Though we live out our lives
Never suspecting its presence.[16]

The crow and I are two bodies, two psyches, with thoughts (it looks from here as though the crow had thoughts, but I have no way of knowing), feelings, sensory experiences. If it seems (except at the rarest of moments) that you have your own consciousness and I have mine, that is because (except at the rarest moments) we are not conscious but are each asleep in his own dream, watching his own movie. "Among those who sleep, each one lives in his own world; only those who are awake have a world in common" (Heracleitus).

This is to distinguish consciousness from thinking, feeling, perceiving, and so forth, all of which are phenomena and hence are as suitable for scientific study as rocks, beetles, and river currents, though one's own psychological phenomena are accessible for direct study only by oneself, which is to say, by consciousness. All those phenomena (thinking, feeling, perceiving) that we usually think of as consciousness can theoretically be produced by computers ("artificial intelligence"), but not the awareness of those phenomena—which, to tell the truth, is usually absent in us unless evoked by reminders or informed, active effort. This awareness is not itself a phenomenon but is the *noumenon*.

"God is not an *object*; God is the absolute *Subject*"[17]—and when the absolute subject is perceiving, it perceives itself and the object as not-two, transcending opposites. There is contemplation and there is action, Mary and Martha. The trick of being human is to be both at once, as Our Lord demonstrated, being both God and man at once, an incarnation of divinity.

Everything is an incarnation of divinity. The trick of being human is to know it—or, better still, to *see* it. "Each life is a representative of God," says Gurdjieff. "Whoever can see the representative will see Him who is represented....Whoever does not love life does not love God."[18]

The Self is one. Unmoving, it moves faster than the mind. The senses lag, but Self runs ahead. Unmoving, it outruns pursuit. Out of Self comes the breath that is the life of all things.

Unmoving, it moves; is far away, yet near; within all, outside all.

Of a certainty the man who can see all creatures in himself, himself in all creatures, knows no sorrow....[19]

I see now that the sun on my right stands for itself but at the same time for the big bang, when time entered in from the halls of the outer heaven. Except in those deep ocean trenches where colonies of giant, headless worms live on energy welling up from within the earth, all the energy of organic life—in the rabbit, in the crow, in me—had its origin in the sun. All the energy in the sun, and in the earth as well, had its origin in the big bang. All the energy in the big bang spilled out of a rupture in the perfect symmetry of the all-powerful stillness that preceded it—if one can use the verb "preceded" to bridge the abyss that separates timelessness from time, for the big bang was the origin of time and space.

The big bang had its origin in the breaking of the symmetry of something altogether unconditioned, unmanifest, perfectly symmetrical, and of contained, unimaginable power. All our energy, therefore, has its origin in timelessness.

The creation of the world, that is to say, the creation of something out of nothing, is itself but the external aspect of something which takes place in God Himself....The primary start or wrench in which the introspective God is externalized and the light that shines inwardly made visible, this revolution of perspective, transforms En-Sof, the inexpressible fullness, into nothingness. It is this mystical 'nothingness' from which all the other stages of God's gradual unfolding in the Sefiroth emanate and which the Kabbalists call the highest Sefirah, or the "supreme crown" of Divinity....It is the abyss which becomes visible in the gaps of existence...every time the status of a thing is altered, the abyss of nothingness is crossed and for a fleeting mystical moment becomes visible. Nothing can change without coming into contact with this region of pure absolute Being which the mystics call Nothing.[20]

These "abysses of nothingness" Gurdjieff symbolizes as the intervals in the octave, especially the interval *si–do*. The aim of an authentic teaching, he says, is the realization of one's own nothingness. This is at the same time an experience of "inexpressible fullness," the reverse of the revolution in perspective that took place in the beginning. It is the "bottom," the crèche underneath the Christmas tree, the opposite pole of a universe that turns inside out. (The return is inner.) The traversal of this interval between levels of being is sometimes symbolized as a bridge across an abyss, "the perilous bridge of welfare," or the death of the old man that has to precede the birth of the new, whereupon, as Saint Paul said, "It is no longer I that liveth, but Christ in me"—the whole human being, partaking of both timelessness and time.

We can know how timelessness relates to time only by experiencing that relationship within ourselves:

> ...to apprehend
> The intersection of the timeless
> With time, is an occupation for the saint...[21]

says T. S. Eliot. Let us scrape the barnacles off the word "saint" and restore it to its original meaning of "whole human being." A whole human being is simultaneously aware of timelessness and time, and not just with the abstract intellect. He "remembers himself," in Gurdjieff's terms. She remembers herself. So long as such a one, woman or man, maintains this state, she or he maintains a connection with timelessness in the midst of time and becomes thereby a bridge between the two.

"Eternity is in love," as William Blake confided to us, "with the productions of time." A whole human being becomes love, just as the rabbit is now becoming warmth, strength, and nourishment. Timelessness and the productions of time nourish each other, and it may be only human beings who can become the site of this exchange.

This gives me another hint of what I am supposed to be doing here on earth, immersed (and usually all the way over my head) in the rich confusion of the productions of time.

Since it is said to be the origin of time, the big bang (which might better be called, as Lewis Thomas remarked, "the great light") may be called one of the points of intersection of the timeless with time, but that point is here and now for Eliot's saint. The simultaneous awareness of the kind of knowledge acquired through the study of science and the kind bestowed at moments in the course of practice of an authentic spiritual discipline would be another such intersection. Pure, unconditioned consciousness imposes no dogma (any more than light does upon whatever it illuminates) but allows phenomena, including the scientific intellect, to be what they are. It feeds on them—not diminishing, but rather enhancing, them—delights in them, is in love with them. You and I are always standing in the way between consciousness and phenomena, with our thinking, talking, judging, theorizing, showing off.

Thinking, talking, and theorizing are also phenomena, but immersed in them I lose consciousness. Thus I am standing here now talking, blocking your view of the crow.

"Real world very big. We very small. When small become big, big disappears." So said Sophia Grigorievna Ouspensky, wife of P. D. Ouspensky, a very great teacher herself. "Once we realized our own nothingness," her pupil, Robert de Ropp, remarks in explanation, "we could emerge into the real world."[22]

Physicists and mathematicians mean something different by "symmetry" than you and I do, but the kind of symmetry we know can serve as an analog or metaphor for theirs. When I sit in meditation in the morning, straightening my back in imitation of the axis of the universe, leaning neither forward nor back, neither to the right nor to the left, balancing out all the stresses and strains so that they add up to zero, pointing the top of my head directly up, toward the Sundoor or North Star—emblems, like the big bang, of the point of intersection of the timeless with time—I imitate the perfect symmetry that was before the world began.

And when I get up and walk, I stumble off-balance into time— as did the universe, in a series of broken symmetries—and move out from unmanifest inner space into my room, my house, my city, and the great, roaring, expanding globe of the out-of-doors under the sky.

In this transition, I imitate the origin of the universe—and discover that as soon as I get up and walk, I forget where I came from and who I am. I forget my Self. I forget the Unmanifest, the Unconditioned. I forget God.

Swept up in time, I lose all touch with timelessness, though by definition, timelessness is always now and here. What was before the big bang "is not in space but in the mind of God." When I sit in inner stillness, breathing in, breathing out, I am a "closed system"—complete but inert and aloof, like one of the noble gases. When I get up and walk, I am partial but active. I participate in a greater whole, which in turn participates in one greater still.

It is a sense of these greater wholes that I am after, so as not to get lost all the time in time.

The crow has waked me up for a moment and reminded me that part of the answer to the question of what I am supposed to be doing here on the earth is: *Wake up*! In the midst of time, that is, wake up to timelessness, and—by becoming inwardly attentive and still and relaxing away from personal ambition and its attendant anxiety—get out of the way, from between God and the object.

Stop blocking eternity's view of the productions of time. Something timeless needs the energy of these minute, particular, evanescent impressions—and in the light of that something timeless, their meaning is revealed, *sub specie aeternitatis.*

"From the age of 13 or 14, I wanted to know how the universe worked, and why," said the cosmologist Stephen Hawking, "and why it is what it is. But now I have some idea of how the universe works, but I still do not really understand—but I still do not really understand why."[23] And Steven Weinberg, one of the world's leading theoretical physicists and author of the best-selling *The First Three Minutes*, wrote, "The more the universe seems comprehensible, the more it also seems pointless."[24]

It is not possible to answer questions like "Why?" (in the sense of "For what purpose?") and "What is the point?" through science because from the beginning, Western science has scrupulously avoided asking those questions. The part of the mind that is used in science is not the right instrument for answering them.

That in oneself that truly asks "Why?" is not the part that wants to "predict and control" (the stated aims of our science) but is something much simpler, that has the capacity to feel the immediate presence of something much greater than oneself, to ask and listen in longing inner stillness—*en hypomene*, as Simone Weil put it: in patience, "waiting for God"—and to recognize an answer when it strikes like lightning, without any words, and is gone again: to see the point of it all when it pierces you like a sword.

This is revelation, which does not cancel out but transcends, sometimes corrects, and often precedes reason, as in moments of scientific inspiration—just as the teaching of Beatrice in Dante's poem does not negate but goes beyond the teaching of Virgil, which is a teaching of self-knowledge and self-rectification, in the sense of straightening out, recovering one's balance and symmetry.

Indeed, his teaching is prerequisite to hers. "The only right way to objective consciousness is through the development of self-consciousness."[25] Reason must encompass self-knowledge as well as knowledge of the world before the ground is prepared for revelation—and the goal of self-knowledge is the realization of one's own nothingness.

This humility is nothing Uriah Heepish but, on the contrary, is a cleansing of the doors of perception—what Zen calls "don't-know mind" and what T. S. Eliot calls, "a condition of complete simplicity"—that early-morning clarity and freshness that Dante evokes so poignantly at the outset of his *Purgatorio*, when he and Virgil issue forth from Hell:

> Sweet hue of oriental sapphire that was gathering in the serene face of the sky, pure all the way to the first circle, restored delight to my eyes as soon as I issued forth from the dead air that had afflicted my eyes and my breast. The lovely planet that prompts to love was making the whole East smile....[26]

Once we realized our own nothingness, we could emerge into the real world.

The big bang had its origin in the breaking of the symmetry of something altogether unconditioned and unmanifest (and therefore, from an outer point of view, "nothing"), perfectly symmetrical, and of contained, unimaginable power. All our energy, therefore, has its origin in eternity and its end, according to the second law of thermodynamics, in "the heat death of the universe"—in those evanescent bits of raveling yellow line on my left.

Or does it?

What about those "ever more intricate and elaborate forms" into which the universe has blossomed? The relationship between evolution and entropy has been a tangle of confusion and controversy since the nineteenth century. While pessimists like Henry Adams were being depressed by the idea of the "heat death of the universe," whose inevitability seemed to be implied by the second law of thermodynamics, optimists were being inflated by the idea of progress, extrapolated from Darwin's theory of evolution.

Where physicists see living things as "dissipative structures," productive of entropy, biologists see them as builders-up of form, and when physicists equate evolution with information or "negentropy," biologists protest:

> There must surely be a misunderstanding here. Order or organization as the biologist understands it means complex regularity, with the extra connotation of stability....Order of this kind is by no means confined to the living world: it is the orderliness of a crystal, of a molecule, or in general of the solid state. But an increase of complex regularity may accompany a *decline* of free energy; for example, in the combination between gaseous hydrogen and oxygen to form molecules of water, which are more highly "organized" in the biological meaning of the word than the parent molecules; or, again, in the phenomena of polymerization and crystallization. In all such cases an increase in the degree of "organization" accompanies an *increase* of entropy—the opposite of what we should expect if biological and thermodynamic order were essentially the same. Willard Gibbs said entropy was "mixedupness"; biological order is not, or not merely, unmixedupness.[27]

From a thermodynamic point of view, living things are dissipative systems, productive of entropy. Enormous quantities of energy are spent in evolving and maintaining them. Just as in chemistry huge excesses of reagent are needed to drive a reaction away from the "attractor" of equilibrium, huge expenditures of energy, productive of entropy, are required for just "stayin' alive." It is like the lavish excesses of nature, wasting billions of acorns to produce one oak tree—but then, the waste of one is the food of another. One man's garbage is another man's gourmet dinner. The decaying acorns fertilize other trees. The sun produces enormous quantities of energy, and a minute fraction of this "waste" suffices to sustain all life on earth.

We living things are like tiny Dixie cups in the magnanimous Niagara of the sun. This huge excess seems to be required to keep us alive. We are expensive. We are bought with a price.

Such lavish expenditure implies that the universe places great *value* upon the evolution of form, the ascent away from the attraction of a lower equilibrium (disintegration and death) to a higher, more inclusive one—from a lower *do* in the octave to a higher one. It seems to place great value upon what Erich Jantsch calls "self-transcendence"—the evolution of the altogether new, what has not existed before. If survival alone were the desideratum, evolution would have come to a halt with the first algae, still going strong after 4 billion years.

In the human realm, what does not evolve degenerates, like a dance repeated and repeated until it becomes mechanical and habitual, and no longer serves as a vessel for effort, aspiration, and self-transcendence—for outdoing oneself. It's too easy. On all scales, evolution is, as Gurdjieff said, "no cheap thing."

> To continue our conversation on the subject of man's nature, man is in essence a passion for understanding the meaning and aim of existence. His work on the planet is to encounter, overcome and create obstacles. His aim is to fulfill the potentiality of his Being. As Gurdjieff says, he is born incomplete, and his task on Earth is to complete himself. That is the position of man on a cosmic scale.[28]

According to Gurdjieff's redaction of the universal myth of creation,[29] before the universe began, His Endlessness ("the one single spirit") had one sole dwelling place (one "window"), the Most Great and Most Most Holy Sun Absolute (that "single seed" from which the universe began), which "was maintained and existed on the basis of the system called 'Autoegocrat'" ("I-myself-power"): that is, "that principle according to which the inner forces which maintained the existence of this cosmic concentration had an independent functioning, not depending on any forces proceeding from outside." It was, that is, in the terminology of thermodynamics, a closed system.

Dante says the same thing of the Empyrean, the first, or highest, heaven: "It has within itself, in every part, that which its matter demands."[30] Plato says the same thing of the Creator's original plan for the body of the world:

> ...it had no need of eyes, as there remained nothing visible outside it, nor of hearing, as there remained nothing audible; there was no surrounding air which it needed to breathe in, nor was it in need of any organ by which to take food into itself and discharge it later after digestion. Nothing was taken from it or added to it, for there was nothing that could be; for it was designed to supply its own nourishment from its own decay.[31]

And modern physics, pursuing its own path in a direction away from tradition, has now come around full circle to the same universal traditional view. According to modern unified field theories, "all the interactions we see in the present world are the asymmetrical remnant of a once perfectly symmetrical world."[32]

In Gurdjieff's body of thought, the two fundamental laws that govern the universe are called the Law of Three ("Triamazikamno") and the Law of Seven, or Law of Octaves ("Heptaparaparshinokh"). The Autoegocratic system is symbolized by the Law of Three in symmetrical union with the Law of Seven, as depicted in a figure called the enneagram.

According to P. D. Ouspensky, Gurdjieff said of this figure:

> The isolated existence of a thing or phenomenon under examination is the closed circle of an eternally returning and uninterruptedly flowing process. The circle symbolizes this process. The separate points in the division of the circumference symbolize the steps of the process. The symbol as a whole is *do*, that is, something with an orderly and complete existence. It is a circle—a completed cycle. It is the *zero* of our decimal system; in its inscription it represents a closed cycle. It contains within itself everything necessary for its own existence. It is isolated from its surroundings. The succession of stages in the process must be connected with the succession of the remaining numbers from 1 to 9. The presence of the ninth step filling up the 'interval' *si-do*, completes the cycle, that is, it closes the circle, which begins anew at this point.[33]

The points 3 and 6 represent intervals where something is needed in order for the process to continue. In this diagram, representing the Autoegocratic, or closed, system, which cannot prevail in our world as we know it but prevails before our world begins ("before the big bang") or when it is complete, at the end of the time ("after the big crunch"), the intervals fall between *mi* and *fa* and between *sol* and *la*. They are filled by the two angles at the bottom of the inner triangle. The angle at the top represents *do*—both low *do* and high *do*. This arrangement of things indicates that the being, or dynamical system, or whole, represented by this enneagram has its own Law of Three within itself. "It contains within itself everything necessary for its own existence."

According to Gurdjieff, our familiar seven-tone major scale is

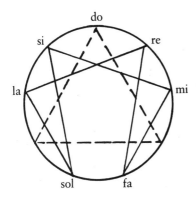

FIGURE 4.1 "The isolated existence of a thing or phenomenon under examination is the closed circle of an eternally returning and uninterruptedly flowing process." Enneagram of a closed system. Drawing by the author, after Ouspensky, *In Search of the Miraculous*, p. 288.

a symbol whose meaning has been forgotten. It represents "the progress and development of phenomena on all planes of the universe observed by us."[34] In this scale, each note of the octave is separated from the next by a whole step, except for *mi* and *fa*, and *si* and *do*, which are separated by a half step. (In musical parlance, these half steps and whole steps are both called "intervals," but Gurdjieff restricts his use of the term "interval" to the half steps—that is, to the places where there is "a missing half tone." In this discussion of his system as I understand it, I am using the term in this second sense.) So from a modern point of view, in this enneagram (figure 4.1) representing the Autoegocratic system, the intervals are in the wrong places.

This discrepancy points to the broken symmetry that lies at the origin of the world as we know it, the transition from Autoegocrat ("I-myself-power") to Trogoautoegocrat ("I-eat-myself-power"), from a closed system to the immense, proliferating network of open systems, feeding and being fed, that constitute the living organism of our expanding universe, which feeds, as a whole, according to Plato, on its own decay.

In the beginning, the Sun Absolute, existing on the basis of the system called Autoegocrat, was a closed system. But a closed system is subject to the second law of thermodynamics:

> The famous Second Law of Thermodynamics affirmed that for any given system conceived as a closed—in fact, an isolated—unit of matter and energy, differences and gradients in concentration and temperature tend to disappear, to be replaced by uniformity and randomness. The universe, at least in its material components, moves from a more organized and energetic state toward states of growing homogeneity and randomness. It ultimately reaches the state of perfect heat distribution in which no irreversible processes can any longer occur....The arrow of time is thus given by the probability that closed systems run down....[35]

The second law is the law of entropy, which Webster defines as "a measure of the degree of disorder in a substance or a system: entropy always increases and available energy diminishes in a closed system, as the universe."[36]

In Gurdjieff's story of the creation of the universe, His Endlessness was constrained to create our world because He noticed that the Sun Absolute was diminishing in volume, and He ascertained that the cause of this was "merely the Heropass, that is, the flow of Time itself," which is to say, entropy. In order to avert the inevitable end, His Endlessness changed the two fundamental laws (of Three and Seven) by which the whole universe was, and still is, maintained, in such a way—and principally by breaking the symmetry of the Law of Seven, of which the musical octave, with its two asymmetrical missing half tones (between *mi* and *fa* and between *si* and *do*), is a diagram—as to make their independent functioning dependent on forces coming from outside.

In thermodynamic terms, He established the principle upon which so-called open systems are maintained and may evolve, and that required the creation of a whole universe of such systems feeding one another. By the changes He made in the lower part of the octave, He made it possible for fresh energy to be imported into a system from outside—energy that enters, in our case, via food, air, and impressions, from our sun, and ultimately from the Sun Absolute, and maintains us (as Lewis Thomas put it) in "a nonequilibrium steady state," "a chancy kind of order, always on the verge of descending into chaos, held taut against probability by the unremitting, constant surge of energy from the sun."[37]

By moving the upper interval close to high *do*, He made it possible for energy descending from above to blend with the energy in the note *si*, in accordance with the Law of Three: "the higher blends with the lower in order to actualize the middle." He thus facilitated evolution from one level of organization to the next—as if a hand reached down from the ledge above and drew the climber up to a higher level of integration, governed by a more penetrating and comprehensive principle.

Atom ascends to molecule, molecule to cell, cell to organism. Each new principle of organization may be said to "eat" the ascending creature, incorporating it into a cosmos of another level, of greater scope in space and in time—larger, longer lasting, more highly organized. The part comes under the laws of a greater

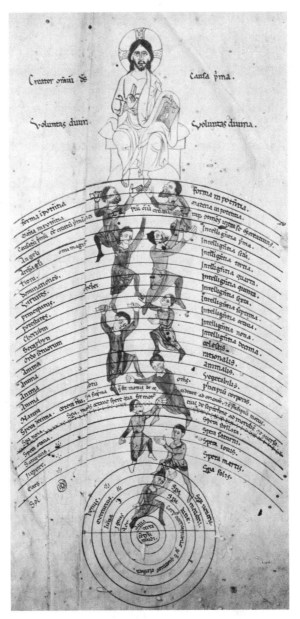

FIGURE 4.2   *...as if a hand reached down from the ledge above and drew the climber up....* Ascent of the soul through the spheres. Hermetic manuscript, anonymous, twelfth century, The National Gallery of Scotland (Jill Purce, *The Mystic Spiral: Journey of the Soul* [New York: Avon Books, 1974] p. 67).

whole, with more *meaning* in it. The creature, on its side, uniting with the higher principle, moves on to a deeper, vaster, and more unified and encompassing sense of who it is.

There is reciprocal feeding on the same level, as it were, and also between adjacent levels of being. Human beings, according to one of the diagrams Gurdjieff gave his pupil Ouspensky, are food for archangels.[38]

The sun is an archangel. The earth eats vertebrates and also ourselves, insofar as we are vertebrates. "The earth that fed you now will eat you," the deceased is told at a Greek funeral. The earth is an angel.

Moon, earth, and sun represent three levels of being, analogous to the levels possible for, but seldom achieved by, human beings. The moon has no atmosphere. It does not breathe. It shows only one side to the earth and keeps the other side hidden, like ourselves when there is no commerce between conscious and subconscious, when we present one face to the world and show another—made "bad," like a rejected child, through deprivation of warmth and light—only in private. The moon does not respond. It is not responsible. It is a dead weight dragging on the earth, like an infant in the womb, not yet able to breathe on its own.

The earth breathes. It revolves on its axis, exposing all sides of itself to the light of the sun. It supports the moon and feeds all organic life, financed, like a wife of the old school, by its husband, the sun. The earth *responds*: it is responsible—"marvelously skilled in handling the sun....You have to be able to catch energy and hold it, storing precisely the needed amount and releasing it in measured shares,"[39] like a good housewife handling money—but is not itself the source of the energy it handles with such skill. The sun, and beyond it the Unconditioned, is the source of that energy.

By analogy, we too can move from the condition of being dead weights within whatever communal group with a common aim we participate in, to become able to respond to what is needed within the group, and maybe even beyond that, to become sources of evolutionary energy for other human beings—sources, like the sun, but not the ultimate source, which is the Unconditioned.

With each step, there is an abyss to be crossed. A system can evolve only when it is open and far from equilibrium.

All the energy in a closed system will eventually become unavailable for useful work. It will end up as heat. "It is not energy that is lost," said Richard Feynman, "but opportunity." But open systems can import energy from outside themselves. In Gurdjieff's terminology, this principle is called (as noted earlier) Trogoautoegocrat ("I-eat-myself-power"), "that true Savior from the law-conformable action of the merciless Heropass." "This Most Great common-cosmic Trogoautoegocratic-process...was established by our Endless Creator to permit the 'exchange of substances,' or 'Reciprocal-feeding' of everything existing, to proceed in the Universe, so that the merciless Heropass would no longer have its maleficent effect on the Sun Absolute."[40]

The rabbit, crow, and I not only stand in the stream of increasing entropy symbolized by the yellow line disintegrating toward the horizon on my left. We are also enmeshed in the reciprocal feeding of everything that exists. The perpetual motion of eating and being eaten on earth is part of the perpetual motion of the whole. "It was designed to supply its own nourishment from its own decay." The activity of the whole universe throughout time feeds God, who created it. It is the Everything of his All, the myself—composite, multiple, in ceaseless motion, change, and transformation—of his I, which is the Self that transcends all opposites ("unmoving, it moves") and is alone immortal.

> I am the food, I am the food, I am the food; I am the eater, I am the eater, I am the eater; I am the link between, I am the link between, I am the link between....
> I am this world and I eat this world. Who knows this, knows.[41]

What I have before me in the form of a road-killed rabbit and a crow (or my own dinner table with my family seated around it) is a vision of, and a feeling of communion with, the common-cosmic Trogoautoegocrat, our true savior from entropy, or time. The crow, in eating the rabbit, is eating himself. He is an emblem of the Trogoautoegocrat.

There is only one I, and insofar as we are awake, we all partake of it. I, in watching rabbit and crow, watch myself. We are all in this together, and what we are in is perpetual transformation. Nothing stands still except the consciousness that contemplates, which at the same time moves (vibrates, revolves, like a quasar) faster than the mind. Unmoving, it moves.

We are all in this together, woven into the fabric of organic life, eating and being eaten. "The earth that fed you now will eat you." The rabbit is now paying his debt to nature, as we all will sooner or later, and it becomes clear that by the large abstraction "nature" we mean *each other*: the whole community of living beings on the earth (Gaia), yes, but also in the whole universe from the beginning of time. Such a vast company is comprehensible to the mind but not to the imagination or the heart, so it is fortunate that in practical terms "each other," representative of the whole, means you and I, a slaughtered rabbit, a jet-black crow, and the great sun himself or herself (our sun), in whom we live, and move, and have our being, and who is, like us, mortal.

When the sun runs out of hydrogen and out of all subsequent, coarser fuels, swells into a red giant, and then collapses into a white dwarf, reducing the earth and us with it back into the stardust from which we were compounded, we will all be eaten by second-generation stars, and so on, until the end of time—the big crunch—when we will all disappear back into the Unconditioned.

But so long as I realize my own nothingness, get out of the way, from between God and the object—from between eternity and the productions of time—I am feeding the Unconditioned even now. "We are the bees of the infinite," said the poet Rainer Maria Rilke, and when we are seeing like this, he said (when we have "emerged into the real world"), we are seeing things as they are within the Angel. Rilke gives El Greco's *Toledo* as an example of how things look from this perspective, as Father Berry gave an example in the passage quoted earlier: "What seemed so opaque and impenetrable suddenly becomes radiant with intelligibility, powerful beyond imagination."

And so we stand here, the crow and I, each one containing (as did the rabbit too, not long ago) a hierarchy of forms within forms within forms, atoms within molecules within cells, reflecting the whole history of the universe. The crow, the rabbit, and I stand at right angles to the yellow line, "held taut against entropy" for a little while, "stayin' alive" (two out of three, in any case); and I, with my upright human posture, extend into another dimension, at right angles to the other two, and thanks to this have the possibility (seldom exercised!) of contemplation. We can think of these as three dimensions of time: the yellow line pointing off to the left with the arrow of entropy; the cycles of eating and being eaten revolving around that line at right angles to it, a temporary stay against disintegration ("cycles for the storage and release of energy," or, as Gurdjieff would say, "the evolution and involution of substances"); and the third coordinate, my upright body, representing the possibility of the connection of time with timelessness, the perfect symmetry anterior to time.

Insofar as we are inwardly passive, inanimate, we are altogether subject to entropy and the yellow line of time; insofar as we are alive, enmeshed in organic life with rabbit and crow, we are "self-organizing," partake of the reciprocal feeding of everything existing, and through cycles for the storage and release of energy hold off dissolution for a while. Insofar as we begin to wake up, we become aware of still another dimension, intersecting every moment of the other two, so that every here and now is a doorway (an op-port-unity) to timelessness: to connect one's seeing, and then one's being, with that which transcends opposites.

What the grand evolutionary synthesis shows us is that we cannot grow toward completion in isolation, as "closed systems," but only by becoming, consciously and voluntarily, part of something greater than ourselves—"a particle, though an independent one, of everything existing in the Great Universe."[42] For this we need to realize, first of all, that we are, willy-nilly, part of Gaia, organic life on earth. And we need to realize it not just with the mind but also with the heart and flesh, with love, gratitude, and sorrow, knowing that we will serve Gaia with the death of our living bodies, as we have been served by her with food, air, and the wealth of impressions lavished upon us by her intricate beauty.

Beyond this we can learn, with joy and adoration, that we also have the possibility to partake of the Unconditioned, insofar as we wake up to it. Then we will be in a position to search for ways to serve both God and nature consciously in action as well as in contemplation, for we are not put on the earth to escape from the earth, as some ascetic religious schools have supposed, but to aid in its transformation: Thy kingdom come...on earth as it is in heaven. To aid in the transformation of the earth does not mean building highways and parking lots; it means becoming oneself the site of a marriage of heaven and earth, timelessness and time. The fruit of this marriage is a love for the productions of time that stems from seeing with new eyes: God is in the details.

> The ancient pond.
> A frog jumps in—
> The sound of the water.
> —Bashō

The fourth dimension ("imaginary time") on Stephen Hawking's diagram of the universe (figure 3.13) had an arrow that pointed in one direction only, the direction of increasing entropy.[43] Dante's fourth dimension, on the other hand—although it too showed this direction (the direction toward the bottom of Hell) and indicated the necessity of descending all the way to that point of the second death, the death of egotism—passed through the zero, the hole Satan is stuck in, beneath that "center of entropy" and made a turn (in that so literally portrayed "conversion" of Dante and Virgil). At this point, his fourth dimension's arrow began to point in the opposite direction: the direction of increasing "speed of revolution"—of light, love, aliveness, intelligence, and unity of being: the direction of evolution.

There is no indication on Hawking's diagram of the whole concern of biologists: the direction of the increasing self-organization of matter throughout time, from the big bang until today, when we ourselves seem to be charged with responsibility for the continuation or noncontinuation of the process, at least on earth.

"How can we explain the fact that matter arrays itself in these successive complexities of form," asks Louise B. Young, that quarks and leptons suddenly materialize out of the cosmic flux—and these fuse into nucleons—and nucleons combine to create compound nuclei? Logically we would expect that the cosmic expansion would have distributed the hot, undifferentiated plasma of matter and energy ever more evenly and more diffusely throughout space....The facts all fall into place...if we make the assumption that there is a natural tendency for self-organized wholes to form.[44]

To assume that "there is a natural tendency" is of course no explanation—but then Newton did not profess to explain gravity either, only to articulate the few beautiful and simple laws of its quantitative behavior. We know what gravity is anyhow, in the sense that we have immediate experience of it in our very flesh, so long as we are on the earth (you have the sensation of it this very minute in your body, pressing the soles of your feet to the earth or your bottom to the seat of the chair—you have "carnal knowledge" of it); and we also have carnal knowledge (though we may be unaware of it, or interpret it as something else) of this "whole-making tendency," as Young calls it.

What does "self-organized" mean? Surely it cannot be supposed that every atom has made a separate decision and, on its own initiative, "by taking thought," organized itself—any more than we can suppose that every stone kicked over a precipice makes an individual decision to fall or not to fall. This whole-making tendency is not personal to any of the entities it organizes, although it is experienced, first of all, as coming from within. We experience it, like gravity, in our very flesh: an aspiration, a sense of there always being something missing, a hunger for we don't know what, a void we are always trying to fill with always ultimately unsatisfying substitutes for whatever it is.

This sensation used to be called "divine discontent" or "the unquiet heart of the Christian." Both Plato and Freud called it *Eros*, but when awareness of the real existence of "a natural tendency for self-organized wholes to form" was thrown out with Aristotle's idea of entelechy and the Christian idea of the possibility of self-completion or self-perfection, we lost all possibility of understanding the meaning of this perpetual dissatisfaction we all suffer from or try to anesthetize through all the dodges of our endlessly inventive psyche: projection, addiction, self-destruction, violence—what used to be called the seven deadly sins, or errors: all the myriad ways of missing the point of life.

This need is innate in us—"a constant and unflagging instinctive need to perfect oneself in the sense of being."[45] It is the motive force of our searching and striving. ("Hunger is our food," say the Sufis.) It needs only to be revived and detoxified and assured by the intellect that it has a real existence in the universe, and a true goal.

I hold, with Louise B. Young (and Dante and Aristotle), that this whole-making tendency, this "instinctive need for self-perfection in the sense of being," is also the motive force of evolution. "There is something within life, within nonliving matter, too, that is not passive—a nisus, a striving that is stimulated by challenge."[46]

We know that; we have always known it. What we need is to be once more intellectually assured that within the whole of things, the whole history of the universe, this instinctive need and striving of ours has a really existent goal.

Merely "stayin' alive" (not to mention evolving toward wholeness) requires constant exchange of substances. We are able to maintain ourselves against entropy for a little while only, thanks to the sacrificed lives of millions of animals and plants, to the whole of organic life on earth, laboriously evolved for 4 billion years, and behind that to the labors of the sun, and behind that to the evolution of the whole universe over 15 billion years, including the labors of the stars in evolving the complex atoms of which we are composed and which we need constantly to import into our bodies. We are also indebted to all the plants of the earth for the air we breathe, and to the whole organization of agriculture and food distribution developed over the centuries through the intelligence and labor of our ancestors and still maintained today by the labors of countless human beings, for our food, its quality, and the quality of the air fought for by still other human beings, sometimes at the risk of their lives.

As for news of our possibility, as human beings, of becoming the channel for the transmission to the earth of an energy that it requires, an energy that passes through us from timelessness into time and is that love of eternity for the productions of time that William Blake spoke of—we owe that to the messengers who have again and again descended throughout history to attempt, indefatigably, to tell us so: Christ, Buddha, Mohammed, Dante, Krishnamurti, Gurdjieff, and no doubt many others whose names I have only read or never knew.

It's really extraordinary that even when I enumerate all these undoubted debts (which amount to only a fraction of the total), no matter how I whip myself up with rhetoric, I still feel no gratitude.

This is for me a waking-up clue to some profound, unconscious illusion we in the West have fallen into since the time of the Renaissance as to who we are and where we belong in the universe. Indian (Native American and Canadian) children are brought up addressing everything in nature as a relative, as did Saint Francis: Grandfather Sun, Mother Earth, Brother Wolf, our little sisters the birds. As children, we saw them that way until, without any words, we learned to be ashamed of our own perceptions. The picture of the real nature of the universe that is emerging in our science today seems to support the prescientific emphasis on *gratitude*: prayers of thanksgiving, acknowledgment of one's debt to sun, earth, rain, seed, harvest, ancestors, parents—and to God, the timeless One who exclaimed, as He created the world, "Let's hope it works."[47]

Whether or not it works on earth is up to us. We are all in this together. "We can no longer accept the old a priori distinction between scientific and ethical values," say Prigogine and Stengers;[48] but the distinction is not so old. No such distinction exists in Dante's *Divine Comedy*. It arose with the scientific revolution, when the arrogant ego blinded itself to our dependency and need for relationship, when the a priori distinction between primary and secondary qualities split the psyche in two and relegated to subconsciousness and contempt our naïve awareness of the immediate presence of divinity and our capacity to perceive life, sensitivity, and personhood in anything but ourselves.

To revive these banished forms of perception will require of us not only humble application for help to those who have not lost them but also individual journeys into the underworld comparable to Dante's—or, rather, Orpheus's. "Every one of us," as Willa Cather said, "has lost an Eurydice"; and my teacher, Jeanne de Salzmann: "You are going on a journey. You can't leave anyone behind. If you leave him behind, you will have to go back and get him."

The Middle Ages left certain aspects of the psyche behind. The Renaissance and scientific revolution had to go back and get them—but in so doing lost hold of the kind of knowledge that had been so long and laboriously accumulated in the East and throughout the Middle Ages.

Now it is time to descend into the underworld in search of the buried maiden, Persephone (Eurydice, Beatrice, Cordelia), our soul, whom each of us left behind when we lurched, off-balance, out of childhood.

We have to go back and get her. And since feeling is hidden in particular sensory impressions, each one of us has to go back and recover her from his or her own memories, his or her own facts.

Nothing is left of the rabbit but the fur. The crow has flown away.

Extrapolating Backward

*"What?" said John and Barbara together in very surprised
voices. "Really? You mean they understood the Starling and
the Wind and—"*

*"And what the trees say and the language of the sunlight
and the stars—of course they did! Once," said Mary Poppins.*

*"But—but how is it that they've forgotten it all?" said
John, wrinkling up his forehead and trying to understand.*

P. L. TRAVERS, *Mary Poppins*

*I myself do not know my own face,
I have forgotten it
In the midst of the market crowd.*

KANZE MOTOKIYO ZEAMI, "Ashikari,"
in Twenty Plays of the Nō Theatre

*...follow autobiographical time until it transcends time and
space. Consciousness then deals with the whole compass
of the universe.* CARY NELSON, *The Incarnate Word*

My sister and I did not find the house, that time. It had long since
burned down in the restless forest fires of California. But we
found the creek and the canyon, and the chimney still standing.

By then we were hot and thirsty. Our clothes were full of dust
and burrs, and our hands and faces were covered with scratches.
Smoke from distant fires made the hot air thick and the light dull.
The sun looked tired, as though it wanted to go out.

My sister crossed the creek, jumping from rock to rock in her
light tennis shoes, and then we walked a little distance upstream—
she on one side of the water, I on the other—and entered the deep
shade of the canyon.

In here, the rushing creek was sending up a cool breeze. There
was a feeling of stirring and breathing. The ferns were bowing

down, springing up, flinging sprays of drops into the darkness. Each of us sat down on a rock on her own side of the creek. We pulled off our battered shoes and socks and, with gasps and groans, lowered our feet into the water. We leaned down and flung icy handfuls of it onto our faces. Then we pulled our feet up, turned around, back to back, each on her separate rock, and wept.

Clinging to my eyelash was a tiny drop across which rainbows swept like clouds. Enclosed within it I saw, in miniature, as if at a great distance, the cabin still whole; the smoke ascending in whorls and throbs from the chimney; and within (as if the house, too, were transparent), the ring of us children around the hearth, passing on stories from one to the next in a game called rigmarole. This tiny drop, containing so much movement, resembled the earth as seen from outer space, or the transparent spherical vesicle within which an embryo thrashes and writhes.

Then I shook my head and it was gone.

I felt alien in the forest, lost, shut out. Some barrier had grown up within me during the fifteen years since, five years old, I had comfortably played all day in this canyon, feeling, without thinking about it, the presences of the great trees around me like guardians—*hearing* their presences like deep organ chords; or played all day in the creek, farther downstream, where the shallow water rippled in perfect transparency over amber pebbles. I would scoop the pebbles up and roll them around in my hands. They were cool and smooth and speckled with darker brown like the eggs of birds. They rattled when I passed them from hand to hand. I would build intricate waterworks out of them—miniature dams, spillways, waterfalls, corrals for salamanders. Flowing over and around these obstacles the water made crystalline shapes—puckers, swellings, dimples, meanders—that were at the same time moving and still. They stood there, quivering a little, while unceasingly the clear water streamed on through them.

Then I would make new shapes, rearranging pebbles, singing to myself, humming, murmuring, muttering, and the creek would do the same.

In the intervening years, I had learned (more by implication than directly) that to feel the trees as living, conscious presences, to feel a companionship with stones and water dogs, a kinship with clear water, was childish error: primitive animism, pathetic fallacy, projection. Such impressions might be considered poetic and charming but were certainly not to be taken as authentic data about what was "really out there."

Now, at twenty, as I sat in these woods, the voices of the trees were drowned out by the idiot chatter inside my own head. Their silent witness made me feel my own nonentity. I no longer knew who I was. Nothing in my head was my own. Every idea, tone of voice, posture, gesture was imitated from somebody else, and the whole machine belt of my actions was driven by the desperate need to impress or to please (so as not to feel cast into outer darkness) whomever I happened to be with at the moment—parent, teacher, member of one or another clique of contemporaries—and each new role was a betrayal of the one before. The harmony of nature made me feel my own disharmony, and I wanted to get out of there.

"Let's go," I said.

We put on our shoes and walked downstream, out of the canyon, past the ruined chimney, through the groves of shimmering aspen (finding with ease, on the way out, the road we had struggled so hard to discover on the way in), back out onto the highway and into our separate lives, our separate marriages, the births and growings up of our separate children: I to my writing, she to her career in organic chemistry.

Now, forty-five years further still down the stream of time, I turn and peer through the darkness, making my way back against Lethe, the river of forgetfulness, entering sphere after sphere of memory, moving, slowly, stage by stage, toward the source—toward the place where I parted from my sister, the soul—the part of us that sees everything as alive, sentient, and a *person*; that sees each life as a representative of God; that sees all creatures in herself, herself in all creatures.

Sonnet to a Scientific Sister

"Now let your vases clear and steadfast be,"
Said Trismosin, "wherein the sulfur seethes,
And, seeking escape, the sophic mercury:
"Else shall you lose the milkfed Pearl who breathes."

So she, nor nun nor alchemist, yet wears
White habits and reactions. She can show
Forests in flasks, birds in ionic pairs;
And sealed herself in silence long ago.

All others suffer fracture, or small leaks
Let seep away the elemental child.
She only wears birth's close transparency,
Within her shimmering envelope still speaks
To animals and snow, and cannot see
She has herself become the sought-for gold.

Just as the building up of form runs counter to the current of entropy, the spatializing of time in active remembering runs counter to Lethe. Houses and landscapes are containers in which memories are stored away in timelessness. There is a geometry to this. Without vessels in which to store what we know—houses with rooms and chests of drawers and shelves with rows of shining jars; remembered spheres of stillness roofed with sky and ringed with lakes and forests—all we have learned and lived through is lost to us.

Our image of the cosmos is the all-inclusive house of our psyche—and vice versa: the house in which we first come to consciousness is our first cosmos. "It is our first universe, a real cosmos in every sense of the word."[1] Strictly speaking, the body is that first house—at the center of the ever-larger spheres of our awareness of the world, as the earth was at the center of the medieval universe—and then the crib, and then the room, and then the house, and then the yard, and then the block, and then the church, and then the school, and then the whole neighborhood—depending on how far the world you know intimately, through your own experience and interaction, can expand and still be held as a whole within your imagination.

But the unspoken world views you absorb, and the different ways you are expected to behave, in these different spheres come into conflict so that the psyche begins to be divided into rooms without doors, and you are cut off from the passageway that leads to that first and innermost room: your sense of inhabiting your own body, firmly established in your own center, yourself.

Only when you are established at this center can you be in communication with the worlds above and below and, indeed, all around you. "Our soul is an abode. And by remembering 'houses' and 'rooms,' we learn to 'abide' within ourselves."[2] Whenever the psyche is out of connection with its center and source, it falls into a heap of broken images, like a ruined house.

> I can connect
> Nothing with nothing.
> The broken fingernails of dirty hands.[3]

Then it's time to extrapolate backward, as the physicists did when they discovered that the universe was expanding, and followed the expansion backward in mathematical imagination to where the four forces were one.

I want to extrapolate backward to where I and my functions were one, where my thinking, feeling, and sensing were my own—and then to that single spark of energy, the source and point of it all, the frontier of the Unconditioned, where the scattered pages of my own particular universe were bound into a single volume by love—and beyond that, to the great darkness and emptiness into which light and fullness turned itself in the beginning, and now, at the end (since the return is inner, and the universe is a great egg that turns inside out perpetually without breaking its shell),

> ...the darkness shall be the light, and the stillness the dancing.[4]

Just as the physical body begins its life as a simple sphere, the fertilized egg, so does our unconscious image of the world. Looking back as far as we can toward the origin of memory, each one of us sees something like the striking of a match in the darkness. A door is thrown open. A wedge of powdery light stabs in, broken by silhouettes haloed in flickering rays of alternate shadow and light. That first moment of consciousness reveals a surrounding world, a "topological sphere" with yourself at the center—a barred crib in a bedroom, a buggy in a backyard dappled with shade, an army cot covered with old, woodsmoke-fragrant quilts in a cabin alive with firelight (where you open your eyes and a mouse runs by along a splintery two-by-four close to your nose)—and joining you within that sphere, appearing and disappearing in accordance with unknown laws, emitting radiations of nourishment or chill, are parents, siblings, and relatives, in attitudes of affection, threat, or indifference. These figures are the archetypes of your inner world, your gods. The quality of your image of the world, and your estimation of your own worth, will depend upon the quality of these people and their attitudes toward you.

Whether I was playing in the creek at the country home or seated on the curb in front of our house in the city watching a sowbug curl itself into a gunmetal sphere when I touched its stomach with a blade of grass, watching my leafboats sail off on the fishscale-rippling rainwater rushing past along the gutter toward the awful Niagara in the culvert at the end of the street (while the ancient palm tree hovered high above me like a huge umbrella, a dusty second celestial vault), I was always in a *temenos*, the sacred enclosure of the sphere of my own perception, a cosmos, with a great palm tree for an *axis mundi* and, at its foot, an inexhaustible well of living energy—a stream sparkling in the light of a sun that warmed me through and through like my father's look of love. ("Ah, the blessed thing," he used to say whenever he saw me—or any child.)

Our first world is spherical. Everything in it is alive. If you sit very still, the animals—even the trees and streams—will begin to speak and tell you what you are to do, what your mission is, the secret meaning of your presence here in this world.

For a brief time after giving birth, a woman may once more experience this sphericality ("that globed feeling," my mother called it), enclosed with her child in a sphere of quietness. Within that *temenos*, she becomes aware, not in the mind but in the wordless thanksgiving of the flesh, of Gaia: of sun, earth, rain, air; of the whole intricate dance of transformations of energy in the bodies of the animals and plants that have given their lives for her and her child, passing on their energy and strength; of all the human beings who have given their labor to the care and cultivation and preparation and transportation of this piece of toast on her tray, this egg, this glass of milk. She is plugged into the whole magnanimous stream of the bestowing of the blessing of nourishment because the circuit is closed: for a short time, like all the other members of Gaia, her body not only is fed, but feeds.

> ...all seemed right to me at that moment. It was one of the few times I felt: this is the way things are and should be.... *I knew where the center of the world was.* A remarkable feeling, in which time turns in a circle, and he who stands at the core has power over everything that takes the form of line and angle and square.[5]

Then the globed moment at the center of the world passes. Things move on. The sphere divides and multiplies, but unlike the cells of the physical body, the many worlds of experience never become a single organism unless at some point in life, impelled by a sensation of dismemberment and inner contradiction, you go in search of a single image that could embrace all these worlds in harmony: a new cosmology. You have to undo your old, fragmented world view, picked up from outside, from here and there, from your fragmented education, and start all over again from your own center, from what you know for yourself. Then the pieces acquired from elsewhere will find their places, not pasted any old how onto the surface of your mind but organically digested into the growing organism of your own understanding.

When I was a premed student, in the display cases outside the zoology lab there was an "exploded skull," with the bones removed at equal distances from the center and fastened to rigid rods so that, thus separated from one another at the sutures, the parts of the skull could be studied and their names learned by heart. The fragmented psyche is like this exploded skull. By moving backward, toward the source and center, we may see the parts come together again and form one whole, enclosed and protected in the first house, as the brain is enclosed and protected within the skull.

Our first real house and cosmos is the body. Whether we grew up in a house with cellar and attic, in an apartment high in the air, or in no house at all—an overturned boat or a cardboard box—we have that first house in common.

> At the very beginning of our individual lives we measure and order the world out from our own bodies: the world opens up in front of us and closes behind. Front thus becomes quite different from back, and we give an attention to our fronts, as we face the world, which is quite different from the care we give to our backs and what lies behind us. We struggle, as soon as we are able, to stand upright, with our heads atop our spines, in a way different from any other creatures in the world, and *up* derives a set of connotations (including moral ones) opposite from *down*. In our minds left and right soon become distinguished from each other in quality as well as in direction, as words like "sinister" and "dextrous" record.
>
> All these qualitative distinctions, based on our own awareness of ourselves, are implicitly called into question once we start our formal education and learn a new system, the Cartesian.…Cartesian coordinates…exhibit no connection with the body-centered, value-charged sense of space we started with.…
>
> One tell-tale sign remains, in modern America, of a world based not on a Cartesian abstraction, but on our sense of ourselves extended beyond the boundaries of our bodies to the world around: that is the single-family house, free-standing like ourselves, with a face and a back, a hearth (like a heart) and a chimney, an attic full of recollections of *up*, and a basement harboring implications of *down*. In children's drawings of houses (sometimes even in countries where the houses do not look like ours) there is generally a door like a mouth, windows like eyes, and a roof like a forehead.…[6]

The idea that Cartesian space is "real" space, like the idea that only the primary qualities are real, is an aspect of the shift in world view that took place in the sixteenth and seventeenth centuries. The development of perspective in painting was another symptom of this shift,[7] removing the observer from the center of the scene—where he had been involved and participant with all his senses, including touch, taste, and smell—to a safe distance, with a Cartesian grid interposed between him and the world and the sense of sight exalted above all the other senses.

At this time, graveyards were removed outside city walls. One senses beneath all these fastidious developments of supposed impersonality and objectivity the fear of death, and hence of one's own mortal body, that must have followed upon the destruction of the medieval image of the cosmos and the loss of hope of human reconnection with timelessness that destruction entailed. (As Evelyn Fox Keller so discreetly points out,[8] and Einstein's famous wish to escape the mess of everyday life testifies, scientists make a considerable personal investment in this impersonality.) The haptic sense, especially, was lost to consciousness. "*The haptic sense is the sense of touch* reconsidered to include the entire body."[9] (In the blind, this sense reemerges, like the stars when the sun sets below the horizon.) Thus historically the faculties were separated from one another and thrown out of balance, and in each of our lives this "exploding of the skull" is recapitulated.

The *axis mundi* connecting us with worlds above and worlds below and defining the center of *this* world is really the sensed vertical axis of our own body.

> The human imagination is spatial and it is constantly constructing an architectonic whole from landscapes remembered or imagined; it progresses from what is closest to what is farther away, winding layers or strands around the single axis, which begins where the feet touch the ground.[10]

Further orientation, establishing front, back, right, and left, implies two other axes, all three axes intersecting at a felt center in the body experienced as *I*. The Cartesian extirpation of the axes of space from within the body has alienated us from our own centers and "exploded" the psyche into disconnected fragments like that skull outside the anatomy class.

Paradoxically, then, the first step on a spiritual path today is to return to a sense of one's own body, to rediscover the central place where the axes cross and to reestablish one's center of gravity there—first at the center of gravity of the physical body in the *hara*, just below the navel (doorway to the world below); then, drawn by the center of attraction of aspiration just above the head (doorway to the world above), establishing the uniquely human center between the two, in the heart (doorway to communion with *this* world). Together, the three centers make a chord: *do–mi–sol*, which Zuckerkandl calls "the holy chord."

Our education has disoriented us, thrown us off balance until we look to outer things and people, trying to get a sense of ourselves by reflection, but every context demands a different persona. When you wake up and find yourself a heap of broken images, the first step toward reintegration is to return again and again to a sense of yourself firmly seated in your own physical body. From there, you can begin to rebuild your psyche, your memory palace.

Wisdom, says the Bible—that "central form which gives meaning and position to all the facts which are acquired by knowledge"[11]—*hath builded her house*,[12] her magical memory cathedral. If that house is your body's sense of itself, which can take the shape of any space you have lived and learned in, it can be carried with you wherever you go, like a magic snailshell that can light up and display any scene from memory you call forth. The Mountain of Purgatory is such a house, with upper stories as yet unexplored. There are scenes displayed in various media on each of its levels to show the aspiring climber the way that he must go toward the summit, where true love awaits him—first the ancient flame, the love of Beatrice, the half of himself that he had lost; then the love of God.

Your body, paradigm of every house, temple, and cosmos, becomes, like Dante's *Divine Comedy*, a cabinet with knowledge and memories filed in order on their proper levels, a reference library with instant access, faster than a computer, to show you where you are and which way to turn at this particular moment, in this particular situation. Your body becomes the house of Wisdom, who will guide you through life.

> Everyman, I will go with thee, and be thy guide,
> In thy most need to go by thy side.[13]

Standing up in the field of gravity, each one of us creates a cosmos: world axis, navel of the world, the six directions and their intersection at a point of no dimension (which I feel as *I*) in the heart. Standing up, we establish heaven above our heads, toward which, with effort, we aspire; standing up, we establish hell below our footsoles—place of roots, fountain of our energy, beloved enemy without whose resistance to our aspiration no muscle fiber could ever grow strong. Those who now revolve weightless in space grew their splendid muscles on the earth, and their dogged determination. As soon as we stand upright, we build a bridge reaching from the earth toward the sky. In the beginning, the bridge reaches up into our parents' arms.

The rectangle of the crib. The vertical bars. I pull myself up. The mattress is soft under the bare soles of my feet. It gives a little but upholds me. I have to keep stepping around on it to keep my balance. Darkness is pressed against my face, against my skin, over my whole body, as if I were tightly packed in black velvet. I scream.

The door opens. Light comes in, and my mother and father are silhouetted, radiant around the edges with the light behind them. Their shadows are cast all the way to the end of the room, which is now entirely filled with mingling, intersecting shafts of light. Light and shadow play like a harp as my mother and father minister to me.

Having laid the foundation stone securely in the sense of one's own physical body, one can then begin to watch one's memory palace—which is really an organism, a second body—regenerate from that root and out from that center. O. W. Holmes's poem "The Chambered Nautilus," which we liked to ridicule in university English classes, turns out to be more apt than we thought. The image of the soul building "statelier mansions" outward from its center in the body, without losing connection with its origin and principle, is a better image than the memory palaces of classical rhetoric, which were static structures. If the statelier mansions the nautilus built were concentric spheres, the image would echo medieval cosmology. The spiral in which it does build, however, may reflect more accurately our image of an expanding universe, distinguished into epochs when conditions (of temperature, pressure, or the like) brought forth the moment when the next level of organization could appear. The nautilus is what the expanding universe would look like if we could see the whole of it at once, extended in time. Einstein, in fact, liked to refer to the shape of the universe as a "mollusk," and on an ancient fresco on the vault of the Parecclesion in the Kariye Museum, Istanbul, called the "Scroll of Heaven,"[14] the universe, borne aloft by an angel at the end of time, is clearly portrayed as this same giant, pearly snail, containing the sun, moon, and stars—an ancient representation of the big crunch:

> And the stars of heaven fell unto the earth, even as a fig tree casteth her untimely figs, when she is shaken of a mighty wind.
> And the heaven departed as a scroll when it is rolled together.[15]

Our memory palace is like the image James Gleick gives us of what it is like to analyze a nonlinear equation: it is "like walking through a maze whose walls rearrange themselves with each step you take." "Nonlinearity means that the act of playing the game has a way of changing the rules"[16]—but this was true of the game Dante was playing too, the "Master Game"[17] of spiritual development: as *he* (his *being*) changed, the way he saw the world around him changed also.

And so with us; from a sense of inhabiting our own bodies, we expand our psychological boundaries to inhabit successively larger spaces: room, house, backyard, front yard, school, church, movie house, exploring farther and farther out from the center of the first house until we include the whole neighborhood within the sphere of familiarity, the well known, and, if we are lucky, predominantly well loved.

There are pockets of dark, evil, and cold in the neighborhood, but also corresponding pockets in which we can take refuge. I cannot speak for those who have been altogether deprived of such protection, but even in the next to worst cases there may be a grandmother, a teacher, a counselor, a sibling—even one person can build around a child a soul-saving sphere of warmth and light.

The next "chamber" of our memory palace–nautilus, after the haptic sense of our body itself, is our haptic sense of the first house we remember.

Go there now, up the path, up the stairs. Set your hand upon the cold doorknob.

As for me, I will walk again up the front walk of my first house, between the rose bushes on the left (upon whose dark green, glossy leaves the snails make silver tracks) and the hydrangeas on the right (under which we will toss our burnt-out Fourth of July sparklers, to make the blossoms turn blue).

> The house we were born in is physically inscribed in us....After twenty years...we would recapture the reflexes of the "first stairway," we would not stumble on that rather high step....We would push the door that creaks with the same gesture, we would find our way in the dark to the distant attic. The feel of the tiniest latch has remained in our hands....The word habit is too worn a word to express this passionate liaison of our bodies, which do not forget, with an unforgettable house.[18]

In my dreams, I walk, run, fly, am swept through corridors, up and down long flights of stairs, into great halls with crystal chandeliers, or caverns where the green light of underground rivers trembles on the rocky ceiling, or over "cliffs of sheer fall"; and I say "*I* was walking down this long corridor" or "running up these stairs." But *I* am also the corridors, flights of stairs, sparkling ballrooms, underground rivers, and precipices—or, rather, the sensation of moving through the space and the sensation of *being* the space are equally myself. The imagination is both still and moving, and because, like the moving part, it is alive, the still part—the "container" (cave, corridor, building, house, cathedral, cosmos)—can change shape, as our imagined cosmos has changed shape over the centuries, achieving, with Dante, globed perfection; bursting shortly thereafter, the contents of our knowledge spilling out into disconnection; flowing, now, toward a center again.

Just so, in memory I become the spaces I am remembering, my imaginary body assuming their shapes, as if—as the sensitive flesh of a mollusk is in contact with its shell at every point—my "topological" skin expanded to touch the remembered spaces at every point.

At the same time, I am the figure who walks through them, like an archaeologist with a flashlight, feeling my way along, shining the light just ahead to see where to place my foot, then moving it all around so that the beam slides over ceilings and down walls, causing one detail after another to leap out of the long darkness.

The first house is like the fertilized egg we once were, containing the whole of us in undifferentiated form. Every subsequent house was partial, because we ourselves became partial, divided. The first house contains the impressions we took in with the whole of ourselves. Like the tree, it was writing a Divine Comedy for us before we could read at all, much less read Dante's. "Verticality is ensured by the polarity of cellar and attic."[19] The first house is that underworld we have to enter to recover our hearts and start over, slowly and carefully reascending so as not to leave anyone—any form of perception, any part of ourselves—behind.

Enter through the cellar, as Dante and Virgil enter the medieval cosmos, which is (like our own first house) at the same time a picture of the psyche and the universe. "With the house image we are in possession of a veritable principle of psychological integration."[20]

On the bottom is the basement. Its floor is just dirt. It smells of earth. The dirt floor slopes upward toward the back, so that you have to squat lower and lower. Don't go back there. There are black widow spiders. That is also where the coal pile is, solar energy imprisoned in blackness at the bottom of the world, waiting for my father to release it in golden fire.

Come out and climb up.

To course over better waters the little bark of my genius now hoists her sails....[21]

The back stairs are rickety. They sway as you climb. The railing is full of slivers. Don't slide your hand along it. Stop at the landing. Look out over a billowing sea of treetops and white shirts snapping on the clotheslines like signal flags, magicians' hands in white gloves.

The back porch has windows all around it. Open the glass door carefully. My brother, who sleeps out here in the freezing cold, keeps a pistol under his pillow. He might mistake us for burglars.

Would he recognize me after sixty years? He himself has been dead five. On this porch he is eternally sixteen. "We travel to the land of Motionless Childhood....Memories are motionless, and the more securely they are fixed in space, the sounder they are....In its countless alveoli space contains compressed time. That is what space is for."[22]

A blast of cat smell hits us as we open the door. Here is my cardboard playhouse, where Goochie had her kittens. Sit down on the cold linoleum. The pattern is worn off in places. We sit, bare underthighs icy, rolling colored marbles down the spiral cornice of the redwood marble-run, paradigm of Purgatory—for backsliders. (My father often says ruefully of himself, "I am a backslider." I picture trying to climb a pile of gravel and how, as soon as you stop exerting effort from within, clawing and scrambling, you slide back down.) Inside, the "Missouri Waltz" is playing on the radio.

No, it is the "Beautiful Blue Ohio."

After a while, we get up and go into the kitchen.

The kitchen is painted orange. It glows like the inside of a pumpkin. It sweats and pulses with earthly love, good smells, and oven warmth. "Give us this day our daily bread" is carved in Gothic letters around the edges of the round breadboard. In the morning, when a navy blue sky ripples against the windows, the kitchen is filled with invisible essence of cocoa and cinnamon toast.

Is Mother sleeping? I cannot see her.

I.

The hollow in the heart my mother left
Contains a world revealed by her removal
And still retains her shape—as does the bed
Whereon my husband laid her gently, dead,
Still warm—and bleeds, a new-delivered womb,
As silent and as empty as her room.

II.

And now her ashes mingle with my father's
In a high place, an urn above a door
Under a skylight. To read the names I look
Up into the sun. Here is the place where
Time stops. I cannot stay. My heels
Tick tick along the corridors of dead.

III.

While you lived, I braced
myself against
your sentiment. I had to be
hard-boiled, to mock
your gentle, self-effacing
hesitations.

The instant you were dead all this dissolved.
The small pulse beating at the base of your throat
stopped.

I lifted your soft limp arms, I laid them
one by one across your chest, I touched
your cheek.

Beautiful bones.

Mother I loved you.

IV.
And didn't know I did. Feeling
has gone on living
a different life
than thought.

How shall I find it?

Be quiet. Wait

in the dark.

V.
The world within the heart is dark. The walls
Are sore. I sit and wait. "What are you feeling
Now?" somebody says. Nothing at all.
And then, far off, a stirring, a feeble
Ripple at the bottom of a well.
"O my dove that art in the clefts of the rock
"In the secret places of the stair,
"Let me see thy face."

She is standing behind my chair, she is braiding my hair, she is pulling. I whine, "Ouch!" I am dunking buttered toast in hot chocolate. When I take a bite, the chocolate streams into the mug. Golden coins of melted butter float on the surface.

At noon, when the outside is golden, the kitchen smells of melting cheese and Campbell's soup. If it is alphabet soup, we carefully pick out the letters of our names and lay them in order on our paper napkins. If it is cream of tomato, we hold our spoons high and then tilt them slightly, letting thin streams pour down. We eat the bubbles.

But the kitchen is not the ultimate source of heat in the house. Its warmth derives from the cast-iron coal stove in the den next door. The small stove bulges with heat until its black cheeks ripple with waves of orange light. It throbs in its rotundity. We hear a sound from within it like the rushing of wings.

My father has made the hero-journey to the cellar, to the kingdom of the black widow spiders, and returned triumphant, his black scuttle heaped with darkly gleaming coal. His strong hand firmly holds the handle. His spotless white shirtsleeve is rolled up high, baring the mighty muscles of his arm. He puts on a striped cotton gauntlet and knocks at the silver coil of the stovedoor handle with his shovel. The door swings open with a shriek. The fire roars horribly, like the anger of grown-ups. My sister and I, who have run downstairs to dress by the stove, jump back—but not too far. That heat does not penetrate far in space—our bedrooms upstairs are freezing.

But it penetrates through sixty years of time. I feel it now, underneath my clothes, radiant on my naked skin.

The reaches of the living room are cooler, dimmer. I see it in black and white and palish green. The overstuffed chairs loom up in the half-light like great rocks whose bases are licked by ripples of rug, its Oriental pattern reduced to vague swirls by the intervening years.

What glows in full color here are the books in two sentinel cases flanking the big front window. Each of these books contains a world. Each of the covers is a door opening on vast spaces that dwarf this living room, the worn velvet cushion of whose window seat has become the color of mist and fog.

Through the patterned lace curtain still shines the streetlight, casting clear, mathematical shadows on the floor. Behind that grid of enlightened precision, blurred shadows of palm fronds mutter and gesticulate, like harmless lunatics talking to themselves. When the wind blows, they go completely mad.

My mother is ironing by the window in the dining room, in the afternoon light. Starched puffed-sleeved dresses hang around the plate rail in the dim room. There is a smell of ironing and of sheets that have hung in the sun, whipped by the fresh wind blowing from the sea.

Push aside the velvet portiere appliqued with leather that shuts off the front hall. It rattles on its brass rings. It goes on undulating ominously, heavily, like something in a story by Edgar Allen Poe, long after you have pushed it aside.

Look along the long, thin, faded carpet. Above you on your left are pegs for coats. Aunt Winnie hangs her fur piece there. The foxes bite each other with their pointy little noses and their sharp little teeth. Their tiny dead-dog feet dangle down.

Rush past them hurriedly. A great wave of perfume emanating from them pursues you. Open the front door. You have to grasp the handle with both hands and press down on the heavy brass thumbpiece with both your thumbs.

Step out onto the front porch.

Straight ahead is the huge palm tree, our *axis mundi*, full of forgotten secret notes tucked into hollowed-out scales. Later, the city will have the tree cut down. Our connection from earth to heaven will be severed. Lost tennis balls will shower down like fruit. *And the stars will fall...*

Summer afternoons
Of childhood. A screen door
Slams. Quick footsteps
Hollow on the wooden stair,
Sharp across the sidewalk, pausing
At the curb. Looking
Down I see my feet are small in scuffed
Red leather sandals, beside them
My sister's feet in ragged tennis shoes.
A river of water ripples down the gutter. Over it
Shadows of the fronds of a great palm tree
Lash and writhe. "Willy Rauch is coming!"
We run back to the front porch. Behind us
Our parents' house stands guard unshakeably.
Safe in a box we sit and hug our knees.
Between us and the violent tree comes lurching
A dark figure staring straight ahead,
Bowl-cut black hair jerking at every step,
Arms hanging down to knees.
Small heads, one dark, one gold, turn slowly
Warily watching. We have heard the tale.
He poured kerosene on his baby sister
And lit a match.

Other figures pass by forever on the memory street, both moving and still, passing and staying:

Rags bottles sacks. Rags bottles sacks.
The rag man is coming.
His ancient horse, head hung down,
Proceeds down the empty street.
Clip.
Clop.

Clip.
Clop.

Mr. Nielson, our next-door neighbor.
In his baggy pants and captain's hat,
ambling home every evening along the middle of
the street, looking down, leaning over now and then
to pick up paperclips, bits of string, anything
lost, dropped in the street, that might prove
useful. He is Danish. He smells of cigar smoke.
His house smells deliciously of coffee
and hot Danish pastries.
In his cellar he has a ball of string
as big as a basketball,
whiskered all over with tiny knots.
He has a ball of tinfoil
bigger than the moon.

Our front hall stairway goes straight up with an open banister on one side, then suddenly makes a ninety-degree turn to the right and continues between solid walls, like the passages Dante and Virgil climb through to get from one ledge of Purgatory to another. The hall light doesn't reach around the corner. I grope my way up here in the dark, being the youngest and hence the first to go upstairs to bed. I feel the cool embossed wallpaper sliding along under the palms of my hands, setting my teeth slightly on edge, like fingernails on a blackboard. Then my fingers move about, delicately probing like spider legs until they find the small, round button of the light switch.

The button has a silky, mother-of-pearl center. I push it in, and the upstairs opens out of darkness like Ali Baba's cave.

The upstairs is tranquil and contemplative. In the front bedroom, my grandmother dies. I climb up onto the foot of the bed and watch the priest administer extreme unction, the only time a priest ever enters our house, for my father has long ago left the Catholic church. I can't understand what the priest says. It is in another language. I turn my head to the left and see the sunlight pouring in the open window and the filmy white curtains rising in the breeze like the vapor that rises from a morning meadow when the dew evaporates.

It is Grandma, waving good-bye.

The lights have all gone out, there has been
a power failure.

In the dark dining room downstairs my mother
is lighting candles. I cannot see her face,
it is high above me.

She hands me a candle in a Jack-be-nimble
candlestick, with a silver ring
to hold it by. Now I

am climbing the stairs, the small living light
quivers over the wallpaper, streaming
shadows of smoke wind up into the dark.
She has made me a new summer nightgown,
pale blue seersucker sprinkled with rosebuds,
bare to the shoulder where a ruffle of lace
makes buds of wings.

Bare feet on the stair treads.

Underfoot the carpet
gives like graveyard grass.

The middle room upstairs is my mother and father's. It is almost completely filled by the big honey-colored Victorian bedstead, carved with flowers and fruits, garlands and urns and undulating grapevines. When I am sick, I am allowed to lie in it. I raise my bare arm languidly full length and run the back of my fingernails along the carved border. If you run along beside the schoolyard fence with a stick it makes a sound like that, but iron and sepulchral. Fingernails along this wooden border make a sound like the buzzing of bees.

Beyond that is the room where my sister and I sleep. There is a broad window that opens inward and looks out over dark pine trees. You can see the school from here. Under the window is a wooden bench. Everything is painted white. My father kneels with me beside my bed and teaches me to say my prayers.

Gentle Jesus, brave and mild,
Look on me, a little child. Ah-
men.

Our folded hands rest side by side on the patchwork quilt. When I fold my hands like this, the dimples on my knuckles disappear. Under my father's thumbnail there is a purple bruise, and a black scab on his knuckle. The straps on the top of his eyeshade make a white cross sunk deep in his thick brown curls, like the cross on a hot cross bun.

The full moon wakes me up, shining straight into that window. The furniture looks full of significance. Everything white is glowing blue. Space itself has turned into something alive and delicately palpable, a mist of light vibrating with an excitement just beyond the pitch of audibility. I throw back the covers, jump out of bed, and begin to dance in the beam that pours into my window. My skin is blue. From the darkness in the next room comes a sound like a stream of silver bells.

It is my mother's laugh. "*Darling,*" *she says,* "*are you dancing by the light of the moon?*"

Out of that window you can see the backyard. Fermenting plums and baby roses. Wasps cling to the stepped-on plums, sucking the juice, which is amber, like pus. The chickenhouse is buried in blackberry vines like the castle of the Sleeping Beauty—or, better still, the hut where the Henwife lives, who will help you on your way. My sister keeps it very clean inside. Warm, beige Banty hens on nests of clean straw, making low, contented purring sounds. Small, warm brown eggs under their soft feathers. Stripes of sunlight and stillness fall through the cracks in the roof.

My brother's clubhouse. No Girls Allowed. The swing set Uncle Roy made us. The glider, the vacant lot behind. One morning I wake up and run to the wide-open window as always, drinking in the delicate morning breeze, the tender light ("pure all the way to the first circle.") Kneeling on the window seat, like the Blessed Damozel leaning out from the porch of heaven, I look down and see that there is a hobo asleep in the backyard glider. Mother will give him food. My father says there is a mark on the front of the house indicating that, poor as we are, she is an easy touch.

Next door, Nielsen's barn. Late afternoon sunlight shines in from the back. Smell of hay, dust, silence, and sun. Powdered dust underfoot. Dust moving in sunlight.

Out that back window, we watch our school burn down, huge orange flames leaping to the zenith of the black sky. Charred pages of primers blow about the streets long after, red balloons black at the edges. See Spot run. If you pick up a page, Spot crumbles to dust and flies away on the wind.

Now my soul expands into the shape of the huge Victorian schoolhouse, fishscaled and turreted, "1888" carved into the triangle above the dark front door (I feel it carved into my forehead). I am at the same time the school and the pilgrim from the future who enters. Inside, there is a smell of oiled floors. Turn left and open a door. Pale grey daylight comes slanting out. This is the room that gets the most light—the kindergarten room. There are red and yellow and blue balloons with flying strings appliquéd onto the unbleached muslin curtains. Under the high windows, there are cupboards full of crayons, clay, poster paints, easels, and acres of paper. If you are good, Miss Helen Jane sends you home with a gold star stuck onto your collar. If you are bad, you have to sit in the Naughty Chair.

I am always good. I never have to sit in that chair.

My friend and I paint a mural as long as the whole wall. We paint a picket fence and a row of flowers, pink, red, yellow, and blue, each with a green stem and two green leaves like donkey ears.

Miss Helen Jane is pretty. She has wavy dark hair and pink cheeks. She sits down on the piano bench and calls us to gather round her. We sit cross-legged on the floor, and she sings to us.

I can't remember any of the songs.

In the back room where supplies are kept is the door to the furnace room, domain of Mr. Jennings, the crippled janitor. He wears overalls of mattress-ticking. He wears a shiny black shoe on his club foot. It looks like a Smith Brothers cough drop or the spherical patent-leather belly of a black widow spider. He is kind. When somebody throws up on the floor, which is the most awful thing that can happen to you, he dumps a bucket of sawdust on the unspeakable mess and sweeps it up with his big push broom. We are enormously relieved and grateful to him.

But when he opens the door of the furnace room, there is a terrible roar. There is a kind of rickety bridge or catwalk over a dark abyss to the huge, pulsing black iron beast in the corner that opens its mouth and belches out flames when he heaves whole scuttlefuls of coal into its maw.

Mr. Jennings is my Virgil. I stand on the narrow catwalk behind him, look down into the dark abyss, and hear the roaring, exactly like Dante entering Hell.

There is a game we children play every day at recess in a kind of cement pit by the basement door. There is a little elevated platform in the corner of the pit. It smells of stale urine in there. Someone stands on the platform ticktocking in a sepulchral voice, in time with a stiff-right-arm pendulum swung rhythmically across the body. Then, without warning, the clock-child begins to strike twelve: DONG, DONG, DONG, DONG...

At midnight, the clock jumps down and kills everybody. We all fall flat on our backs, shrieking with terror and delight.

And now I become the Congregational church, a bigger building still, red brick with leaded windows and a bowling alley in the basement.

It is my first day of Sunday school. I'm five years old. My sister takes me to the kindergarten room. She holds my hand. We climb the dark stairs together (as I hope we shall after death). The door opens. It is just like entering the sun. The room is so full of light that its walls dissolve in radiant mist. Everybody is singing "Jesus Wants Me for a Sunbeam."

I sing too. I want to be a sunbeam. My body feels transparent, powdery and golden, giving off light. On an easel to the left is a big tablet of paper with words printed on it in large black type. I can already read. When my eyes stop dazzling, I make out the words: "The Lord is my shepherd, I shall not want...." I see peaceful meadows with green velvet grass. I want to be a soft, white lamb and lie down there. I can smell the earth and the dew-wet grass. I cannot see the Lord, but His presence feels like my father. I know He is kind and will take care of me.

Now we sing "Jesus loves me, that I know, for the Bible tells me so." The Sunday school teacher has a voice as sweet and viscous as the Log Cabin syrup we had for breakfast, pouring it out of the chimney of a little tin house.

I am not a Catholic, since my father left the church, but on weekday afternoons I go to catechism with my friend. The nun wears a voluminous black dress with a big, black rosary slung around her hip at an angle, like a cowboy's ammunition belt. Her forehead is tightly bandaged with a white bandage, to keep her brains from spilling out. We chant in singsong: "Who made the world?" "God made the world." "What is God?" "God is a spirit." We don't know what it means, but it makes us feel pious and secure to know all the answers.

Afterward, we explore the parish hall. It smells of chalk dust. In an upper room we find a wheel of fortune. When we give it a turn, it makes a flipping sound, like my brother's bicycle wheel when he clips a playing card to the spoke with a clothespin.

My friend informs me that since I am not a Catholic, I will go to hell, but when they need little girls to march in white veils, I am pressed into service anyhow. There is a little pink satin ribbon to hold the veil on, with a pink rosette over each ear. I love to march with hands pressed together and head bowed. We look down at our white Mary Janes and carefully set down each white-stockinged foot in time with our partner. As the double row of little girls moves slowly and rhythmically down the aisle, a wave of murmuring follows us on either side—the old ladies, all in black, saying "Sweet, sweet!"

If we enter the church without a hat on, they swoop down upon us like a flock of crows and grab us fiercely, pinching our arms. They lay their sodden hankies on the tops of our heads.

Alone, I go to the chapel of the Little Flower. There is a bank of votive candles on the right in little ruby glasses. The red candle flames stand erect inside, writhing and twitching when a draft blows over them. I put a nickel in the slot of the brass candlestick and light a candle. I like to hear the nickel rattle loudly all the way down inside the hollow brass tubes. I kneel at the creamy marble rail, look up at the statue of the Little Flower, and pray fervently, "Make me a Catholic!" I do not want to go to hell. The Little Flower smiles down sweetly. She looks like a department store dummy.

The Catholic church is large and dark and hollow, full of echoes. It smells of smoke and incense. There are rustlings and whisperings in the corners, "Pss pss pss pss. Forgive me father, for I have sinned." Mea CULpa, mea CULpa, mea MAXima CULpa. I love to say this, beating my chest four times, in rhythm, hard. The priest walks solemnly across the front of the church, kneels in front of the altar, crosses himself, rises, and walks on. There is a hole in the sole of his shoe. He is going outside for a cigarette. "Good afternoon, Father," we say as we go out into the blinding afternoon sunlight. We love making this pious greeting, aware of how little and good we look. The priest keeps his pack of cigarettes somewhere deep in his voluminous black robes. As we pass him we feel, little as we are, the blast of his huge, dark virility.

When there is mass, the priest lifts up a golden monstrance shaped like a sun shooting out crystallized, golden rays, and at that moment there is the littlest, tiniest ringing of a bell. It pierces through the church like a flash of light along a golden wire. There is such a stillness. Something has entered the vast, dark barn of a church from some other dimension, some source even higher than the high stained glass windows through which, sometimes, a dusty beam of multicolored sunlight spills down onto the floor. The sound of the little bell transfixes me—stiletto stab of a memory of something I have forgotten. With my whole body, I listen to the vibrant stillness.

In the Protestant church, where I go with my sister after Sunday school, nobody seems worried about not being a Catholic and going to hell. Above the altar, in place of the huge naked man on a cross with his forehead all scratched and bleeding and a ragged diaper slung around his loins, there is a peaceful painting of green meadows stretching off into the distance, groves of trees, a tranquil river. This painting scares me more than the naked man with his agonized face because there are no people in it. It reminds me of the well-groomed cemetery where we go to play or pass through on our way to the hills. It makes me feel alone, abandoned, as if I might evaporate into the empty air. Whoever painted the picture must have been a man of the Enlightenment—one, that is, who had forgotten that the trees know us.

But the whole congregation sings enthusiastically together:

This is my Father's world
And to my list'ning ears
All Nature sings and round me rings
The music of the spheres...

and outdoors, when the wind blows over the treeless, empty hills, I remember:

In the rustling grass
I hear him pass.

I lift my eyes unto the California hills, which are always there at the end of our street, briefly green in the springtime, splashed with orange poppies. All the rest of the year, the grass is golden.

And then, the dark cave of the Piedmont Theater.

Dusty carpets, burgundy with huge, writhing yellow vine pat-

terns on them, saturated with stale cigarette smoke, leading you on past dim, ornate mirrors flecked with black; dusty, elaborate golden sconces and chandeliers with crystals hanging down like water drops or stalactites. (We steal the ones we can reach— hanging down from the candle-shaped sconces in the ladies' room— and wear them dangling from our ears.) Dusty, burgundy velvet draperies you push aside and—armed with small white paper bags bulging with penny candy (red and black licorice whips, Hershey kisses, Necco wafers, jujubes, root beer barrels, green leaves, round white peppermints)—enter the dark.

Oh, now forgotten are mother and father, Christ on the cross, the little bell, the sound of God in the rustling grass, your father's prayers and your mother's laughter, the maple syrup sweetness of the Sunday school teacher's voice, the pious procession of us white-veiled prepubescent virgins down the central aisle of the Catholic church. There is only Tyrone Power, Clark Gable, Gary Cooper, the way a man and woman look at each other, magnetized toward the moment at the end of the movie when they will melt into each other in profound embrace, two becoming one, and then the darkness. Our bodies sit there rattling paper bags and cellophane candy wrappers, sucking on peppermints, drooling a little, but we are not there. We are mesmerized, sucked into the screen. We have become Rita Hayworth, Lana Turner, Madeleine Carroll. We can't remember wanting anything in life but this.

Our parents come in and find us in the front row. We have sat through two double features, with newsreel, cartoons, and two Saturday afternoon serials. They lead us, pale, slack-mouthed, blankly staring, out into the murderous sunlight that will show us, reflected in shop windows, as still-awkward kids, one fat, one skinny, in plaid flannel shirts and overalls, ragged sneakers and orthopedic shoes.

Now let me expand to encompass the whole neighborhood. I can handle that. I can handle the whole neighborhood, our house, our block, bordered in sidewalks etched with fading chalk hopscotch courts, the school, the two churches, the movie house.

Standing in front of my parents' house, under the great palm tree, centered in myself and touching the shaggy scales of that living world axis, no abstraction but a tangible reality as intimately known and loved as a pet mammoth, I am surrounded by a sphere I can encompass in imagination—haptically. The sense of touch, coterminous with my body—with my skin—can expand and occupy the whole—*become* the whole, as if it were a larger body, with my sense of *I* burning at the quick of it, like the intense spot of light that springs into being when we hold our ten-cent magnifying glasses (Made in Japan) between sun and sidewalk or between sun and skin, until involuntarily the hand springs back, having experienced wordlessly the power, murderous and life-giving, of the source of our energy.

Inside me, the neighborhood is enclosed in a hemisphere of light, like Dante's Limbo, with the earth for a floor, our street as a horizontal axis, and the darkness of the not-yet-explored all around it. The cemetery lies at one end of the street, the hospital where some of us were born at the other end, and beyond that, "downtown," a region of chaos and crashing streetcars erupting sparks from trolley and tracks, where we go sometimes but only when holding for dear life onto a grown-up's hand. The sphere is bounded by hills over which I can't see.

This sphere, with known areas mapped out, each with its place on the surface, is like the frog embryo Dr. Eakin wanted me to study with him: a sphere with areas defined in different colors, indicating which would become leg, gut, eye, lung, stomach, skin, brain—the embryonic tissues of my future world. Differential speeds of cell division would shift them around on the surface, cause outside to grow into the inside, cause wrinkles and bifurcations, expansions, invaginations, foldings over, and foldings under, until this smooth sphere had become my grown-up brain and the fragmentary images of the world it projected.

We are going to go to the country home. It will be the first time I have been there, the first time I have traveled beyond these hills, the limits of the known world. I squat under the palm tree and wonder: will the sky be a different color than it is here? Will the trees be purple and pink? To go there, we will have to get up at four o'clock in the morning.

> At break of day
> I seek a path
> To a world unknown.[23]

*I wake up in the dark. My nose
is cold, it feels like a mushroom.*

*Squeak-click, squeak-click, my father is sharpening
his razor blades in his sharpening machine.*

Wake up!

Beat it through the outer darkness. Find him.

Pat pat, bare feet over icy linoleum.

Knock on the bathroom door. O joy!

it opens.

*A burst of blazing light and clouds
of billowing steam, my arms are immediately
wet with it and the sweet flower smell
of shaving cream. Through the bright mist
Father I begin
to see you.*

*Rosy in your white summer BVDs and baggy
trousers, on either side a U
of suspenders hanging down, you lean above
the basin. I am just tall enough
to see the bits of white scum floating
on the surface of the water.
You scoop up water in both your hands and*

dash it in your face, blowing like a whale.
"Merciful father!" That was your favorite
oath. Father,
my hair and shoulders
sparkle with your bright water-
drops. "Ah,
the blessed thing," you say, and you mean

me.

O Christmas Tree

We are really making the universe in a likeness.
BLACK ELK, speaking of the Sun Dance,
in *The Sacred Pipe*

With an ornament in my hand, I get down on elbows and knees
and then slither like a snake, flat on my belly, under the Christmas
tree, trying to reach one of the bottom branches in the back that
still remains bare. Old and arthritic, I cannot reach it by myself.
Husband, children, and grandchildren are off somewhere watching television.

All at once, I lose the will to continue, let the ornament drop,
and lie there on the floor, face down, at the bottom of the tree.

My husband walks into the room.

"Next year," I mumble into the carpet, "I am not going to have
a tree."

"Why not?" he says, surprised.

Every year, for the forty years of our marriage, we have had a
tree, and before that, my parents—one a lapsed Catholic, one a
Protestant—and his—marginal Jews—always had one.

"Nobody cares about it," I say. "It doesn't mean anything to
anybody."

"*I* care," he says, and begins to help.

One by one, the others wander in, and each hangs something
on the tree until the boxes are empty and all the ornaments (too
many!—according to my family's tradition; not enough!—according to my husband's) have miraculously found their places.

Once more, not knowing why—just repeating what our parents and grandparents did—we have produced something magical. It makes us all keep silence before it. Moreover, it has brought
us together, as if the conical shape of the fir tree were an inverted

vortex, exerting a centripetal force, drawing us at the same time upward and toward the center. It draws us together both in time and in space. It is reuniting us with our parents, who passed the custom on to us, and with one another. The children have returned here from all over the continent—one from overseas.

All at once, I hear myself speak.

"Do you know what it is?" I say. "It is the whole universe, with stars and planets and plants and fruits and birds and animals.

"Up there"—I point to the space above the tree—"is the invisible, out of which everything comes.

"And the point at the top is the big bang, the singularity where everything enters into space and time.

"And then it expands downward, producing everything that is: stars and planets and fruits and animals and birds."

"C'mon, Maw," protests my son the engineer. "Those old Teutonic tree-worshippers didn't know about the big bang."

I can't answer him just now, because the image is astonishing me—lights for stars and baubles for planets. Someone must have intended that. I never thought about the meaning before but just blindly repeated the ritual, spurred on by the wish that my children should experience what I myself experienced as a small child.

When you went to bed, there was the ordinary old living room. But in the morning—what had happened during the night, while we all slept?

A magic, a transformation. The room was filled with a finer substance—something vibrating at a higher frequency, many-colored, fragrant, softly glowing, exciting, more alive. A wonderful intelligence was at work behind the appearances. Exciting things were in store for us—not just presents but unimaginable possibilities. The magnanimity of it! We were experiencing the overwhelming gratuitousness, the undeservedness, of divine grace.

And now I see that there was something in it for the intellect as well. This is the true meaning of esoteric knowledge: that the way you have seen things done every day all your life has an inner, psychological and cosmological, meaning that will be revealed to you at the proper time, when you are ready to make use of it to order your inner world into one harmonious whole, world within world, in preparation for conscious and voluntary service of His Endlessness, the Unconditioned.

"The smallest gadget contains a whole world view," and the smallest ancient ritual holds a complete teaching about why we are on earth, what we are supposed to be doing in order to go on striving for self-perfection, and why. It was not possible for this healing to begin until the cosmology of science could once more be harmonized with the ancient, universal, and unchangeable cosmologies of the religions of the world.

A tree recalls the opposing gyres of the Breath of Brahma, which grow into a sphere that expands and contracts at the same time when you sit in attentive stillness at the center of your heart, waiting for God. It expands from above, from the big bang, entering in from the halls of the outer heaven. And how does the Breath of Brahma turn around at the bottom, at the end of the world, and return toward the source? At the bottom of the tree we place the crèche, with the ox and the ass, and with the son of God lower even than these, in the animals' manger, the place of their food. Our own breath turns around at the bottom of the belly, at the *hara*, and there is the place where Dante and Virgil made their turn—were converted—and the place of the Virgin, "a condition of complete simplicity." *Behold, the handmaid of the Lord.* Having become zero, she was open to infinity, the Holy Spirit, the whole-making force. Once we realized our own nothingness, we could emerge into the real world.

There is the tree of creation and the ladder of souls, each higher one reaching down a hand to help the lower one up, the chain of teacher and pupil reaching down from the founder of each great tradition, lifting up those who strive to follow his or her indications until, having fallen into the power of time, the Merciless Heropass, the teaching succumbs to entropy like everything else that enters the conditioned world, the world of space and time.

And then the son or daughter of God becomes incarnate in another form, another place, another time, and the current is renewed, breathing out, breathing in, cycles for the storage and release of energy supporting new creations, new heavens, and new earths—new visions of the order of the universe, new understandings of our obligation to maintain, as those we are pleased to call "primitive" people have never ceased to maintain, the health of our mother the earth and the sensitivity of her organ of perception, which is organic life, including ourselves who participate in it and extend above it only insofar as we become receivers and transmitters between the earth and the sun and beyond it, between the earth and the world of timelessness.

Eternity is in love with the productions of time, and we are children of earth and heaven, of time and timelessness, vessels and channels of their mutual adoration. Only when the familiar, particular, and beloved is fused with the universal and intelligible does "the desire of your mind become the desire of your heart"[1]— the desire for meaning. It remains then to live your thought—to live in accordance with what you have seen in a cosmological context to be what you are supposed to be doing here on the earth, so that "the desire of your heart may become the reality of your being."[2]

How lovely are thy branches.

Notes

PREFACE

1. Today, this aspect of my vague dissatisfaction is being answered in the new science that studies the global behavior of dynamical systems. Those dances no human body could perform are being accomplished with the greatest of ease by computer images. "Changes in embryos ...have to be symbolized by trajectories in multidimensional phase space" (Conrad H. Waddington, "Concluding Remarks," in *Evolution and Consciousness: Human Systems in Transition*, ed. Erich Jantsch and Conrad H. Waddington [Reading, MA: Addison-Wesley Publishing Company, 1976], p. 244). See also James Gleick, *Chaos: Making a New Science* (New York: Viking, 1987), p. 47: "Linking topology and dynamical systems is the possibility of using a shape to help visualize the whole range of behaviors of a system.... If you can visualize the shape, you can understand the system."

   But at the time I speak of, dynamical systems theory did not yet exist, and if computers did, I had not heard of them. Besides, as should become apparent in the course of this book, there were other aspects to my dissatisfaction with the method of "dissect and label" that no computer could ever address.

2. T. S. Eliot, "Burnt Norton," 1:1–3, in *Four Quartets* (New York: Harcourt, Brace and Company, 1943), p. 3.

3. Eliot, "Burnt Norton," 2:10–11.

4. P. D. Ouspensky, *In Search of the Miraculous: Fragments of an Unknown Teaching* (New York: Harcourt, Brace and Company, 1949).

5. G. I. Gurdjieff, *Beelzebub's Tales to His Grandson: An Objectively Impartial Criticism of the Life of Man (All and Everything, First Series)*, (New York, Viking Arkana, 1992).

6. The passages on Gurdjieff's teaching in this book are expressions of my own attempts to assimilate it and should not be taken as objective expositions of his methods or ideas.

7. This paragraph is adapted from Jacques Merleau-Ponty and Bruno Morando, *The Rebirth of Cosmology*, trans. Helen Weaver (New York: Alfred A. Knopf, 1976), pp. xii ff.

8. W. B. Yeats, "The Double Vision of Michael Robartes," 1:7–8. Re-

printed with permission of Macmillan Publishing Company from *The Poems of W. B. Yeats: A New Edition*, edited by Richard J. Finneran, p. 170. Copyright 1919 by Macmillan Publishing Company, renewed 1947 by Bertha Georgie Yeats.

9. Ouspensky, *In Search of the Miraculous*, p. 299: "...religion is doing; a man does not merely *think* his religion or feel it, he 'lives' his religion as much as he is able, otherwise it is not religion but fantasy or philosophy."

10. William James, lecture 17 in *The Varieties of Religious Experience: A Study in Human Nature, Being the Gifford Lectures on Natural Religion Delivered at Edinburgh in 1901–1902* (New York: Random House, The Modern Library, 1902), p. 419.

11. Quoted by Peter Matthiessen in *Nine-Headed Dragon River: Zen Journals 1969–1985* (Boston: Shambhala Publications, 1986), p. 133, from Kazuaki Tanahashi, *Moon in a Dewdrop* (Berkeley, CA: North Point Press, 1985).

12. *Scientific American*, September 1980. Review of Mark A. Peterson, "Dante and the 3-Sphere," *American Journal of Physics* 47, no.12 (December 1979), pp. 1031–1035.

13. See chapter 4.

14. See, for example, Jyri Paloheimo, "Superforce and Beelzebub," *A Journal of Our Time* (Traditional Studies Press, Box 984, Adelaide Street P.O., Toronto, Canada M5C 2K4), no. 4, p. 13.

15. See Brian T. Swimme, "The Resurgence of Cosmic Storytellers," in *ReVision* 9, no. 2 (Winter–Spring 1987), pp. 83–88.

THE DARK WOOD

1. Joseph Campbell, *The Masks of God: Creative Mythology* (New York: Penguin Books, 1976), p. 611.

2. Czeslaw Milosz, *Visions from San Francisco Bay*, trans. Richard Lourie (New York: Farrar, Straus & Giroux, 1982), p. 32.

3. Ibid., p. 221.

4. William Shakespeare, *The Merchant of Venice*, act 5, sc. 1, lines 60–65.

5. C. S. Lewis, *The Discarded Image: An Introduction to Medieval and Renaissance Literature* (Cambridge: Cambridge University Press, 1964), pp. 98–100.

6. Dante Alighieri, "Epistola 10," in *Dantis Alagherii Epistolae: The Letters of Dante*, ed. Paget Toynbee (Oxford: Oxford University Press, 1966), p. 202.

7. Frances A. Yates, *The Art of Memory* (Chicago: University of Chicago Press, 1966), p. 95.

8. Dante, *Paradiso*, 33:145, in *The Divine Comedy*, Bollingen Series, no. 80, trans., with a commentary, by Charles S. Singleton (Princeton, NJ: Princeton University Press, 1970–1975). Copyright © 1970, 1973, 1975 by Princeton University Press. All quotations from the *Divine Comedy* in Italian or in translation by Professor Singleton in this book are reprinted by permission of Princeton University Press.

    Unless otherwise indicated, all English translations of passages from the *Divine Comedy* are by Singleton. I have altered his translation of this line from *Paradiso* slightly. Singleton has "the Love which moves the sun and the other stars."

    The translation of lines 1–3 of *Inferno* that stands at the head of this chapter is mine.

9. Arthur O. Lovejoy, *The Great Chain of Being: A Study of the History of an Idea* (New York: Harper & Brothers, first Harper Torchbook edition, 1960), p. 109.

10. Blaise Pascal, *Pensée* 206, in *Pensées; The Provincial Letters* (New York: The Modern Library, 1941), p. 75.

    Alexander Koyré (in *From the Closed World to the Infinite Universe* [New York: Harper & Brothers], 1958, p. 43, n. 29) attributes the famous statement *"Le silence éternel de ces espaces infinis m'effraye"* ("The eternal silence of those infinite spaces terrifies me") not to the famous seventeenth-century physicist, mathematician, and God-seeker himself but to the *libertin* Pascal imagines speaking in *Pensée* 194:

    > "I see those frightful spaces of the universe which surround me....I see nothing but infinites on all sides, which surround me as an atom, and as a shadow which endures only for an instant and returns no more...from all this I conclude that I ought to spend all the days of my life without caring to inquire into what must happen to me." (p. 68)

    > "Who," asks Pascal, "could desire to have for a friend a man who talks in this fashion?" (p. 69)

11. Quoted in Marjorie Hope Nicolson, *The Breaking of the Circle: Studies in the Effect of the "New Science" upon Seventeenth Century Poetry* (Evanston, IL: Northwestern University Press, 1950), pp. 147–148.

12. Evelyn Fox Keller, *Reflections on Gender and Science* (New Haven, CT: Yale University Press, 1985), p. 100.

13. Gaston Bachelard, *The Poetics of Space*, trans. Maria Jolas (Boston: Beacon Press, 1969), p. 51.

14. Ibid., pp. 234, 217.

15. Lewis, *Discarded Image*, p. 221.

16. See Thomas S. Kuhn, *The Copernican Revolution: Planetary Astronomy in the Development of Western Thought* (Cambridge: Harvard University Press, 1957), pp. 233–234; and Koyré, *From the Closed World*, pp. 35–38.

17. E. J. Dijksterhuis, *The Mechanization of the World Picture: Pythagoras to Newton*, trans. C. Dikshoorn; foreword by D. J. Struik (Princeton, NJ: Princeton University Press, 1986).

18. Carolyn Merchant, *The Death of Nature: Women, Ecology and the Scientific Revolution* (San Francisco: Harper & Row, Publishers, first Harper & Row paperback edition, 1983).

19. Dijksterhuis, *Mechanization*, p. 310.

20. Nicolson, *Breaking of the Circle*, p. 130.

21. Dijksterhuis, *Mechanization*, pp. 337, 338.

22. Edwin Arthur Burtt, *The Metaphysical Foundations of Modern Physical Science* (Garden City, NY: Doubleday & Company, Anchor Books edition, 1954), pp. 98–99.

23. Ibid., p. 85.

24. Ibid., p. 84.

25. Dijksterhuis, *Mechanization*, p. 431.

26. Erwin Schrödinger, "The Mystery of the Sensual Qualities," in *What Is Life?; Mind and Matter* (Cambridge: Cambridge University Press, 1967), pp. 176–177:

> So we come back to this strange state of affairs. While the direct sensual perception of the phenomenon tells us nothing as to its objective physical nature (or what we usually call so) and has to be discarded from the outset as a source of information, yet the theoretical picture we obtain eventually rests entirely on a complicated array of various informations, all obtained by direct sensual perception.

27. Ilya Prigogine and Isabelle Stengers, *Order out of Chaos: Man's New Dialogue with Nature* (New York: Bantam Books, 1984), p. 45.

28. M. C. Cammerloher, "The Position of Art in the Psychology of Our Time," in *Spiritual Disciplines: Papers from the Eranos Yearbooks*, Bollingen Series, no. 30:4 (Princeton, NJ: Princeton University Press, 1960), p. 424.

29. Ravi Ravindra, "The Mill and the Mill-Pond," *American Theosophist* 74, no. 9 (October 1986): 303.

30. Dante, *Purgatorio*, 3:73.

31. Alfred North Whitehead, *Science and the Modern World* (New York:

New American Library, first Pelican Mentor Books edition, May 1948), p. 56.

32. Louise B. Young, *The Unfinished Universe* (New York: Simon & Schuster, 1986), p. 55.

33. Swimme, "Resurgence of Cosmic Storytellers," p. 85.

34. Ibid.

35. Thomas Berry, *The Dream of the Earth* (San Francisco: Sierra Club Books, 1988).

36. Richard Tarnas, "The Transfiguration of the Western Mind," *ReVision* 12, no. 3 (Winter 1990): 16.

37. Erazim Kohák, in transcript of Canadian Broadcasting Corporation series "The Age of Ecology," *Ideas*, June 18–21, 25–28, 1990. (A printed transcript of this series can be obtained by writing to CBC Ideas, Box 500, Station A, Toronto M5W 1E6.)

38. Erazim Kohák, *The Embers and the Stars: A Philosophical Inquiry into the Moral Sense of Nature* (Chicago: University of Chicago Press, 1984).

39. Milosz, *Visions*, p. 77.

40. Norman O. Brown, *Life Against Death: The Psychoanalytical Meaning of History* (New York: Vintage Books, 1959), p. 316.

41. Morris Berman, *The Reenchantment of the World* (New York: Bantam Books, 1984).

42. Heinrich Zimmer, *The King and the Corpse: Tales of the Soul's Conquest of Evil*, 2d ed., Bollingen Series, no. 11, ed. Joseph Campbell (New York: Pantheon Books, 1956).

43. Martha Heyneman, introduction to *Place of Birth*, by David Kherdian (Portland, OR: Breitenbush Books, 1983), pages unnumbered.

44. William Shakespeare, *As You Like It*, act 2, sc. 1, line 12.

45. S. K. Heninger, Jr. *Touches of Sweet Harmony: Pythagorean Cosmology and Renaissance Poetics* (San Marino, CA: The Huntington Library, 1974), p. 14.

46. Jamake Highwater, *The Primal Mind: Vision and Reality in Indian America* (New York: Harper & Row, Publishers, 1981), p. 61.

47. Lewis, *Discarded Image*, p. 14.

48. Kuhn, *Copernican Revolution*, p. 54.

49. Stephen W. Hawking, *A Brief History of Time: From the Big Bang to Black Holes* (New York: Bantam Books, 1988), p. 138. Quotations from this work are reprinted by permission of the publisher.

50. Peterson, "Dante and the 3-Sphere" (see Preface, n. 12).

51. Joseph Campbell, *The Masks of God: Primitive Mythology* (New York: Penguin Books, 1969), p. 199.

52. William Morris, *The Collected Works of William Morris with Intro-*

ductions by His Daughter May Morris, vol. 12, *The Story of Sigurd the Volsung and the Fall of the Niblungs* (London: Longmans Green and Company, 1911), pp. 1–4:

> Thus was the dwelling of Volsung, the King of the Midworld's Mark,
> As a rose in the winter season, a candle in the dark;...
> So therein withal was a marvel and a glorious thing to see,
> For amidst of its midmost hall-floor sprang up a mighty tree,
> That reared its blessings roofward, and wreathed the roof-tree dear
> With the glory of the summer and the garland of the year....
> And when men tell of Volsung, they call that war-duke's tree,
> That crownëd stem, the Branstock; and so was it told unto me....
> So round about the Branstock they feast in the gleam of the gold;
> And though the deeds of man-folk were not yet waxen old,
> Yet had they tales for songcraft, and the blossomed garth of rhyme;
> Tales of the framing of all things and the entering in of time
> From the halls of the outer heaven; so near they knew the door.

53. Joseph Campbell, in PBS television series "Joseph Campbell and the Power of Myth: with Bill Moyers," part 2, "The Message of Myth."
54. Berry, *Dream of the Earth*, p. 69.
55. Quoted in Timothy Ferris, *Coming of Age in the Milky Way* (New York: William Morrow & Company, 1988), p. 177.
56. Ken Wilber, ed., *Quantum Questions: Mystical Writings of the World's Greatest Physicists* (Boulder, CO: Shambhala Publications, New Science Library, 1984), p. 20.
57. Ravi Ravindra, "Experience and Experiment: A Critique of Modern Scientific Knowing," in *Science and Spirit*, ed. Ravi Ravindra (New York: Paragon House, 1991), p. 134.
58. Hawking, *Brief History*, p. 116.

THE MEANING OF MEANING

1. See Rupert Sheldrake, *The Presence of the Past: Morphic Resonance and the Habits of Nature* (New York: Times Books, 1988).
2. Ernest Fenollosa, *The Chinese Written Character as a Medium for Poetry: An Ars Poetica,* with foreword and notes by Ezra Pound (Washington, DC: Square Dollar Series, n.d.), p. 75.
3. Amy Lowell, "Patterns," in *Modern American Poetry; Modern British Poetry: A Critical Anthology,* combined ed., ed. Louis Untermeyer (New York: Harcourt, Brace and Company, 1942), pp. 188–190.
4. Lawrence Weschler, "Profiles (Nicolas Slonimsky—Part II); Boy Wonder—II," *The New Yorker,* November 24, 1986, p. 75.

Slonimsky, one of the world's foremost musical lexicographers, was ongoing editor of both *Baker's Biographical Dictionary of Musicians* and *Music Since 1900.* Ninety-two years old at the time, he was lecturing to an undergraduate music appreciation class at the University of California, Los Angeles. Weschler describes the scene (p. 73):

> "I really should play you some Villa-Lobos. Let's see." He pulled up the piano bench and sat down. "This is his 'Alma Brasileira.' I hope I can remember it. I haven't played it in over twenty years." He could have fooled us: he tore into the piece with astonishing vigor, negotiating the intricate rhythmic patterns with absolute authority. When he finished, the room was still.

5. "A Conversation with Robert Bly," *Material for Thought* 10 (Fall 1983): 18. Published and distributed by Far West Editions, 3231 Pierce Street, San Francisco, CA 94123.
6. I copied this statement, ascribed to Rabbi Eliezer, from an English translation displayed in an exhibition of Hebrew books and manuscripts at the New York Public Library, November 1988.
7. *Webster's New World Dictionary of American English,* 3d college ed., s.v. "rote²."
8. T. S. Eliot, "The Waste Land," 3:301–302, in *Collected Poems 1909–1935* (New York: Harcourt, Brace and Company, 1936), p. 83.
9. *Black Elk Speaks: Being the Life Story of a Holy Man of the Oglala Sioux,* as told through John G. Neihardt (*Flaming Rainbow*); illustrated by Standing Bear (New York: Simon & Schuster, Washington Square Press, 1972).
10. Lewis, *Discarded Image,* p. 5.
11. Dante, *Purgatorio,* 24:52–54. The translation of this passage is mine.
12. Loren Eiseley, *The Immense Journey* (New York: Random House, Vintage Books, 1959), p. 26.
13. Quoted in Malcolm W. Browne, "Chemistry Is Losing Its Identity," *New York Times,* December 3, 1985.
14. Richard N. T-W-Fiennes, ed., *Biology of Nutrition: The Evolution and Nature of Living Systems; The Organisation and Nutritional Methods of Life Forms* (Elmsford, NY: Pergamon Press, 1972), p. 182.
15. Ludwig von Bertalanffy, *Perspectives on General System Theory: Scientific-Philosophical Studies,* ed. Edgar Taschdjian, with forewords by Maria von Bertalanffy and Ervin Laszlo (New York: George Braziller, 1975), p. 157.

Bertalanffy makes a distinction between "systems science" and "general system theory":

> "Systems science" [is] scientific exploration and theory of "systems" in the various sciences.... This requires, first, the exploration of the many systems in our observed universe in their own right and specificities. Secondly, it turns out that there are general aspects, correspondences, and isomorphisms common to "systems." This is the domain of *general system theory.*

16. See chapter 3, p. 75.
17. See Prigogine and Stengers, *Order out of Chaos.*
18. See, for example, Ludwig von Bertalanffy, *Systems Theory: Foundations, Development, Applications* (New York: George Braziller, 1968); Jantsch and Waddington, *Evolution and Consciousness*; Erich Jantsch, *The Self-Organizing Universe: Scientific and Human Implications of the Emerging Paradigm of Evolution* (Elmsford, NY: Pergamon Press, 1980); Prigogine and Stengers, *Order out of Chaos,* foreword by Alvin Toffler; Ervin Laszlo, *Evolution: The Grand Synthesis,* foreword by Jonas Salk (Boston: Shambhala Publications, 1987); Gleick, *Chaos*; Young, *Unfinished Universe.*
19. T. S. Eliot, "The Dry Salvages," 2:45–48, in *Four Quartets*, p. 24.
20. *The Confessions of St. Augustine,* trans. E. B. Pusey (New York: E. P. Dutton & Company, Everyman's Library, 1907), p. 20, n.1.
21. Julian Huxley, *Evolution in Action* (New York: Harper & Brothers, 1953), p. 127.
22. See Giorgio de Santillana and Hertha von Dechend, *Hamlet's Mill: An Essay on Myth and the Frame of Time* (Ipswich, MA: Gambit, 1969), p. 161.
23. Martin Buber, *I and Thou,* 2d ed., trans. Ronald Gregor Smith (New York: Charles Scribner's Sons, 1958).
24. Samuel Copley, *Portrait of a Vertical Man: Maurice Nicoll, An Appreciation* (London: Swayne Publications, 1989), p. ii (unnumbered): "He defined Hell as 'absolute meaninglessness.'"
25. Thomas Berger, *Little Big Man* (New York: Delacorte Press, Seymour Lawrence, 1964), p. 91.

See also Jaime de Angulo, *Indian Tales* (New York: Hill & Wang, 1953), pp. 241–242. The conversation is between de Angulo and Wild Bill, a Pit River Indian (California):

> "People are living, aren't they?"
> "Sure they are! That's what I am telling you. Everything is living, even the rocks, even that bench you are sitting on. Somebody *made that bench for a purpose,* didn't he? Well, then, *it's*

alive, isn't it? Everything is alive. That's what we Indians believe. White people think everything is dead...."

"Listen, Bill. How do you say 'people'?"

"I don't know...just *is,* I guess."

"I thought that meant 'Indian.'"

"Say...ain't we *people?*!"

"So are the whites!"

"Like hell they are!! We call them *inilaaduwi,* 'tramps,' nothing but tramps. They don't believe anything is alive. They are dead themselves. I don't call that 'people.' They are smart, but they don't know anything."

26. Berger, *Little Big Man,* p. 213.

27. Ananda K. Coomaraswamy, "Eastern Wisdom and Western Knowledge," in *Am I My Brother's Keeper?* (New York: John Day Company, an Asia Press book, 1947), p. 60:

> ...the West will have to abandon what [René] Guénon calls its "proselytizing fury," an expression that must *not* be taken to refer only to the activities of Christian missionaries...but to those of all the distributors of modern "civilization" and those of practically all those "educators" who feel that they have more to give than to learn from what are often called the "backward" or "unprogressive" peoples; to whom it does not occur that one may not wish or need to "progress" if one has reached a state of equilibrium that already provides for the realization of what one regards as the greatest purposes of life. It is as an expression of good will and of the best intentions that this proselytizing fury takes on its most dangerous aspects. To many this "fury" can only suggest the fable of the fox that lost its tail, and persuaded the other foxes to cut off theirs.

THE BREATHING SPHERE

1. David Wagoner, "Lost," in *The Forgotten Language: Contemporary Poets and Nature,* ed. Christopher Merrill (Layton, UT: Peregrine Smith Books, 1991), p. 155. Copyright by David Wagoner. Quoted by permission of the author.

2. Lewis Thomas, "The World's Biggest Membrane," in *The Lives of a Cell: Notes of a Biology Watcher* (New York: Bantam Books, 1975), p. 170. "Viewed from the distance of the moon, the astonishing thing about the earth, catching the breath, is that it is alive."

3. Frithjof Schuon, *The Transcendent Unity of Religions,* trans. Peter Townsend (London: Faber & Faber, 1953), p. 81.

4. Euripides, prologue to *Ion*, quoted in Jane Harrison, *Prolegomena to the Study of Greek Religion* (New York: Meridian Books, 1922), p. 320.
5. Daisetz T. Suzuki, *Zen and Japanese Culture*, Bollingen Series, no. 64 (Princeton, NJ: Princeton University Press, 1973), p. 185 and n. 30.
6. Mircea Eliade, in Roger Cook, *Tree of Life: Image for the Cosmos* (New York: Thames & Hudson, 1988), p. 9.
7. Cook, *The Tree of Life*, pp. 38–39.
8. Milosz, *Visions*, pp. 13–14.
9. Maria-Gabriele Wosien, *Sacred Dance: Encounter with the Gods* (New York: Avon Books, 1974), p. 23.
10. Ananda K. Coomaraswamy, "The Symbolism of the Dome," in *Coomaraswamy: Selected Papers*, vol. 1, *Traditional Art and Symbolism*, Bollingen Series, no. 89, ed. Roger Lipsey (Princeton, NJ: Princeton University Press, 1977), p. 421.
11. S. K. Heninger, Jr., *The Cosmographical Glass: Renaissance Diagrams of the Universe* (San Marino, CA: The Huntington Library, 1977), p. 13.
12. See N. Max Wildiers, *The Theologian and His Universe: Theology and Cosmology from the Middle Ages to the Present* (New York: Seabury Press, 1982), p. 158: "...Catholic theologians continued to defend the medieval interpretation of Christian doctrine long after the world picture from which it derived its credibility had been discarded by the discoveries of the natural sciences."
13. Ouspensky, *In Search of the Miraculous*, pp. 205–213.
14. Heinz R. Pagels, *The Cosmic Code: Quantum Physics as the Language of Nature* (New York: Bantam Books, 1982), p. 233.
15. "Tzar Saltan," in Post Wheeler, *Russian Wonder Tales* (New York: Century Company, 1912), p. 15.
16. Paul Valéry, quoted in Jantsch, *The Self-Organizing Universe*, p. 157.
17. W. B. Yeats, *A Vision*, (New York, Collier Books, 1966), p. 70.
18. William Shakespeare, *Sonnet 73*.
19. See especially Jantsch, *The Self-Organizing Universe*, and Prigogine and Stengers, *Order out of Chaos*.
20. Victor Zuckerkandl, *Sound and Symbol: Music and the External World*, Bollingen Series, no. 44, trans. Willard R. Trask (Princeton NJ: Princeton University Press, 1956), pp. 35–36. Copyright © 1956 by Bollingen Foundation, Inc., New York, NY. Reprinted by permission of Princeton University Press.
21. Ibid., pp. 96–98, 101–102.
22. Eliot, "The Waste Land," lines 37–41, in *Collected Poems 1909–1935*, p. 70.

23. de Santillana and von Dechend, *Hamlet's Mill*, p. 2. Reprinted with permission from the Harvard Common Press.

24. Coomaraswamy, "On the Loathly Bride," in *Coomaraswamy*, vol. 1, *Traditional Art and Symbolism*, p. 368.

25. *The I Ching or Book of Changes*, Bollingen Series, no. 19, Richard Wilhelm translation, rendered into English by Cary F. Baynes, with foreword by C. G. Jung (New York: Pantheon Books, 1950).

26. Gurdjieff, *Beelzebub's Tales*, p. 381.

27. de Santillana and von Dechend, *Hamlet's Mill*, p. 3. Reprinted with permission from the Harvard Common Press.

28. Richard Nelson, *The Island Within* (New York: Vintage Books, 1991), p. 13.

29. de Santillana and von Dechend, *Hamlet's Mill*, pp. 58–59. Reprinted with permission from the Harvard Common Press.

30. See *Black Elk Speaks*.

31. Marcel Griaule, *Conversations with Ogotemmêli: An Introduction to Dogon Religious Ideas* (New York: Oxford University Press, 1975).

32. Coomaraswamy, "Two Passages in Dante's *Paradiso*," in *Coomaraswamy*, vol. 2, *Metaphysics*, p. 248.

33. Lewis, *Discarded Image*.

34. Eliot, "Burnt Norton," 3:26, in *Four Quartets*. The preceding quotations in parentheses are from the Bible (King James Version), Song of Sol. 2:14, 2:9, with "countenance" modernized to "face" and "shewing" to "showing."

35. From "I syng of a mayden," anonymous medieval lyric, in *An Oxford Anthology of English Poetry*, ed. Howard Foster Lowry and Willard Thorp (New York: Oxford University Press, 1935), p. 2. ("Ther"= where; "moder"=mother.)

36. Kuhn, *Copernican Revolution*, p. 7: "The astronomer may on occasions destroy, for reasons lying entirely within his specialty, a worldview that had previously made the universe meaningful for the members of a whole civilization, specialist and nonspecialist alike."

37. *Staying Alive* written by Barry Gibb, Robin Gibb, and Maurice Gibb. © 1977 Gibb Brothers Music. All rights reserved. Used by permission.

38. Wallace Stevens, "Things of August," from *Collected Poems of Wallace Stevens* (New York: Alfred A. Knopf, 1965), p. 490. Copyright 1947 by Wallace Stevens. Reprinted by permission of Alfred A. Knopf, Inc. for US, Canada and elsewhere except the British Commonwealth (excluding Canada); and by permission of Faber & Faber Ltd for the rest of the British Commonwealth.

39. Timothy Ferris, "The Creation of the Universe: A Science Special for

Television" (transcribed and published by PTV Publications, P. O. Box 701, Kent, OH 44240), p. 15. Quoted by permission of Timothy Ferris.

40. Description of the beginning of creation from the *Book of Zohar*, quoted in Cook, *Tree of Life*, p. 19.

41. The two quotations are from *Paradiso* 28:16–18, 41–42. The second selection is translated by Dorothy Sayers and Barbara Reynolds in Dante, *The Divine Comedy*, vol. 3, *Paradise* (New York: Penguin Books, 1962), p. 302. Courtesy of David Higham Associates, Ltd.

42. Stephen W. Hawking corrects this popular misconception in *Brief History*, p. 8:

> ...the concept of time has no meaning before the beginning of the universe. This was first pointed out by St. Augustine. When asked: What did God do before he created the universe? Augustine didn't reply [as is popularly supposed]: He was preparing Hell for people who asked such questions. Instead, he said that time was a property of the universe that God created, and that time did not exist before the beginning of the universe.

All quotations from *A Brief History of Time* are by permission of Bantam Books.

43. Stephen Hawking, in Ferris, "Creation of the Universe," p. 15. Quoted by permission of Timothy Ferris.

44. Peterson, "Dante and the 3-Sphere," p. 1031. Courtesy of the *American Journal of Physics*.

45. Edwin A. Abbott, *Flatland: A Romance of Many Dimensions* (New York: Harper & Row Publishers, Perennial Library, 1983), p. 84.

46. T. S. Eliot, "Little Gidding," 2:27, in *Four Quartets*, p. 33.

47. Steven Weinberg, *The First Three Minutes: A Modern View of the Origin of the Universe* (New York: Bantam Books, 1979), p. 2.

48. Henry David Thoreau, *Walden, or Life in the Woods* (New York: New American Library, a Signet classic, 1960), p. 71.

49. Yeats, "Sailing to Byzantium," in *Poems: New Edition*, p. 193. Reprinted with permission of Macmillan Publishing Company. Copyright 1928 by Macmillan Publishing Company, renewed 1956 by Georgie Yeats.

50. Yeats, *A Vision*, p. 67.

51. Peterson, "Dante and the 3-Sphere," p. 1031. Courtesy of the *American Journal of Physics*.

52. Hawking, *Brief History*, p. 116.

53. Ibid., p. 137–139.

54. Dante, *The Banquet (Il Convito)*, trans. Katharine Hillard (London: Kegan Paul, Trench & Company, 1889), pp. 63–66.

55. Peterson, "Dante and the 3-Sphere," p. 1033. Courtesy of the *American Journal of Physics*.

56. Hawking, *Brief History*, pp. 149–150.

57. Johann Sebastian Bach, Cantata no. 4, "Christ Lag in Todesbanden," "Christ Lay in the Bonds of Death."

58. Charles S. Singleton, "The Vistas in Retrospect," *Modern Language Notes* 81 (1966): 55–60.

59. Ouspensky, *In Search of the Miraculous*, pp. 207, 209.

60. Plato, *Timaeus*, in *Plato: Timaeus and Critias*, trans. Desmond Lee (New York: Penguin Books, 1971), pp. 44–45. The italics in the quotation are mine.

61. Gurdjieff, *Beelzebub's Tales*, p. 696.

62. Heracleitus, quoted in Yeats, *A Vision*, p. 68.

63. *Encyclopaedia Britannica*, s.v. "Empedocles."

64. Yeats, *A Vision*, p. 33.

65. "The Dancing Master" [G. I. Gurdjieff], anonymous interview in Paris *Magazine Littéraire*, December 1977.

66. See Yates, *The Art of Memory*, p. 95.

67. "Katha Upanishad," in *The Ten Principal Upanishads*, trans. Shree Purohit Swami and W.B. Yeats (London: Faber & Faber, 1937), p. 33. Reprinted with permission of Macmillan Publishing Company for sale in the United States, its territories and dependencies, copyright 1937 by Shree Purohit Swami and W.B. Yeats, renewed 1965 by Bertha Georgie Yeats and Anne Yeats; and by permission of A.P. Watt Ltd on behalf of Michael Yeats and Benares Hindu University for sale throughout the British Commonwealth.

68. See Mark Johnson, *The Body in the Mind: The Bodily Basis of Meaning, Imagination, and Reason* (Chicago: University of Chicago Press, 1987).

69. Jantsch, *The Self-Organizing Universe*, p. 75.

THE GRAND EVOLUTIONARY SYNTHESIS

1. Eliot, "East Coker," 1:5–8, in *Four Quartets*, p. 11.

2. Quoted in Laszlo, *Evolution*, p. 16.

3. Gurdjieff, *Beelzebub's Tales*, p. 696.

4. Thomas, "The Music of *This* Sphere," in *Lives of a Cell*, pp. 27–28.

5. Quoted in Young, *Unfinished Universe*, p. 34.

6. Ferris, "Creation of the Universe," p. 13. Quoted by permission of Timothy Ferris.

7. Young, *Unfinished Universe*, p. 39.

8. Ferris, "Creation of the Universe," p. 13. Quoted by permission of Timothy Ferris.

9. Stephen Spender, "I think continually of those," in *Collected Poems 1928–1953* (New York: Random House, 1955), p. 32:

> I think continually of those who were truly great.
> Who, from the womb, remembered the soul's history
> Through corridors of light where the hours are suns,
> Endless and singing.

Copyright 1934 and renewed 1962 by Stephen Spender. Reprinted by permission of Random House, Inc. for English language publication in the United States, its dependencies and the Philippine Republic; and for English language publication elsewhere in the world by Faber & Faber Ltd.

10. Saint Augustine, in *Confessions*, p. 20, n. 1.

11. Young, *Unfinished Universe*, p. 55.

12. Quoted ibid., pp. 41–42.

13. Ferris, "Creation of the Universe," p. 18. Quoted by permission of Timothy Ferris.

14. Schrödinger, "Oneness of Mind," in *What Is Life?*, p. 140.

15. Aziz Nasafi, Persian mystic of the thirteenth century, quoted ibid., p. 139.

16. Kanze Motokiyo Zeami, "Hanjo," trans. Royall Tyler, in *Twenty Plays of the Nō Theatre*, ed. Donald Keene and Royall Tyler (New York: Columbia University Press, 1970), p. 137. Copyright © 1970 Columbia University Press, New York. All quotations from *Twenty Plays* in this book are reprinted with the permission of the publisher.

17. Henry Corbin, *The Man of Light in Iranian Sufism*, trans. Nancy Pearson (Boston: Shambhala Publications, 1978), p. 88.

18. G. I. Gurdjieff, *Views from the Real World: Early Talks in Moscow, Essentuki, Tiflis, Berlin, London, Paris, New York and Chicago, As Recollected by His Pupils* (New York: E. P. Dutton & Company, 1973), pp. 251–252.

19. "Eesha-Upanishad," in Purohit Swami and Yeats, *Upanishads*, p. 15. For permissions, see THE BREATHING SPHERE, note 67, p. 195.

20. Gershom G. Scholem, *Major Trends in Jewish Mysticism* (New York: Schocken Books, 1961), p. 217.

21. Eliot, "The Dry Salvages," 5:17–19, in *Four Quartets*, p. 27.

22. Robert S. de Ropp, *Warrior's Way: The Challenging Life Games* (New York: Delta/Seymour Lawrence, a Merloyd Lawrence book, 1979), p. 114.

23. In Ferris, "Creation of the Universe," p. 18. Quoted by permission of Timothy Ferris.
24. Weinberg, *The First Three Minutes*, p. 144.
25. Ouspensky, *In Search of the Miraculous*, pp. 141–142.
26. Dante, *Purgatorio*, 1:13–18. (I have slightly modified Professor Singleton's translation.)
27. P. B. Medawar, *The Art of the Soluble* (London: Methuen & Company, 1967), p. 54.
28. A. R. Orage, quoted in Louise Welch, *Orage with Gurdjieff in America* (Boston: Routledge & Kegan Paul, 1982), p. 51.
29. Gurdjieff, "The Holy Planet Purgatory," in *Beelzebub's Tales*, pp. 681–742.
30. Dante, *The Banquet*, p. 63.
31. See chapter 3, n. 60.
32. See chapter 3, n. 14.
33. Ouspensky, *In Search of the Miraculous*, p. 288.
34. Ibid., pp. 126–127.
35. Laszlo, *Evolution*, pp. 15–16.
36. *Webster's New World Dictionary*, p. 454.
37. See n. 4.
38. "The Diagram of Everything Living," in Ouspensky, *In Search of the Miraculous*, p. 323.
39. Thomas, *Lives of a Cell*, p. 170.
40. Gurdjieff, *Beelzebub's Tales*, pp. 719; 129.
41. "Taittireeya-Upanishad," in Purohit Swami and Yeats, *Upanishads*, p. 78. For permissions, see THE BREATHING SPHERE, note 67, p. 195.
42. Gurdjieff, *Beelzebub's Tales*, p. 171.
43. Hawking, *Brief History*, p. 145.
44. Young, *Unfinished Universe*, p. 41.
45. Gurdjieff, *Beelzebub's Tales*, p. 352.
46. Young, *Unfinished Universe*, p. 85.
47. Prigogine and Stengers, *Order out of Chaos*, p. 313.
48. Ibid., p. 312.

EXTRAPOLATING BACKWARD

1. Bachelard, *Poetics of Space*, p. 4.
2. Ibid., p. xxxiii.
3. Eliot, "The Waste Land," lines 301–304, in *Collected Poems 1909–1935*, p. 8.
4. Eliot, "East Coker," 3:28, in *Four Quartets*, p. 15.
5. Berger, *Little Big Man*, p. 240.

6. Kent C. Bloomer and Charles W. Moore, *Body, Memory and Architecture* (New Haven, CT: Yale University Press, 1977) pp. 1–2.
7. See Robert D. Romanyshyn, *Technology as Symptom and Dream* (London: Routledge, 1989).
8. Keller, *Gender and Science*, p. 10.
9. Bloomer and Moore, *Body, Memory and Architecture*, p. 34.
10. Milosz, *Visions*, pp. 6–7.
11. Northrop Frye, *Fearful Symmetry: A Study of William Blake* (Princeton, NJ: Princeton University Press, 1947), p. 23.
12. Proverbs, 9:1.
13. Motto of Everyman's Library, from the medieval play *Everyman*. As a matter of fact, it was Good Deeds who said this to Everyman and who alone could be counted upon to accompany him through the dark door of Death—but Everyman's Library seems to be implying that Wisdom said it.
14. Reproduced on the cover of *Parabola* 16, no. 4 (November 1991).
15. Revelation 6:12–13.
16. Gleick, *Chaos*, p. 24.
17. Title of a book by Robert S. de Ropp (New York: Dell Publishing Company, 1968).
18. Bachelard, *Poetics of Space*, pp. 14–15.
19. Ibid., p. 17.
20. Ibid., p. xxxii.
21. Dante, *Purgatorio*, 1:1–2.
22. Bachelard, *Poetics of Space*, pp. 5–6, 8.
23. Komparu Zenchiku, "Yōhiki," trans. Carl Sesar, in *Twenty Plays of the Nō Theatre,* ed. Donald Keene and Royall Tyler (New York: Columbia University Press, 1970), p. 211. Copyright © 1970 Columbia University Press, New York. The lines are spoken by a sorcerer preparing to search for the emperor's departed beloved in the afterworld.

O CHRISTMAS TREE

1. The "old Tamil" to Prince Yuri Lubovedsky, in G. I. Gurdjieff, *Meetings with Remarkable Men* (New York: E. P. Dutton & Company, 1963), p. 158.
2. Prince Lubovedsky to Gurdjieff, in *Meetings with Remarkable Men,* a film directed by Peter Brook with screenplay by Jeanne de Salzmann and Peter Brook. A Corinth video release. Copyright 1978 Remar Productions, Inc; copyright 1987 Corinth Films, Inc.

Index